GOETHE
FAUST I & II

GOETHE

Selected Poems
Faust I & II
Essays on Art and Literature
From My Life: Poetry and Truth (Parts One to Three)
From My Life: Campaign in France 1792 • Siege of Mainz (Part Four)
Italian Journey
Early Verse Dramas and Prose Plays
Verse Plays and Epic
Wilhelm Meister's Apprenticeship
Conversations of German Refugees & Wilhelm Meister's
Journeyman Year or The Renunciants
The Sorrows of Young Werther • Elective Affinities • Novella
Scientific Studies

Collected Works in 12 Volumes

Goethe's Collected Works, Volume 2

Johann Wolfgang von
GOETHE

Faust I & II

Edited and Translated by Stuart Atkins

Princeton University Press
Princeton, New Jersey

Published by Princeton University Press, 41 William Street,
Princeton, New Jersey 08540
In the United Kingdom by Princeton University Press, Chichester, West Sussex
Copyright © 1984 by Suhrkamp/Insel Publishers, Boston, Inc.

Reprinted in paperback by arrangement with Suhrkamp Verlag

Library of Congress Cataloging-in-Publication Data

Goethe, Johann Wolfgang von, 1749–1832.
[Works. English. 1994]
Goethe's collected works
p. cm.
Originally published: Cambridge, Mass. : Suhrkamp, 1983–1989.
Includes indexes.
Contents: v. 1. Selected poems—v. 2. Faust I & II—v.
3. Essays on art and literature.
ISBN 3-518-03055-8 (v. 2 hardback)
ISBN 0-691-03656-X (v. 2 paperback)
I. Title.
PT2026.A1C94 1994
831'.6—dc20
93–27617

First Princeton Paperback printing, 1994

Printed in the United States of America

9 10 8

http://pup.princeton.edu

ISBN-13: 978-0-691-03656-4

ISBN-10: 0-691-03656-X

CONTENTS

GOETHE
FAUST I & II

FAUST
A Tragedy

DEDICATION

Once more you hover close, elusive shapes
my eyes but dimly glimpsed when I was young.
Shall I now try to hold you captive?
Do these illusions still attract my heart?
Nearer yet you crowd! So be it! Do your will   5
as forth from mist and fog you rise about me—
the breath of magic that surrounds your train
stirs in my breast a youthful strength of feeling.

Images of happy days accompany you,
and many dear familiar shades emerge,   10
first loves and early friendships too,
like ancient tales whose words are half forgotten;
pain is renewed, lament reiterates
life's perplexing labyrinth
and names kind friends, cheated of joy by fortune,   15
who have disappeared ahead of me.

The souls for whom I sang my early songs
will never hear the songs that follow;
those many friends are all dispersed,
their first response, alas! is long since muted.   20
My tragic song will now be heard by strangers
whose very praise must cause my heart misgivings,
and those to whom my song gave pleasure,
if still they live, roam scattered everywhere.

I feel the spell of long-forgotten yearning   25
for that serene and solemn spirit realm,
and like an aeolian harp my murmuring song
lets its uncertain tones float through the air.
I feel a sense of dread, tear after tear is falling,
my rigid heart is tenderly unmanned—   30
what I possess seems something far away
and what had disappeared proves real.

PRELUDE ON THE STAGE

Enter MANAGER, POET-PLAYWRIGHT, *and* PLAYER OF COMIC ROLES.

MANAGER. You two who have so often been of help
   to me in trial and tribulation,
   tell me, now that we're here in Germany,   35
   how well you think our enterprise will fare.
   I'd greatly like to satisfy the public—
   not least because they're easy-going.
   The posts are set, the boards are laid,
   and everyone expects a splendid show.   40
   Already in their places, quiet and expectant,
   they're hoping to be pleasantly surprised.
   I know what counts for popularity,
   and yet I've never been quite so uneasy—
   of course they are not used to anything first-rate,   45
   but still they've done an awful lot of reading.
   How shall we offer only what is fresh and new
   yet won't offend because it's just absurd?
   As well you know, I like to see the public
   when they are surging towards our tent   50
   and, with a litany of groans and grumbling,
   squeeze through the narrow gate of grace;
   when in broad daylight, not yet four o'clock,
   they shove and fight to reach our cash-box
   and, as at the bakery-door for bread in time of famine,   55
   they nearly break their necks to get a ticket.
   With people of such different kinds, poets alone
   perform this miracle—your task, my friend, today!
POET. Spare me your public and its varied kinds—
      to glimpse it is enough to put our thoughts to rout!   60
      Don't let me see the surging crowd that can,
      against our wills, draw us into its whirl.
      Take me instead to some celestial refuge
      where nothing blights the poet's quiet joy
      and where with godlike bounty love and friendship   65
      create and nurture the blessings of our hearts.
         Alas! what had its source in depths of feeling
      and timid lips could only stammer,
      defective here, but here perhaps successful,
      is brutally engulfed by the tempestuous moment.   70
      Often it is expressed in perfect form
      only after many years of effort.
      What glitters, lives but for the moment;
      what has real worth, survives for all posterity.

PLAYER. Don't talk about posterity to me!   75
    Suppose *I* chose to preach posterity,
    who'd entertain the present generation?
    Amusement's what they want, and what they'll get.
    A fine young fellow here and now is not,
    in my opinion, altogether worthless.   80
    If you know how to say your say and be relaxed,
    you aren't embittered by the public's whims—
    one even wants a good-sized audience,
    to be more sure of getting a response.
    So don't be shy or hide your excellence: 85
    let us hear Phantasy with all her choirs,
    hear Reason, Good Sense, Sentiment, and Passion,
    and take good care that Folly too is heard.
MANAGER. The main thing, though, is having lots of action!
    Spectators come expecting something they can see.   90
    If you unreel enough before the public's eyes
    to make them marvel open-mouthed,
    a quantitative triumph is already won,
    and you're the man they idolize.
    Only by mass can you subdue the masses—   95
    there's then enough for all to have their pick.
    Offer a lot, and lots get what they want,
    and no one leaves the theater uncontented.
    Don't wait because your piece is still in pieces!
    Whatever you've concocted is sure to be a hit,   100
    and simple recipes are simple to serve up.
    Nor does it help to offer anything complete—
    your audience will only tear it all apart.
POET. You don't appreciate how low such hackwork is,
    or how unworthy of a genuine artist.   105
    I see that you derive your principles
    from the fine efforts of incompetents.
MANAGER. Your accusation doesn't hurt my feelings:
    a man who wants to be effective
    must know the worth of proper tools.   110
    Remember that the wood you have to split is soft,
    and don't lose sight of whom you're writing for!
    If one is driven here by boredom,
    another's come from gorging at the table;
    and worst of all, for many we are but   115
    a change from reading magazines.
    It's curiosity that makes them rush our way,
    as mindless as if to a masquerade;
    the ladies displaying themselves and their finery

take supporting parts at no expense to us. 120
What do you poets dream of on Parnassus?
Why should a full house make you happy?
Take a close look at the patrons you have,
half are indifferent, the rest are boors!
After the play, *he* counts on playing cards, 125
and *he* on a wild night in some girl's arms—
why, in a cause like this, must you poor fools
so sorely try the Muses' kindness?
If you just give them more and more, and then still more,
I guarantee you'll never miss the mark. 130
Just try to keep your audience distracted;
to please them is no easy task. . . .
But what's this paroxysm—ecstasy or pain?
POET. Go find yourself another hireling
if you expect that merely for your sake the poet 135
shall wantonly forfeit the fundamental right
with which he and all men are endowed by Nature!
What is the force that lets him move all hearts
and even make the elements obey him?
The consonance between what surges from his heart 140
and what that heart in turn takes from the world!
When Nature, unconcerned, twirls her endless thread
and fixes it upon the spindle,
when all creation's inharmonious myriads
vex us with a potpourri of sound, 145
who then divides the strand monotonously unreeling
and gives it life and rhythmic motion,
who summons single voices to the general choir
where music swells in glorious accord?
Who endows the storm with raging passions 150
or lets the sunset glow in somber mood?
Who bestrews the paths of those we love
with all the fairest blooms of spring?
Who plaits from humble leaves of green
garlands that honor merit however achieved? 155
Who preserves Olympus and keeps the gods assembled?—
The Poet who incarnates this human power!
PLAYER. In that case, put your fine abilities to use
and manage your literary business
the way a love affair's conducted. 160
Two meet by chance, are smitten, don't go on,
and bit by bit they get involved;
there's growing happiness, with trials to test it;
joy knows no bounds, and then there's misery,

and so before you know it you have got a novel.   165
Let the play we give be just like that!
From the whole store of human life just grab some bit—
we all live life, and yet to most it's something strange,
so that it is of interest, whatever you may pick.
Lively scenes that aren't too lucid—   170
much confusion, a glimmer of truth—
best let you brew the drink that satisfies
and yet refreshes one and all.
If that's provided, then your play will draw
the young élite, alert for any revelation,   175
and from your work more tender souls
will suck the nourishment of melancholy,
and in the various emotions you arouse
all then will recognize what they themselves have felt.
They're still as prone to weeping as to laughter,   180
still like fine turns of speech, delight in make-believe—
there is no pleasing those who are adult and know it,
but those who're young won't fail to show appreciation.
POET. Then give me, too, those days again
when I was young and life still lay ahead,   185
when one new song after the other
welled forth in an unceasing stream,
when through a veil of fog I saw the world,
and every bud still promised miracles,
when I gathered the myriad flowers   190
profusely filling every vale.
I had no worldly goods, yet had enough:
desire for truth and joy in make-believe.
Give me again my untamed passions: 195
the power to hate, the strength to love—
give me back my youth again!
PLAYER. Perhaps, my friend, you may need youth
when you're beset by enemies in battle,
when all-too-charming girls insist   200
on throwing their arms about your neck,
when in a race the victor's wreath
beckons afar from the hard-sought goal,
or when the frenzied whirl of dancing
ends in a night of revelry and wassail.   205
It's up to you old gentlemen, however,
to play with sure and pleasing touch
whatever instrument you've mastered
and to meander gracefully
toward the goals you've set yourselves—   210

do that, and we won't think the less of you.
The saying, age makes childish, is not true;
it only finds us really children still.
MANAGER. This altercation's gone on long enough,
   it's time I saw some action too!   215
While you are polishing fine phrases
something useful could be going on.
What's the point of harping on the proper mood?
It never comes to him who shilly-shallies.
Since you pretend to be a poet,   220
make poetry obey your will.
You know that what we need
is a strong drink to gulp down fast,
so set to work and brew it!
What's left undone today, is still not done tomorrow;   225
to every day there is a use and purpose;
let Resoluteness promptly seize
the forelock of the Possible,
and then, reluctant to let go again,
she's forced to carry on and be productive.   230
   As well you know, these German theaters
let everyone do exactly as he wants;
since that's the case, this is no time to stint
on scenery or stage effects.
Put both the sun and moon to use,   235
be lavish with the stars and planets—
nor are we short of fire or water,
of precipices, birds, or beasts.
So now upon our modest stage act out
creation in its every aspect,   240
and move with all deliberate haste
from heaven, through the world, to hell!   [*Exeunt.*

PROLOGUE IN HEAVEN

Heaven opens, revealing the LORD *and* HEAVENLY HOSTS;
three ARCHANGELS *step forward.*

RAPHAEL. In ancient rivalry with fellow spheres
    the sun still sings its glorious song,
    and it completes with tread of thunder   245
    the journey it has been assigned.
    Angels gain comfort from the sight,
    though none can fully grasp its meaning;
    all that was wrought, too great for comprehension,
    still has the splendor of its primal day.   250
GABRIEL. The earth as well revolves in splendor
    with speed beyond all comprehending;
    brightness like that of paradise
    alternates with deep and awesome night;
    the sea's vast floods surge up and break   255
    in foam against the rocks' deep base,
    and rock and sea are hurled along
    in the eternal motion of the spheres.
MICHAEL. Contending storms sweep onward too
    from sea to land, from land to sea,   260
    and in their rage create a causal chain
    whose power is far-reaching and profound.
    Lo! a flash of devastation
    lightens the path of coming thunder.
    But still Your messengers, o Lord,   265
    revere the quiet movement of Your light.
THE THREE. Angels gain comfort from the sight,
    though none can fully grasp Your Being,
    and all the grandeur You have wrought
    still has the splendor of its primal day.   270

Enter MEPHISTOPHELES.

MEPHISTOPHELES. Since, Lord, You once again are come
    to ask us how we're getting on,
    and before have often welcomed me,
    You see among Your servants me as well.
    I'm sorry I can't offer high-flown language,   275
    not even though all here assembled may deride me;
    pathos from me, in any case, would make You laugh
    if You had not stopped laughing long ago.
    I've no remarks to make about the sun or planets,
    I merely see how mankind toils and moils.   280
    Earth's little gods still do not change a bit,

are just as odd as on their primal day.
Their lives would be a little easier
if You'd not let them glimpse the light of heaven—
they call it Reason and employ it only   285
to be more bestial than any beast.
Saving Your Grace's presence, to my mind
they're like those crickets with long legs
who won't stop flying though they only hop, and promptly
sing the same old song down in the grass again.   290
And if they'd only keep on lying in the grass—
they stick their noses into every dirty mess!
LORD. Do you have nothing else to tell me?
   Do you ever come except to criticize?
   Is nothing ever right for you on earth?   295
MEPHISTOPHELES. No, Lord! I find things there, as always, downright bad.
   I am so sorry for mankind's unending miseries
   that even I am loath to plague the wretches.
LORD. Do you know Faust?
MEPHISTOPHELES.   The doctor?
LORD.   And my servant!
MEPHISTOPHELES. Indeed? He serves You in a curious way.   300
   The fool is not content with earthly food or drink.
   Some ferment makes him want what is exotic,
   yet he's half conscious of his folly;
   from heaven he claims as his the brightest stars,
   and from the earth all of its highest joys,   305
   but nothing near and nothing far away
   can satisfy a heart so deeply agitated.
LORD. Though now he only serves me blindly and ineptly,
   I soon shall lead him into clarity—
   the gardener knows, when the sapling turns green,   310
   that blossoms and fruit will brighten future years.
MEPHISTOPHELES. What'll You bet? You'll lose him yet
   if You grant me permission
   to guide him gently along my road.
LORD. So long as he is still alive on earth,   315
   nothing shall prohibit your so doing—
   men err as long as they keep striving.
MEPHISTOPHELES. You have my thanks—as for the dead,
   I never did much care to bother with them.
   Full healthy cheeks are what I best prefer.   320
   I'm not at home to any corpse,
   and like the cat prefer my mouse alive.
LORD. So be it! Do as you are minded!
   Divert this spirit from its primal source,

and drag him, if you can keep hold of him,   325
along your downward path,
and stand abashed when you must needs admit:
a good man, in his groping intuition,
is well aware of what's his proper course.
MEPHISTOPHELES. Agreed! The business won't take long.   330
As for my bet, I'm not the least bit worried.
When I achieve my purpose,
let me beat my breast triumphantly.
Dust shall he eat, and greedily,
like my celebrated serpent-cousin.   335
LORD. When that occurs, again come uninvited.
I have no hate for creatures of your kind.
Of all the spirits of negation
rogues like you bother me the least.
Human activity slackens all too easily,   340
and people soon are prone to rest on any terms;
that's why I like to give them the companion
who functions as a prod and does a job as devil.
   But may, true sons of heaven, you delight
in beauty's living richness!   345
May the power of growth that works and lives forever
encompass you in love's propitious bonds,
and may you give the permanence of thought
to that which hovers in elusive forms.
            Heaven closes; exeunt ARCHANGELS, *severally.*
MEPHISTOPHELES. (*Solus*) I like to see the Old Man now and then,   350
and take good care to keep on speaking terms.
It is quite decent of a mighty lord to chat
and be so human with the very devil.   [*Exit.*

PART ONE OF THE TRAGEDY

NIGHT

A high-vaulted, narrow Gothic room. FAUST, *sitting restless at a desk.*
FAUST. I've studied now, to my regret,
  Philosophy, Law, Medicine,   355
  and—what is worst—Theology
  from end to end with diligence.
  Yet here I am, a wretched fool
  and still no wiser than before.
  I've become Master, and Doctor as well,   360
  and for nearly ten years I have led
  my young students a merry chase,
  up, down, and every which way—
  and find we can't have certitude.
  This is too much for heart to bear!   365
  I well may know more than all those dullards,
  those doctors, teachers, officials, and priests,
  be unbothered by scruples or doubts,
  and fear neither hell nor its devils—
  but I get no joy from anything, either,   370
  know nothing that I think worthwhile,
  and don't imagine that what I teach
  could better mankind or make it godly.
  Then, too, I don't have land or money,
  or any splendid worldly honors.   375
  No dog would want to linger on like this!
  That is why I've turned to magic,
  in hope that with the help of spirit-power
  I might solve many mysteries,
  so that I need no longer toil and sweat   380
  to speak of what I do not know,
  can learn what, deep within it,
  binds the universe together,
  may contemplate all seminal forces—
  and be done with peddling empty words.   385
    O radiant moon for whom I have
  so often, waking at this desk,
  sat at midnight watching until
  I saw you, melancholy friend, appear
  above my books and papers—would that this   390
  were the last time you gazed upon my grief!
  If only I, in your kind radiance,

could wander in the highest hills
and with spirits haunt some mountain cave,
could rove the meadows in your muted light   395
and, rid of all learned obfuscation,
regain my health by bathing in your dew!
   Alas! I'm still confined to prison.
Accursed, musty hole of stone
to which the sun's fair light itself   400
dimly penetrates through painted glass.
Restricted by this great mass of books
that worms consume, that dust has covered,
and that up to the ceiling-vault
are interspersed with grimy papers,   405
confined by glassware and wooden boxes
and crammed full of instruments,
stuffed with the household goods of generations—
such is your world, if world it can be called!
   And still you wonder why your heart   410
is anxious and your breast constricted,
why a pain you cannot account for
inhibits your vitality completely!
You are surrounded, not by the living world
in which God placed mankind,   415
but, amid smoke and mustiness,
only by bones of beasts and of the dead.
   You must escape from this confining world!
And will not this mysterious book
from Nostradamus' very hand   420
amply provide the guidance you need?
If you can read the courses of the stars
and take from Nature your instruction,
you will understand the psychic power
by which the spirit world communicates.   425
But arid speculation won't explain
the sacred symbols to you. –
Spirits that hover near to me,
give me an answer if you hear my voice!
   (*Opening the book and seeing the sign of the Macrocosm.*)
Ha! as I gaze what rapture suddenly   430
begins to flow through all my senses!
I feel youth's sacred-vital happiness
course with new fire through every vein and fiber.
Did some god inscribe these signs
that quell my inner turmoil,   435
fill my poor heart with joy,

and with mysterious force unveil
the natural powers all about me?
Am I a god? I see so clearly now!
In these lines' perfection I behold   440
creative nature spread out before my soul.
At last I understand the sage who says:
"The spirit world is not sealed off—
your mind is closed, *your* heart is dead!
Go, neophyte, and boldly bathe   445
your mortal breast in roseate dawn!''
                    (*Contemplating the sign.*)
How all things interweave as one
and work and live each in the other!
Lo! heavenly forces rise, descend,
pass golden urns from hand to hand,   450
crowd from on high through all the earth
on pinions redolent of blessings,
and fill the universe with harmony!
   How grand a show! But, still, alas! mere show.
Infinite Nature, when can I lay hold of you   455
and of your breasts? You fountains of all life
on which the heavens and earth depend,
towards which my withered heart is straining—
you flow, you nurse, and yet I thirst in vain!
   (*Turning the pages angrily, he sees the sign of the Earth Spirit.*)
How different is this sign's effect on me!   460
You, Spirit of Earth, are closer—
I feel my faculties becoming more acute,
I know the quickening glow of new-made wine.
I now feel brave enough to venture forth
and bear earth's torments and its joys,   465
to grapple with the hurricane
and not to quail although the creaking ship break up. –
The sky becomes overcast —
the moon hides its light —
my lamp's flame vanishes!   470
Mists arise! – Beams of red flash
about my head — a dread chill
flows down from the ceiling-vault
and has me in its hold!
Spirit to whom I pray, I feel you hover near.   475
Reveal yourself!
How my heart is torn asunder!
Strange feelings
stir my entire being!

My heart is now completely yours!   480
Obey! Obey, although my life should be the price!
>*He takes the book and mysteriously utters the sign of the spirit.*
>*In a flash of reddish flame the* EARTH SPIRIT *appears.*

SPIRIT. Who calls to me?

FAUST (*turning away*). A fearful apparition!

SPIRIT. You've used great efforts to attract me,
have long exerted suction on my sphere,
and now –

FAUST.   Alas, I lack the strength to face you!   485

SPIRIT. You beg and pant to see me,
to hear my voice, to view my face;
your urgent prayer has made me well disposed,
so here I am! What paltry fear
now cows a demigod! Where is the summoning soul,   490
the breast that in itself conceived a world
it bore and cherished, the breast that swelled
in trembling joy to reach our spirit-plane?
Where are you, Faust, whose ringing voice I heard,
who strove with all his faculties to reach me?   495
Can he be you who in my aura
tremble in all your depths of being—
a worm that writhes away in fright?

FAUST. I stand my ground before you, shape of flame!
I am that Faust, I am your peer!   500

SPIRIT. In the tides of life, in action's storm,
I surge and ebb,
move to and fro!
As cradle and grave,
as unending sea,   505
as constant change,
as life's incandescence,
I work at the whirring loom of time
and fashion the living garment of God.

FAUST. How close I feel to you, industrious spirit,   510
whose strands encompass all the world!

SPIRIT. Your peer is the spirit you comprehend;
mine you are not!   [*Disappears.*

FAUST (*collapsing*). Not yours?
Whose then?   515
I, made in God's image,
not even your counterpart!
>(*A knocking is heard.*)
Damnation! I know the sound of my assistant—
my happiest moment is destroyed.

Why must that humdrum plodder
disturb this plenitude of visions!   520
    Enter WAGNER, *in dressing-gown and nightcap, a lamp in his
      hand.* FAUST *turns, irritated.*
WAGNER. Excuse me, but I hear you are declaiming;
  no doubt you've been reciting some Greek tragedy?
  That's a skill I wish I could improve,
  since it's so useful nowadays.   525
  I've often heard it said, with no disparagement,
  that actors could give preachers useful lessons.
FAUST. They can, if the preachers are only performers,
  which I suppose may sometimes be the case.
WAGNER. Still, confined to one's study so much,   530
  even on holidays hardly seeing people
  and getting only distant glimpses with a spyglass,
  how can one hope to affect them with rhetoric?
FAUST. That can't be done unless you feel some passion,
  unless there's something bursting from within   535
  that by its easy innate force
  conquers the hearts of all who hear you.
  You may sit and compile forever,
  concoct a stew of morsels left by others,
  and from your feeble heap of ashes   540
  fan paltry flames,
  if you've an appetite for adulation
  from children and from simpletons;
  and yet, unless your heart is where all starts,
  your efforts won't affect the hearts of others.   545
WAGNER. Delivery alone can make a speech a hit—
  I'm well aware how much I've still to learn.
FAUST. Just try to make an honest living,
  and don't put on a cap and bells!
  Intelligence and proper sense   550
  need little art to be expressed;
  if you have something that you really want to say,
  is there a need to hunt for words?
  Let me be blunt: those sparkling speeches you admire,
  those paper baubles for mankind's amusement,   555
  give no more solace than fog-laden winds
  that sough through withered autumn leaves!
WAGNER. Alas, that art is long,
  and human life so short!
  Even when I'm involved in critical endeavors   560
  my heart and mind will often have misgivings.
  How hard it is to get the tools

that let one get back to the sources—
and even before one's halfway there
he's very likely to be dead.   565
FAUST. Is parchment then the sacred fount,
and does one drink from it forever slake our thirst?
There's nothing you can gain refreshment from
except what has its source in your own soul.
WAGNER. Excuse me if I think it a great treat   570
to put oneself into the spirit of past ages;
we see how wise men thought before our time,
and to what splendid heights we have attained at last.
FAUST. Oh yes, we've reached the very stars!
My friend, for us the ages that are past   575
must be a book with seven seals.
What's called the spirit of an age
is in the end the spirit of you persons
in whom past ages are reflected.
And then it often is a sorry sight—   580
one look's enough to make you run away!
A trash bin and a lumber-garret;
at most, a grand-historical display
with excellent pragmatic maxims
well suited to the mouths of puppet-actors!   585
WAGNER. Still, the world, the human heart and mind—
everyone wants some knowledge of these things!
FAUST. Yes, what they choose to call knowledge!
Who dares give the child its proper name?
The foolish few who, with such knowledge, failed   590
to keep their wealth of intuitions in their hearts,
revealed their feelings and their visions to the rabble,
have in all times been crucified and burned. –
Excuse me, friend, the night is far advanced;
we'll have to stop for now.   595
WAGNER. I would have gladly stayed up longer
discussing such learned matters with you.
But tomorrow's Easter Sunday, when I hope
you'll let me ask a few more questions—
I've been assiduous in my pursuit of learning;   600
true, I know much, but all is what I'd like to know.   [*Exit.*
FAUST. How can a person still have any hopes
who is addicted to what's superficial,
who grubs with greedy hand for treasures
and then is happy to discover earthworms!   605
    Is it right to let that voice be heard
where inspiration compassed me about?

And yet, this once you have my gratitude,
you sorriest of mortals—
you snatched me from a desperation 610
that threatened to destroy my mind.
So gigantic was the apparition
that I, alas, could only think myself a dwarf.
    I, made in God's image, who fancied
that I was close to truth's eternal mirror, 615
who, sloughing off mortality,
reveled in clear celestial radiance;
I, more than Cherub, whose presentient powers then
dared flow untrammeled through the veins of Nature
and share the gods' creative life— 620
how I am punished!
One thundered word has been my death.
    It's arrogance to claim I am your peer.
Although I had the power to attract you,
I lacked the strength to hold you fast. 625
In that blest moment
I felt so small and yet so great;
ruthlessly you thrust me back
into the uncertainties that are man's lot.
Who will now teach me? What am I to shun, 630
is there an impulse that I must obey?
Alas, the things we do, no less than those we suffer,
impose restraints upon our lives.
    More and more that is extraneous
obtrudes upon what's noblest in our minds; 635
When we attain this world's material goods,
all better things are called a madman's fancies.
Feelings that before were glorious and vital
grow torpid in the mundane hurly-burly.
    Sustained by hope, Imagination once 640
soared boldly on her boundless flights;
now that our joys are wrecked in time's abyss,
she is content to have a narrow scope. –
Deep in our heart Care quickly makes her nest,
there she engenders secret sorrows 645
and, in that cradle restless, destroys all quiet joy;
the masks she wears are always new—
she may appear as house and home, as wife and child,
as fire, water, dagger, poison;
we live in dread of things that do not happen 650
and keep bemoaning losses that never will occur.
    No peer of gods! I suffer from that truth—

my counterpart's the worm that grovels in the dust
and, as in dust it eats and lives,
is crushed and buried by a vagrant foot.   655
   What else but dust is cramped within
these high and multi-alcoved walls of mine—
the heap of countless, useless things
that in this world of moths beset me?
Is this the place to find the help I need?   660
Should I perhaps peruse a thousand books to learn
that people everywhere have suffered,
that now and then someone was happy? –
You empty skull, why bare your teeth at me
unless to say that once, like mine, your addled brain   665
sought buoyant light but, in its eagerness for truth,
went wretchedly astray beneath the weight of darkness.
You instruments are only mocking me
with wheel and cogs, with cylinder and bridle—
you were to be my key when I stood at the gate,   670
but though it's intricate, the key will lift no bolts.
Nature, mysterious in day's clear light,
lets none remove her veil,
and what she won't discover to your understanding
you can't extort from her with levers and with screws.   675
You ancient implements I've never used are here
only because you served my father's needs. –
You, ancient scroll, have gotten ever grimier
since the dim lamp beside this desk first smouldered.
Far better to have squandered the little I have   680
than to sweat here beneath that little's burden!
If you would own the things your forebears left you,
you first must earn and merit their possession.
What serves no use becomes a heavy burden;
the moment can use only what it itself creates.   685
   But what is there that holds my gaze—
does that vial act as magnet on the eye?
Why do I sense a sudden gentle brightness,
as when in some dark forest moonlight stirs about us?
   Hail, vial of vials! With reverence   690
I take you down—my homage to
the human wit and skill embodied in you.
You essence of kind soporific forces,
you extract of all subtle poisons,
bestow your favors on your master!   695
I see you, and my pain is eased,
I hold you, and my striving lessens—

my turbulence of spirit slowly ebbs away.
I am transported to the open sea,
its surface sparkles down below,   700
and a new day beckons to new shores.
    On airy wings a chariot of fire
sweeps towards me! I am now ready
for the fresh course that lets me pierce the sky
and reach new spheres of pure activity. –   705
Yet, you but now a worm, do you deserve
this grand existence, this celestial joy?
Yes, if you will but turn with firm resolve
your back upon the sun-lit earth!
Be bold and fling the doors asunder   710
which mortals all prefer to pass in silence!
The time has come to prove by deeds that a brave man
is not intimidated by celestial grandeur;
to stand and not to quake before the pit
in which imagination damns itself to torment;   715
to strive on toward that passageway
about whose narrow mouth all hell spouts flame
and, even at the risk of total dissolution,
to take this step with firm serenity.
    Now, long-forgotten cup of flawless crystal,   720
come you down—
forth from your ancient case!
You glistened at ancestral celebrations,
enlivening the solemn guests
who raised you as they pledged each other.   725
The lavish splendor of the artist's pictures,
the drinker's duty to make verses on their meaning
and in one draught to drain the bowl,
bring many memories of nights when I was young.
I shall not offer you to some companion now,   730
nor use your art to demonstrate my wit.
Here is a juice that soon intoxicates,
and whose brown stream now rises to your brim.
The last drink that I have prepared and that I take,
let me with all my heart now pledge it,   735
in solemn salutation, to the Morrow!
    As he places the cup to his lips, church bells and a choir are heard.
CHOIR (*Angels' chorus*). Christ is arisen!
                          Joy to the mortal
                          freed from the baneful,
                          insidious ills   740
                          that man is heir to.

FAUST. What depth of resonance, what clarity of tone,
  can drag the goblet from my lips?
  Do you announce so soon, you muffled bells,
  the first solemnities of Eastertide?   745
  Do you sing now, you choirs, the hymn of consolation
  that by the darkened tomb, from angels' lips,
  proclaimed the certainty of a new covenant?
CHOIR (Women's chorus).
                    With balm and spices
                    we ministered to Him,   750
                    we who were faithful
                    laid down His body,
                    carefully wrapped it
                    in pieces of linen—
                    lo! we discover   755
                    Christ is not here.
CHOIR (Angels' chorus).   Christ is arisen!
                    Blessed the Loving One,
                    He has sustained
                    the grievous ordeal   760
                    that bringeth salvation.
FAUST. Celestial tones, so gently strong,
  why do you seek me here amid the dust?
  Be heard where tender mortals dwell!
  Although I hear your gospel, I lack your faith,   765
  a faith whose dearest child is the miraculous.
  I do not dare aspire to the spheres
  from which your word of grace peals forth,
  and yet these sounds, familiar since my youth,
  summon me now again to life.   770
  There was a time when in the sabbath's solemn quiet
  the kiss of heaven's love would overcome me,
  when there were portents in the choiring chimes,
  and when a prayer was fervent pleasure;
  some strange sweet longing would compel me   775
  to rove through wood and meadow,
  and to a flood of ardent tears
  I'd feel a world arise within me.
  This hymn announced the lively games of youth,
  the happy freedom of spring celebrations;   780
  the memory of childlike feelings now
  keeps me from taking the last, solemn step.
  O sweet celestial songs, sound on—
  my tears well forth, and I am earth's again!

CHOIR (*Disciples' chorus*).

Sublime in this life,   785
He who was buried
now has ascended
to glory on high,
joyous to live again
and still to be active.   790
But we, to our sorrow,
remain on earth's breast;
abandoned disciples,
we languish and suffer—
Master, your happiness   795
makes us shed tears!

(*Angels' chorus*).

Christ is arisen
from the womb of corruption.
Be of good cheer
and get rid of your bonds!   800
You whose deeds praise Him,
who demonstrate charity,
nourish your brethren,
wander and teach them,
promise them bliss—   805
to you is your Master near,
for you He is here!

OUTSIDE THE CITY GATE

A variety of people, coming from the city.

SOME APPRENTICES. Why are you going that way?

OTHERS. We're off to Hunter's Lodge.

THE FIRST. And we're heading out toward the Mill.   810

ONE. I'd recommend the River Tavern.

A SECOND. That's not a very pleasant walk.

THE OTHERS. And what will you do?

A THIRD.   Go with the others.

A FOURTH. Come on up to Burgdorf—there you can count on
   the prettiest girls, the best of beer,   815
   and picking a first-class quarrel too.

A FIFTH. You have a strange idea of fun—
  do you want to be tanned a third time?
  That's not the place for me—it makes me queasy.
SERVANT GIRL. No, no! I'm going back to town.   820
ANOTHER. We'll surely find him near those poplars.
THE FIRST. As if I cared!
  He'll walk with you, and on the green
  he'll only dance with you.
  Your good time is no help to me!   825
THE OTHER. I'm sure he won't be by himself today;
  he said that Curly would come with him.
STUDENT. See that stride! those girls have some life in them!
  Come on, it's up to us to give them company!
  I'm all for good strong beer, tobacco with real flavor—   830
  and maids who have put on their Sunday best.
BURGHER'S DAUGHTER. Do you see those fine looking fellows!
  It really is a shame—
  they could keep perfectly nice company,
  and go running after those servant girls!   835
SECOND STUDENT (to the First).
  Take your time! Back there two more are coming;
  they are not flashily dressed.
  And one is from next door—
  she's someone I really like.
  They may be walking most sedately,   840
  but in the end they'll let us come along.
THE FIRST. Not me! I'd rather not be on my best behavior.
  Hurry now, or we won't catch anything!
  The hand that plies the broom on Saturday
  you'll find on Sundays has the softest touch.   845
BURGHER. No, our new burgomaster doesn't suit me!
  Now he's in, he gets more high-handed every day.
  And what is he doing for the city?
  Aren't things getting steadily worse?
  More than ever we're told what we must do,   850
  and it all costs more than ever before.
BEGGAR (singing).
            Kind gentlemen and ladies fair,
            in handsome clothes and rosy-cheeked,
            please condescend to look at me
            and ease this misery you see!   855
            Don't let me turn my crank in vain!
            Who gladly gives, alone is glad.
            Today, when everyone is idle,
            I hope my work will reap a harvest.

SECOND BURGHER.
    Sundays and holidays there's nothing I like more   860
    than to discuss a war and military matters
    when armies far away—off there in Turkey—
    engage in battle with each other.
    You can stand at the window, drinking
    and watching all the ships that move downstream,   865
    then go cheerfully home in the evening,
    thankful for peace and its advantages.
A THIRD. Neighbor, amen! That goes for me as well—
    let them crack each other's skulls
    and everything be topsy-turvy,   870
    if only nothing changes here at home.
OLD WOMAN (*to the Burghers' Daughters*).
    Oh, how dressed up you are, you pretty young things!
    Who could fail to find you adorable? –
    Don't be so haughty—no offense was meant!
    You know that I can get you what you want.   875
BURGHER'S DAUGHTER. Agatha, come! I don't want anyone to see
    a witch like that and me together—
    though on Saint Andrew's night she let me see
    with my own eyes the man I am to marry.
AGATHA. In her crystal she showed me mine,   880
    one in a group of daring soldiers—
    I keep on looking for him everywhere,
    but he refuses to show up.
SOLDIERS.   Fortresses raising
                battlements high,   885
                girls unrelenting
                in their proud scorn—
                these would I capture!
                Boldness of effort
                pays splendid rewards!   890
                  We let the trumpet
                announce our intention,
                be it love's pleasure
                or be it grand ruin.
                To the assault—   895
                that's how to live!
                The girls and the castles
                will surely surrender.
                Boldness of effort
                pays splendid rewards!   900
                And then the soldiers
                are off and away.

Enter FAUST *and* WAGNER.

FAUST. River and brooks are released from their ice,
   are given new life by the soft gleam of Spring,
   and verdure in valleys gives hope of bliss;   905
   deprived of his strength, old Winter withdrew
   into rugged, unfriendly mountains.
   From them, retreating, he only can launch
   impotent showers of sleet
   over the lands that begin to be green,   910
   but the Sun is hostile to whiteness
   and seeks to enliven with color the forms
   that everywhere strive to develop;
   yet the countryside still has no flowers,
   and so he takes smartly dressed people instead.   915
   Turn around, now we're up here,
   and look back down at the city!
   Out from the depths of its gloomy gate
   a teeming mass of color is surging—
   everyone's eager to get into the sun.   920
   They celebrate the resurrection of their Lord,
   for they themselves are risen;
   from wretched houses and dreary rooms,
   from the bonds of their crafts and professions,
   from the pressing weight of roof and gable,   925
   from the narrow, cramping streets,
   from their churches' night-like solemnity—
   they all have been brought forth into the light.
   Look and see how quickly the crowd
   disperses through the gardens and fields,   930
   how the whole expanse of the river
   carries colorful vessels along,
   and how, so crowded that it almost sinks,
   the last small boat is pushing off.
   Even on distant hillside paths   935
   clothing affords us flashes of color. –
   But now I hear the bustle of the village;
   here is the common man's true heaven,
   here great and small exult contented—
   here I am human and can be myself.   940
WAGNER. To take a walk with you, Professor,
   is a great honor, and edifying too;
   but on my own I wouldn't stray this way,
   detesting as I do whatever's vulgar.
   Fiddling, shouts, the noise of the bowls   945
   are sounds that I do much abhor;

the people carry on as if the fiend possessed them,
then call it entertainment, call it singing.

VILLAGERS (*dancing and singing beneath a linden tree*).

When for the dance the shepherd dressed
in ribbon, wreath, and colored vest   950
he was the height of fashion.
Beneath the tree no room remained,
and all were dancing madly.
Hey-day! hey-day!
and a hey-nonny hey!   955
was what the fiddle played.
    He quickly pushed into the whirl,
but as he did so hit a girl
ungently with his elbow;
a sturdy lass, she turned and said,   960
"You, must you be so clumsy?"
Hey-day! hey-day!
and a hey-nonny hey!
"Pretend you have some manners!"
    But in the ring their feet were light,   965
they danced to left, they danced to right,
with skirt and coat-tail flying.
They got all flushed, were over-warm,
and rested panting arm in arm—
Hey-day! hey-day!   970
and a hey-nonny hey!—
and hips in elbow-hold.
    "And don't you make so free with me—
how many girls as brides-to-be
are victims of deceivers!"   975
He coaxed her nonetheless aside,
but from afar they still heard shouts:
hey-day! hey-day!
and a hey-nonny hey!
and the fiddle under the linden.   980

OLD PEASANT. Professor, it is good of you
  to deign to be with us today
  and, learned doctor though you are,
  to mingle with us ordinary folk.
  And so accept our finest tankard,   985
  which we have filled afresh for you;
  I pledge it to you, and I voice the wish
  that it not only slake your thirst,
  but also that each drop it holds
  be one more day that's added to your life.   990

FAUST. Your tankard I accept and its refreshment
    with thanks and wishes of good health to all.
        The VILLAGERS *form a circle about* FAUST *and* WAGNER.
OLD PEASANT. It is indeed appropriate
    that on this festive day you come among us;
    as well we know, when times were bad   995
    you always were disposed to help us!
    Many a man is here alive
    who, at the time your father stopped the plague,
    was snatched by him at the last moment
    from the burning frenzy of his fever.   1000
    You too—you were a young man then—
    would enter every stricken house
    and yet, although they carried off so many corpses,
    you always would come out unharmed,
    surviving every trial and test—   1005
    by the Helper above our helper was helped.
VILLAGERS. Good health to one who's tried and true,
    and may he be our help for many years to come!
FAUST. Offer your homage to the Helper above
    Who teaches that we all should help each other.   1010
        FAUST *and* WAGNER *resume their walk.*
WAGNER. What feelings, sir, you must derive
    from the respect of all these people for your greatness!
    How happy is the man who is allowed
    to turn his talents to such good account!
    Some father points you out to his young boy,   1015
    and people ask your name, stand still and crowd about you,
    the fiddle stops, the dancers pause.
    As you move on, they stand in rows
    and fling their caps into the air—
    a little more, and they would genuflect   1020
    as if the blessed sacrament were going by!
FAUST. It's but a few more steps up to that stone;
    here we can rest a while from walking.
    I've often sat alone here with my thoughts
    and agonized in prayer and fasting.   1025
    Still full of hope and firm of faith,
    I wept and sighed and wrung my hands
    believing that such efforts could extort
    from God in heaven termination of the plague.
    Now, in the people's praise I only hear derision.   1030
    If you could read my soul and see
    how little either son or father
    deserved such approbation!

My father was a worthy commoner
who in good faith, but in his own eccentric way,   1035
labored at fanciful speculations
about the mystic spheres of nature,
and who, together with his adepts,
would shut himself within his blackened kitchen
and mix contrary elements   1040
according to recipes that never seemed to end.
There a mercurial suitor, the Red Lion,
would in a tepid bath be married to the Lily,
then both be driven by tormenting flames
out of one bridal chamber to another;   1045
when in the beaker the Young Queen
at last appeared, a mass of color,
that was our medicine—the patients died,
and no one thought to ask if anyone was healed.
And so, with diabolical electuaries,   1050
we ravaged in these hills and valleys
with greater fury than the plague.
I have myself dosed thousands with the poison;
they wasted away—and I must live to hear
the brazen murderers adulated.   1055
WAGNER. How can you be disturbed by that!
Is it not sufficient for an honest man
to practice with punctilious exactness
the skills of the profession he's been taught?
If, in your youth, you venerate your father,   1060
you're pleased to take what he can give you;
if you, as man, augment our knowledge,
your son may reach an even higher mark.
FAUST. Happy the man who still can hope
to swim to safety in this sea of error.   1065
What we don't know is what we really need,
and what we know fulfills no need at all. –
But we must not let such dark thoughts spoil
the wealth of beauty that this hour can afford!
See how, against the green about them,   1070
cottages gleam in the blazing sunset.
The sun moves on, retreats, and, after day is done,
hastens away to nurture life elsewhere—
if only I had wings to raise me from the ground
so that I might pursue it on its course forever!   1075
I'd see the silent world below
in an eternal evening-radiance,
all peaks aflame, all valleys hushed,

the silver brook debouching into golden rivers;
no savage mountain or its many gorges   1080
would then impede my godlike passage—
astonished eyes survey the ocean now
and inlets that the sun has warmed.
At last the sungod seems about to sink from view,
but then my urge to follow is again aroused;   1085
I hasten on, to drink its everlasting light,
the day before me and, behind me, night,
the sky above me and, beneath, the sea.
A glorious dream—meanwhile the sun is gone!
Alas! it is so hard to find corporeal wings   1090
that match those of the human mind.
Yet in us all there is an innate urge
to rise aloft and soar along
when, lost in the blue space above us,
the lark pours forth its vibrant song,   1095
when high above fir-covered crags
the eagle floats on outspread wing,
and when above the plains and lakes
the crane seeks out its native place.

WAGNER. I've often had my momentary fancies,   1100
    but that's an urge I never yet have felt.
    One quickly gets his fill of seeing woods and fields,
    and I shall never envy any bird its wings.
    How different is the way the pleasures of the mind
    transport us from book to book, from page to page!   1105
    Then winter nights are pleasant and congenial,
    a vital happiness gives warmth to your whole being,
    and if you do unroll some precious manuscript
    celestial joy is yours on earth.

FAUST. You only know one driving force,   1110
    and may you never seek to know the other!
    Two souls, alas! reside within my breast,
    and each is eager for a separation:
    in throes of coarse desire, one grips
    the earth with all its senses;   1115
    the other struggles from the dust
    to rise to high ancestral spheres.
      If there are spirits in the air
    who hold domain between this world and heaven—
    out of your golden haze descend,   1120
    transport me to a new and brighter life!
    If I but had a magic cloak

that could bear me away to exotic places,
I'd not exchange it for the choicest garments,
not even for the mantle of a king.   1125
WAGNER. Do not invoke the too familiar host
that floods the murky air,
threatening mankind from every quarter
with danger in a thousand forms.
Out of the North the fanged spirits   1130
come to press upon you with their pointed tongues;
from the East they make their withering advance
to feed upon your lungs;
and if the South should send them from the desert
to heap fire upon fire about your head,   1135
the West will bring a troop that first refreshes,
then drowns you and your fields and meadows.
They are all ears and eager to do harm,
gladly obey because they gladly cheat us,
pretend that they are sent from heaven,   1140
and murmur like angels when telling their lies.
   But let us go! Already all is gray,
the air grown cool, the fog descending:
when evening comes, we know a home's full worth. –
Why are you standing still and staring off there?   1145
What can so impress you in this failing light?
FAUST. Do you see the black dog scour the grain that sprouts
                                    from the stubble?
WAGNER. I saw it long ago, but thought it unimportant.
FAUST. Observe it well! What do you think the creature is?
WAGNER. A poodle that in the usual way   1150
   goes to the trouble of tracking its master!
FAUST. Do you notice how it races around us
   in a great spiral, getting closer and closer?
   And unless I'm mistaken, an eddy of fire
   follows closely wherever it goes.   1155
WAGNER. A mere black poodle is what I see—
   you, I suspect, some optical illusion.
FAUST. It's my impression that, with quiet magic, the dog
   is laying about our feet the snares of future bondage.
WAGNER. I see it run around us, timid and unsure   1160
   because it sees two strangers, not its master.
FAUST. The circle is narrowing, the dog's close at hand!
WAGNER. You see a dog, there's no spectre there.
   It snarls and hesitates, lies down on its belly,
   it wags its tail—all just what dogs do.   1165

FAUST. Come and join us! Come here!
WAGNER. It's a silly sort of creature:
  if you stand still, it sits attentive;
  speak to it, and it's all over you;
  let something drop, and it will fetch it—   1170
  even jump in the water for your cane.
FAUST. No doubt you're right: I find
  no trace of mind—it's only training.
WAGNER. When a dog has been well taught,
  even a man of sense can like it.   1175
  So apt a pupil of our students
  indeed deserves to be in your good graces.   [*Exeunt through city gate.*

FAUST'S STUDY

          Enter FAUST, *with the poodle.*
FAUST.   I've left behind the fields and meadows
          that night now veils in darkness—
          night, whose presentient holy dread   1180
          awakes in us our better soul.
          Forces of passion are lulled to sleep
          as restless action ceases;
          love of our fellow man is rousing,
          and with it love of God as well.   1185
Easy, Poodle! Stop running about!
Why are you sniffing the sill of that door?
Lie down behind the stove—
here's my best cushion!
Your running and jumping along the road   1190
entertained us out on the hillside,
now let me entertain you in my turn—
a welcome guest if you'll stay quiet.
          Ah, when within our narrow chamber
          the friendly lamp again is lit,   1195
          our inner being too is brightened—
          our heart, that then can know itself.
          The voice of reason is heard again,
          and hope again begins to flower;
          we thirst for life-giving waters,   1200
          we long for life's fountainhead.
Poodle, don't growl! that animal sound
jars with the sacred harmonies

that now encompass my whole being.
We take it for granted that people jeer   1205
at what they do not understand,
and groan in the presence of goodness and beauty,
which often just makes them embarrassed.
Must a dog, like them, snarl at such things?
    Alas! despite the best intentions, I feel   1210
contentment ebbing in my breast already.
Why must its stream run dry so soon
and leave us thirsting once again,
as has been the case with me so often?
Still, this want can be supplied: 1215
we have been taught to find great worth in what's celestial;
we pine and yearn for revelation,
whose fire burns in the New Testament
with dignity and beauty not elsewhere matched.
I feel impelled to open the text on which all rests   1220
and, deeply moved, properly translate
the sacred Greek original
into my own dear native tongue.
            (*Opening a large volume and preparing to write.*)
It is written, "In the beginning was the *Word.*"
How soon I'm stopped! Who'll help me to go on?   1225
I cannot concede that *words* have such high worth
and must, if properly inspired,
translate the term some other way.
It is written: "In the beginning was the *Mind.*"
Reflect with care upon this first line,   1230
and do not let your pen be hasty!
Can it be *mind* that makes all operate?
I'd better write: "In the beginning was the *Power!*"
Yet, even as I write this down,
something warns me not to keep it.   1235
My spirit prompts me, now I see a solution
and boldly write: "In the beginning was the *Act.*"
    If I'm to share the room with you,
Poodle, stop your baying,
stop that barking!   1240
In these close quarters I can't bear
to keep so bothersome a companion.
One of us—either you or I—
will have to leave the room:
I'm sorry to be no longer hospitable,   1245
the door is open, you're free to go.
But what do I see!

Is that a natural occurrence,
illusion or reality?
How long and broad my poodle's becoming!   1250
It's rising prodigiously—
that is not a canine form!
What a ghastly thing I've brought into the house!
Hippopotamus-like it looks,
with fire-red eyes and frightful jaws.   1255
But I will master you!—
for such a hybrid spawned in Hell
Solomon's Key will do quite well.

SPIRITS (*in the passage*). One of us inside is caught—
                stay outside and join him not!   1260
                Like the fox in an iron snare,
                a sly old devil's quivering there.
                Now take good heed:
                hover high, hover low,
                to and fro,   1265
                and from durance he'll get free!
                You can assist him,
                don't leave him victim—
                long we owe him, every one,
                many favors he has done.   1270

FAUST. Merely to challenge the creature
I must employ the Spell of Four:
                Glow, Salamander!
                Undine, meander!
                Sylph, disappear!   1275
                Gnome, toil away here!
None who lacks knowledge—
of the Elements,
of their powers
and attributes—   1280
ever should claim
to be master of Spirits.
                O vanish in fire's gleam,
                Salamander!
                Merge with a murmuring stream,   1285
                O Undine!
                In meteoric beauty shine,
                O Sylph!
                Help about the house as friend,
                Incubus, Incubus! –   1290
                Spirit, emerge, that I may end.

None of the Four
hides in the creature.
It lies all still and sneers disdain—
till now I've failed to cause it pain.   1295
   But you shall hear me
cast a stronger spell:
         Fellow, if you be
         a fugitive from Hell,
         behold the Sign   1300
         before which incline
         the legions of darkness!
It starts to swell—its hair's on end.
         Being damned and reprobate,
         can you read this token?—   1305
         Him that never was create,
         Him whose name must not be spoken,
         Who pervades the universe,
         though transpierced by lance accursed.
Driven back of the stove by the spell,   1310
it is dilating to elephant size;
filling every bit of space,
it's now about to melt away as mist.
   Stop ascending to the ceiling!
Lie down at your master's feet!   1315
Now you know I make no empty threats.
I can scorch you with sacred fire!
Do not wait until you see
the glowing light of the Trinity,
do not wait until you see   1320
the mightiest of all my arts!

Enter MEPHISTOPHELES *from behind the stove as the mist subsides; he is*
dressed as a goliard.

MEPHISTOPHELES. What's all the noise? Sir, how can I be of service?
FAUST. So that is what was hidden in the poodle:
   a wandering scholar! The *casus* is amusing.
MEPHISTOPHELES. My compliments to your learning, sir!   1325
   you made me sweat profusely.
FAUST. What is your name?
MEPHISTOPHELES.   That seems a petty question
   from one who is so scornful of the Word
   and who, aloof from mere appearance,
   only aspires to plumb the depths of essence.   1330
FAUST. The essence of such as you, good sir,

can usually be inferred from names
that, like Lord of Flies, Destroyer, Liar,
reveal it all too plainly.
But still I ask, who are you?

MEPHISTOPHELES.   A part of that force   1335
  which, always willing evil, always produces good.

FAUST. That is a riddle. What does it mean?

MEPHISTOPHELES. I am the Spirit of Eternal Negation,
  and rightly so, since all that gains existence
  is only fit to be destroyed; that's why   1340
  it would be best if nothing ever got created.
  Accordingly, my essence is
  what you call sin, destruction,
  or—to speak plainly—Evil.

FAUST. You call yourself a part, yet stand before me whole?   1345

MEPHISTOPHELES. I only speak the sober truth.
  You mortals, microcosmic fools,
  may like to think of yourselves as complete,
  but I'm a part of the Part that first was all,
  part of the Darkness that gave birth to Light—   1350
  proud Light, that now contests the senior rank
  of Mother Night, disputes her rights to space;
  yet it does not succeed, however much it strives,
  because it can't escape material fetters.
  Light emanates from matter, lends it beauty,   1355
  but matter checks the course of light,
  and so I hope it won't be long
  before they both have been annihilated.

FAUST. Now I see your meritorious function!
  You can't achieve wholesale destruction   1360
  and so you've started out at retail.

MEPHISTOPHELES. And to be candid, the business doesn't thrive.
  This awkward world, this Something
  which confronts as foe my Nothing—
  despite all efforts up to now,   1365
  I've failed to get the better of it:
  in spite of tempest, earthquake, wave, and fire,
  ocean and land are unperturbed!
  And as for that stupid stuff, the spawn of beast and man,
  there's no way to make inroads on it.   1370
  To think how many I've already buried,
  yet fresh young blood still keeps on circulating.
  On and on—it could make anyone see red!
  From air, from water, and from earth
  a myriad of germs crawl forth   1375

in dryness, moisture, heat, or cold!
If I had not kept fire for myself,
there would be nothing I could call my own.

FAUST. And so you raise your frigid fist,
    clenched in futile diabolic malice,   1380
    against the power of ever-stirring,
    beneficent creativity!
    You would do well, strange Son of Chaos,
    to try some other enterprise.

MEPHISTOPHELES. We'll really have to give some thought to this;   1385
    let's talk about it more at our next meetings.
    May I assume that I am now excused?

FAUST. I don't see why you ask permission.
    Now that I've made your acquaintance,
    you may pay me a visit whenever you wish.   1390
    The window's here, and here the door;
    a flue would suit you quite as well.

MEPHISTOPHELES. There's a confession I must make.
    A little obstacle prevents my walking out:
    the incubus-foot on the sill of your door!   1395

FAUST. You are distressed by the pentagram?
    Well, tell me then, you Son of Hell,
    how you got in while subject to its spell,
    and how a spirit such as you was tricked.

MEPHISTOPHELES. Look carefully and you will find it's badly drawn: 1400
    one point (the one that faces outward)
    is, as you see, not quite completely closed.

FAUST. That is indeed a lucky chance,
    and so—you claim—you are my prisoner?
    This is a triumph that was not intended!   1405

MEPHISTOPHELES. The poodle noticed nothing when it bounded in,
    but now the situation's changed:
    the demon's caught inside your house.

FAUST. Why don't you go through the window, then?

MEPHISTOPHELES. For demons and for spectres there's a rule: 1410
    where they've got in is where they must go out.
    The former's up to us, the latter's not in our control.

FAUST. So even Hell is bound by laws?
    I like your implication that one could
    safely make contracts with you gentlemen!   1415

MEPHISTOPHELES. You can be sure of getting all we promise,
    without a single niggardly deduction.
    But it takes time to work out such arrangements,
    so let's discuss the matter fairly soon.
    Right now, however, I urgently request   1420

that this one time you give me leave to leave.
FAUST. Do stay another moment and, before you go,
  let me hear more of your fine stories.
MEPHISTOPHELES. It's time you let me go! I'll call again soon,
  and then you can ask any question you wish.   1425
FAUST. I didn't lay a snare for you!
  You put yourself into the trap.
  A devil in hand is well worth keeping:
  it takes a good while to catch one again.
MEPHISTOPHELES. If it's your wish, of course I'm glad to stay   1430
  and keep you company—but only if
  you'll let me use the arts in which I'm skilled
  to entertain you in a proper way.
FAUST. I've no objection, and leave the choice to you.
  Just see to it your arts are entertaining!   1435
MEPHISTOPHELES. My friend, from this conjuncture you'll obtain
  more pleasure of a sensuous kind
  than from a whole monotonous year.
  What you hear these gentle spirits sing,
  the lovely pictures that they bring,   1440
  are more than empty magic-show.
  Your sense of smell will be delighted,
  your palate, too, will be excited,
  and then your sense of touch ecstatic glow.
    For preparation there's no need;   1445
  you have me here, so just proceed!
SPIRITS.   Vanish, dark arches,
                     high but confining!
                     Let azure blueness,
                     brighter, more friendly,   1450
                     show from on high!
                     Would that the dark clouds
                     quickly departed!
                      Little stars twinkle;
                     planets among them   1455
                     gleam in the sky.
                     Beauty ethereal—
                     youths truly heavenly,
                     gracefully bending—
                     floats lightly past.   1460
                     Fond yearnings follow
                     them on their paths:
                     fluttering bits
                     of garments abandoned
                     brighten the landscape,   1465

brighten the bower
where lost in illusion
lover unites
with lover for ever.
   Bowers are vineyards!   1470
Tendrils luxuriate!
Grapes hanging heavy
hasten to fill
the vats that will press them;
wines, effervescent,   1475
hasten as brooks
through crystalline rocks
that never are sullied,
soon leave behind
the arbors above,   1480
becoming broad lakes
that mirror and nurture
hills and their verdure.
   Birds of the air,
imbibing delight,   1485
fly on toward the sun,
fly off to far islands,
brilliant and bright,
deceptively rocking   1490
on cradling waters—
islands with meadows
where we see dancers
gathered in groups
and finding amusement   1495
out in the country.
Lo! some are climbing
over the highlands,
others are swimming
in quiet lakes   1500
or float through the air—
all seeking life's fullness,
hoping to find
the far-distant star
of rapture and bliss.   1505

MEPHISTOPHELES. The rest, my insubstantial lads, can keep;
  you've done your duty, he's lulled to sleep,
  and for your concert I am much obliged. –
  But you're not yet the man to hold a demon captive! –
  Encompass him with lovely apparitions,   1510
  plunge him into a sea of mad illusion!

But to undo this doorsill-magic,
tooth of rat is what I need.
I will not have to conjure long;
the one I hear scurrying will quickly hear me.   1515
    The Lord of Rats and Lord of Mice,
Lord of the Flies, Frogs, Bugs, and Lice,
summons you to venture forth
and, at the spot he dabs with oil,
to nibble away the wood of the sill.   1520
So soon you come bounding into view!
To work, at once! The point that cast the spell
to keep me here is on the very outer edge.
Just one more bite and you'll be done. –
Now, Faustus, till we meet again, dream on!   [*Exit.*   1525
FAUST (*awakening*). Have I been duped once more?
    Are life-giving forces so quickly spent—
    did a lying dream invent my devil,
    and did a poodle simply run away?

FAUST'S STUDY

FAUST *and, heard offstage,* MEPHISTOPHELES.

FAUST. A knock? Come in! Who bothers me this time?   1530
MEPHISTOPHELES. It's me.
FAUST.   Come in!
MEPHISTOPHELES.   That must be said three times.
FAUST. Come in, then!
MEPHISTO (*entering*). Now you've done it right!
    I hope we may get on well together;
    to cure you of your anxious fancies,
    I've come as a young nobleman   1535
    in scarlet suit with golden trim;
    my cloak is heavy corded silk,
    there's a cock's-feather on my hat
    and, at my side, a long, sharp sword.
    Take my advice and get yourself   1540
    an outfit similar to mine,
    so that, released from bondage, you can learn
    what life and freedom really are.
FAUST. No matter what I wear, I hardly can escape
    the torment of a life confined to earth.   1545
    I am too old to live for pleasure only,

too young to be without desire.
What can I hope for from this world?
You must abstain, refrain, renounce—
this is the everlasting song in every ear,   1550
one that, our whole life long,
we hear each hour hoarsely singing.
When morning comes, I always wake in terror
and feel like shedding bitter tears   1555
because the day I see will not fulfill
a single wish of mine before it's over,
will dampen any faintest hope of pleasure
by its capricious strictures,
and with a thousand petty matters   1560
will stifle the creative urge that stirs my heart.
At nightfall, too, I'm filled with apprehension
when it is time to go to bed,
for there as well I'll fail to gain repose
and will be frightened by wild dreams.   1565
The god that dwells within my breast
can deeply stir my inmost being;
the one that governs all my faculties
cannot realize its purposes;
and so for me existence is a burden,   1570
death to be welcomed, and this life detested.
MEPHISTOPHELES. And yet Death never is a wholly welcome guest.
FAUST. Happy the victor on whose brow
Death binds the blood-flecked wreath of laurel!
And happy he who, after the mad dance,   1575
is found by Death in love's embrace!
What ecstasy to feel that lofty spirit's might—
if only, then, my soul had left this body!
MEPHISTOPHELES. Still, someone, on that Easter night,
failed to imbibe a certain brownish fluid.   1580
FAUST. You seem to like to play the spy.
MEPHISTOPHELES. I may not be omniscient, but I do know quite a lot.
FAUST. Though, then, sweet music long familiar
rescued me from a host of terrors,
and echoes of an earlier, happier time   1585
confused what still remained of childhood feelings,
now I can only curse all the enticements
that delude my soul with cheating visions,
all powers of persuasion and deception
that hold it here within its dreary cave!   1590
Cursed be, to start, the high opinion
that the mind has of itself!

Cursed be what as appearance
intrudes on and deludes our senses!
and cursed be the falseness of our dreams,   1595
their empty promise of a lasting name!
Cursed be what flatters us as things we own,
as wife and child, as fields our workmen plow!
Cursed be Mammon too, both when he, with his treasures,
incites us to bold enterprise   1600
and when, to provide us idle pleasure,
he cushions us a bed of ease!
A curse upon the nectar of the vine!
A curse upon love's highest favors!
A curse on hope! a curse on faith!   1605
but cursed be patience most of all!

CHORUS OF SPIRITS (invisible).
          Grief and woe!
          A beautiful world
          that, by your violence,
          has been destroyed,   1610
          collapses and shatters,
          crushed by a demigod!
          Into the Void
          we bear off the fragments,
          singing a dirge   1615
          for beauty now lost.
          Build it again,
          O great child of Earth,
          within your own bosom
          build it anew   1620
          in still greater splendor!
          Take a fresh course
          and, no longer despairing,
          start a new life;
          and may other songs   1625
          welcome it in!

MEPHISTOPHELES. Those little creatures
          are my young dependents,
          wise for their years;
          fun and action—that's their counsel!   1630
          They'd like to get you
          out into the world,
          away from a solitude
          that stifles all life. –
Be done with toying with your sorrows   1635
that, vulture-like, consume your being;

the worst society there is could show you
that you are just another human being.
Not that I mean you should be thrust
among the rabble!   1640
I'm not one of the great myself;
but should you wish
to make your way through life with me,
I'll gladly place myself at your disposal
here and now.   1645
I will be your companion
and, if I suit you,
become your servant and your slave!
FAUST. And in return for this, what am I to do?
MEPHISTO. You've lots of time until that needs to be considered.   1650
FAUST. Oh no! The devil is an egoist
    and is not apt, for love of God,
    to offer anyone assistance.
    State in clear terms what you expect—
    there's trouble in the household otherwise.   1655
MEPHISTOPHELES. I'll bind myself to serve you *here,*
    be at your beck and call without respite;
    and if or when we meet again *beyond,*
    then you will do the same for me.
FAUST. With the Beyond I cannot be much bothered;   1660
    once you annihilate this world,
    the other can have its turn at existing.
    This earth's the source of all my joys,
    and this sun shines upon my sorrows;
    if ever I can be divorced from them,   1665
    it cannot matter what then happens.
    I do not want to hear still more discussion
    of whether there'll be future loves and hates,
    and whether also, in those spheres,
    there's an Above or a Below.   1670
MEPHISTOPHELES. You can, on these conditions, take the risk.
    Commit yourself, and you'll soon have the pleasure
    of seeing here what my skills are;
    I'll give you things no mortal's ever seen.
FAUST. And what have you to give, poor devil!   1675
    Has any human spirit and its aspirations
    ever been understood by such as you?
    Of course you've food that cannot satisfy,
    gold that, when held, will liquify
    quicksilverlike as it turns red,   1680
    games at which none can ever win,

a girl who, even in my arms, will with her eyes
pledge her affections to another,
the godlike satisfaction of great honor
that like a meteor is gone at once.   1685
Show me the fruit that, still unplucked, will rot
and trees that leaf each day anew!
MEPHISTOPHELES. These commissions don't dismay me,
  I can oblige you with such marvels.
  But, friend, there also comes a time when we prefer   1690
  to savor something good in peace and quiet.
FAUST. If on a bed of sloth I ever lie contented,
  may I be done for then and there!
  If ever you, with lies and flattery,
  can lull me into self-complacency   1695
  or dupe me with a life of pleasure,
  may that day be the last for me!
  This is my wager!
MEPHISTOPHELES.   Here's my hand!
FAUST.   And mine again!
  If I should ever say to any moment:
    Tarry, remain!—you are so fair!   1700
  then you may lay your fetters on me,
  then I will gladly be destroyed!
  Then they can toll the passing bell,
  your obligations then be ended—
  the clock may stop, its hand may fall,   1705
  and time at last for me be over!
MEPHISTOPHELES. Consider well your words—we'll not forget them.
FAUST. Nor should you! What I've said
  is not presumptuous blasphemy.
  If I stagnate, I am a slave—   1710
  why should I care if yours or someone else's?
MEPHISTOPHELES. This very day at the doctoral banquet,
  I'll do my duty as your servant.
  One other matter!—as insurance
  I must request a line or two in writing.   1715
FAUST. So you want something written, too, you pedant?
  Have you not ever known a man whose word was good?
  Is it not enough that my spoken word
  grants perpetual title to my days?
  Do not the tides of life race on unceasing—   1720
  how could a promise obligate me!
  But still our hearts have their illusions,
  and who would care to live without them?
  Happy the man whose heart is loyal to his pledges—

he'll not be grieved by any sacrifice they ask.   1725
And yet, a parchment document that bears a seal—
that is a spectre that all people shun.
The word begins to die before it's left the pen,
and wax and goatskin take control.
What do you, evil spirit, want from me—   1730
marble or brass, foolscap or parchment?
Am I to write with chisel, stylus, pen?
You are at liberty to choose.
MEPHISTOPHELES. How can you work yourself up so quickly
to this heat of rhetorical exaggeration?   1735
Any small scrap of paper is all right.
A tiny drop of blood will do to sign your name.
FAUST. If this is all that you require,
we may as well go through with the tomfoolery.
MEPHISTOPHELES. Blood is a very special juice.   1740
FAUST. You need not fear that I will break this contract!
It is to strive with all my might
that I am promising to do.
My self-esteem was overly inflated—
my proper place is on your level.   1745
The Great Spirit rejected me with scorn,
and Nature's doors are closed against me.
The thread of thought is torn asunder,
and I am surfeited with knowledge still.
Let us sate the fervors of passion   1750
in depths of sensuality!
May your magic be ready at any time
to show me miracles whose veil cannot be lifted!
Let's plunge into the torrents of time,
into the whirl of eventful existence!   1755
There, as chance wills,
let pain and pleasure,
success and frustration, alternate;
unceasing activity alone reveals our worth.
MEPHISTOPHELES. You are not limited in any way.   1760
You can sample whatever you like
and snatch what suits your passing fancy—
nothing you like will give you indigestion.
I urge you: help yourself and don't be bashful!
FAUST. You heard me say that pleasure doesn't matter.   1765
Excitement, poignant happiness, love-hate,
quickening frustration—to these I'm consecrated!
Henceforth my heart, cured of its thirst for knowledge,
will welcome pain and suffering

and I'm resolved my inmost being   1770
shall share in what's the lot of all mankind,
that I shall understand their heights and depths,
shall fill my heart with all their joys and griefs,
and so expand my self to theirs
and, like them, suffer shipwreck too.   1775
MEPHISTOPHELES. Take someone's word who has been chewing
on this tough morsel many thousand years:
no one, from cradle to the bier,
is able to digest that stale and sour dough!
This universe—believe a devil—   1780
was made for no one but a god!
God lives surrounded by eternal glory,
He cast us into utter darkness,
and you must be content with day-and-night.
FAUST. I've told you what I want!
MEPHISTOPHELES.   Then well and good!   1785
Yet, there's one point that troubles me:
that human life's so short, and art is long.
I think that you could use a bit of guidance.
Go get yourself a poet-partner
and let his fancy have free rein   1790
to heap upon your honored head
all virtues and distinctions:
a lion's heart,
the quickness of the stag,
hot Italian blood,   1795
the North's reliability.
Let him provide you with the secret arts
of wedding magnanimity to malice,
of scheming how to fall in love
with the impulsive ardor of the young.   1800
I wouldn't mind meeting such a fellow myself
and would grant him the title of Sir Microcosm.
FAUST. What am I, then, if there is no attaining
those crowning heights of humanness
toward which my every fiber's straining?   1805
MEPHISTOPHELES. The upshot is: you are just what you are.
Pile wigs with countless curls upon your head,
wear shoes that lift you up an ell,
and still you will remain just what you are.
FAUST. How futile it has been to have amassed   1810
a treasury of human thought and knowledge!
Even when I finally stop and rest,
I feel no source of renewed strength within me;

I have not grown one whit in stature,
I am no nearer to the Infinite.   1815
MEPHISTOPHELES. You're looking at these matters, my dear sir,
  the way that ordinary people do;
  we've got to be a bit more clever,
  to get some joy from life before it's fled.
  Good heavens! It is obvious your hands and feet,   1820
  your head—and other parts—belong to you;
  but all the things I have free use of,
  don't they belong to me as fully?
  If I can pay for six strong horses,
  do I not own their power?—   1825
  as if my legs were twenty-four
  I run about and am important.
  So don't be glum! Stop all this brooding,
  be off with me at once into the world!
  Take my word for it, anyone who thinks too much   1830
  is like an animal that in a barren heath
  some evil spirit drives around in circles
  while all about lie fine green pastures.
FAUST. How do we start?
MEPHISTOPHELES.   We simply leave.
  What sort of torture chamber have we here?   1835
  What kind of life do you call this,
  boring yourself and your beardless youths?
  Leave that to your colleague Paunch!
  Why knock yourself out making bricks of straw?
  If any case, you cannot risk   1840
  telling the boys the best of what you know. –
  I hear one now out in the hall.
FAUST. I cannot bring myself to face him.
MEPHISTOPHELES. The poor fellow has had a long wait,
  he mustn't leave without some consolation.   1845
  Just let me have your cap and gown—
(*Changing clothes.*) this costume's certain to become me—
  and rely on my common sense!
  A quarter of an hour's all I need;
  meanwhile, get ready for our glorious expedition!   1850
                                          [*Exit* FAUST.
MEPHISTOPHELES. Scorn learning, if you must, and reason,
  the highest faculty mankind possesses,
  let your fondness for self-deception
  involve you deeper still in magic and illusion,
  and it's dead certain you'll be mine! –   1855
  Fate has endowed him with a spirit

that cannot curb its onward rush
and that, precipitately striving,
overleaps the joys that this world affords it.
I'll drag him through a life of riot,   1860
through meaningless inanities;
he'll writhe, be paralyzed, and when he's stuck,
before his avid, starving lips
I'll dangle food and drink;
he'll plead in vain for nourishment,   1865
and even if he had no contract with the devil,
he'd end up ruined anyhow!
                    Enter a STUDENT.
STUDENT. I've only been here a short time,
    and come to pay you my respects,
    and to consult a man whose name is mentioned   1870
    in tones of reverence by all.
MEPHISTOPHELES. Your courtesy is much appreciated!
    As you can see, I'm just a man like all the rest.
    Have you paid any other calls as yet?
STUDENT. I hope you'll please be my advisor.   1875
    I'm here with all the best intentions,
    am energetic and in no great need of money;
    my mother hesitated to send me away;
    now I'm out here, I really want to learn.
MEPHISTOPHELES. Then you have come to the right place.   1880
STUDENT. To tell the truth, I'd like to go on somewhere else:
    I really don't feel comfortable
    inside these walls, within these halls.
    It's awfully cramped, and one can't see
    a bit of green, a single tree,   1885
    and in those classrooms with their benches
    I can no longer hear or see or think.
MEPHISTOPHELES. It's simply a matter of what you're used to.
    Just as an infant is at first
    reluctant to take its mother's breast,   1890
    at which it soon feeds eagerly,
    so will you, with each successive day,
    be happier at Wisdom's breasts.
STUDENT. I'm eager to be at her bosom;
    but tell me, please, how can I get there?   1895
MEPHISTOPHELES. Before you go on, would you first say
    in what faculty you intend to study?
STUDENT. I'd like to be a proper scholar
    and have a comprehensive knowledge
    of what there is on earth and in the sky,   1900

of nature and all the branches of learning.
MEPHISTOPHELES. You certainly are on the right track;
  but you must be sure that nothing distracts you.
STUDENT. Body and soul I'm bent upon it;
  and yet, I must admit, I wouldn't mind   1905
  some free time and recreation
  when there's a pleasant summer holiday.
MEPHISTOPHELES. Don't waste your time, it's gone so fast,
  but arranging it right will save you plenty of it.
  Accordingly, dear friend, my first advice   1910
  is that you hear the *Collegium Logicum.*
  The course will discipline your mind
  and lace it tight in iron-boots
  so that it will no longer rush
  headlong along the paths of thought   1915
  or, like a will-o'-the-wisp perhaps,
  wander at random everywhere.
  Days on end will be used to teach you
  that what you once did as a single act,
  as easily as you eat or drink,   1920
  must really be done as one-two-three.
  Although in fact the fabric of thought
  is like a masterpiece of weaving,
  for which one treadle moves a thousand threads
  as back and forth the shuttles fly   1925
  and threads move quicker than the eye
  and a single stroke makes a thousand ties,
  nonetheless the philosopher comes
  and proves to you it had to be thus:
  the first was so, the second so,   1930
  and hence the third and fourth are so;
  but if there were no first and second
  the third and fourth could never exist.
  Students applaud this everywhere,
  but fail to master the weaver's art.   1935
  To understand some living thing and to describe it,
  the student starts by ridding it of its spirit;
  he then holds all its parts within his hand
  except, alas! for the spirit that bound them together—
  which chemists, unaware they're being ridiculous,   1940
  denominate *encheiresin naturae.*
STUDENT. I don't quite follow what you're saying.
MEPHISTOPHELES. It will be much easier very soon,
  when you have learned the use of syllogisms
  and how to put all things in their right classes.   1945

STUDENT. I am as stupefied by this
   as if there were a mill-wheel turning in my head.
MEPHISTOPHELES. After this, and before anything else,
   you've got to tackle metaphysics!
   Make sure you grasp in all its profundity   1950
   what never was meant for the human brain;
   but whether it was or whether it wasn't,
   there's always some high-sounding word available.
   But in your first semester, most of all,
   you must be faithfully methodical!   1955
   You'll have five classes every day;
   when the bell rings be in your seat!
   Be well prepared before you go
   and memorize each section you're assigned
   so that, once you are there, you can make sure   1960
   nothing is said but what is in the book;
   but by all means keep diligently writing
   as if you heard the Holy Ghost dictating!
STUDENT. That's nothing you need tell me twice!
   I see how useful it will be—   1965
   what you've got down in black and white
   you can take home and then be sure of it.
MEPHISTOPHELES. Now tell me what's the faculty you've chosen!
STUDENT. I can't quite bring myself to take up law.
MEPHISTOPHELES. Nor can I blame you very much for that,   1970
   knowing as I do the state it's in today.
   Statutes and laws, like inherited sickness,
   are languidly transmitted
   from one generation to the next
   and slowly shift from one place to another.   1975
   Sense becomes nonsense, or a benefit a nuisance—
   it's just too bad you're a descendant!
   As for the right that's ours by birth,
   alas! that never is at issue.
STUDENT. You make my own aversion greater.   1980
   Happy he, who has you as teacher!
   Now I'm almost willing to study theology.
MEPHISTOPHELES. I wouldn't want you to be led astray.
   To tell the truth about this branch of learning,
   it's hard to keep from taking the wrong course,   1985
   and there's a lot of latent poison in it
   that hardly differs from the medicines it offers.
   Here, too, it's best to listen to a single teacher
   and swear by every word he utters.
   Make it a principle to give words your allegiance!   1990

You then will enter by the one safe gate
into the temple of certitude.
STUDENT. But there must be ideas behind the words.
MEPHISTOPHELES. That's true, but do not fret too much about it,
since it's precisely when ideas are lacking   1995
that some word will appear to save the situation.
Words are perfect for waging controversies,
with words you can construct entire systems,
in words you can place perfect faith,
and from a word no jot or tittle may be taken.   2000
STUDENT. Pardon my detaining you with so many questions,
but I must trouble you still further.
Would you be willing to provide me, too,
with a few helpful words on medicine?
Three years are a short time, alas!   2005
and yet the subject is so vast.
If one could only get a pointer,
he wouldn't have to grope so in the dark.
MEPHISTOPHELES (*aside*).
I've had enough of a sober tone,
it's time to play the real devil again.   2010
(*Aloud.*) The essence of medicine's easily grasped:
you study nature, you study man,
but in the end you let things take
the course God wills.
It's pointless to waste time by being scientific—   2015
you learn only as much as you possibly can;
but if you profit from your opportunities
you're a made man.
You have a rather pleasing figure, too,
and no doubt the assurance to go with it,   2020
so if you only have self-confidence,
others will place their confidence in you.
Above all, learn to handle women;
their myriads of aches and pains,
that never never cease,   2025
can all be cured if you know the right spot—
and if your behavior is halfway discreet
they all will be at your beck and call.
A title's needed first, to reassure them
that you have greater skill than other men,   2030
and right away you're welcome to investigate
what someone else needs years to reconnoiter;
you will know how to take a dainty pulse
and, with a cautious ardent glance,

to put your arms about her slender hips 2035
and see how tightly she is laced.
STUDENT. Now that's more like it—and it's practical!
MEPHISTOPHELES. All theories, dear friend, are gray;
the golden tree of life is green.
STUDENT. I'd swear I'm in some sort of daze. 2040
Perhaps you'll let me bother you again,
to hear the rest of all your wisdom?
MEPHISTOPHELES. I'm always glad to be of service.
STUDENT. I cannot bear to take my leave
until you've written in my album. 2045
Grant me, I beg, that token of your favor!
MEPHISTOPHELES. With pleasure.
He writes, and returns the album.
STUDENT (*reading*).
Eritis sicut Deus, scientes bonum et malum.
Closing the album reverently, the STUDENT *bows and withdraws.*
MEPHISTOPHELES. Follow the ancient saw, and my cousin the serpent,
and I warrant your likeness to God will some day perplex you. 2050
Enter FAUST.
FAUST. And now, where are we going?
MEPHISTOPHELES.   Where you please.
Let's first see ordinary life, the *grand monde* later;
you'll find this course—don't pay the registrar a fee—
both practical and entertaining!
FAUST. Yet as you see from my long beard 2055
I lack all nonchalance of manner.
I know that this experiment won't work;
I never could adapt to people.
When I'm with them I feel so insignificant;
I'll never be at ease at all. 2060
MEPHISTOPHELES. Everything will work out fine, my friend;
once you gain confidence, your manners will be easy.
FAUST. But how are we to start our travels?
Where have you horses or a coach and groom?
MEPHISTOPHELES. We'll simply lay my cloak out flat; 2065
it will carry us through the air.
But just be sure, since there's a certain risk,
that you don't carry too much luggage.
Some heated air that I'll concoct
will lift us off the ground with ease, 2070
and if we're light enough, we'll quickly be high up.
Congratulations on your new career!   [*Exeunt.*

AUERBACH'S WINE-CELLAR IN LEIPZIG

A lively drinking-party.

FROSCH. Why aren't you drinking? Why is nobody laughing?
 I'll teach you not to make long faces!
 Today you're like wet straw,   2075
 although you normally are scintillating.
BRANDER. It's all your fault; you haven't contributed
 anything silly or piggishly bawdy.
FROSCH (*emptying a glass of wine on* BRANDER'S *head*).
 There's both for you!
BRANDER.   You pig twice over!
FROSCH. That's what you wanted, isn't it!   2080
SIEBEL. Kick anyone out who starts to quarrel!
 Now drink, let's fill our lungs and sing a good loud round!
 Wake up! Hey there! Halloo!
ALTMAYER.   Ouch! he's done me in!
 Some cotton, quick! The fellow's splitting my ears.
SIEBEL. It's only when the ceiling echoes   2085
 that you feel the full power of the bass.
FROSCH. That's right, kick anyone out who doesn't approve!
 Trala, trala, trala!
ALTMAYER. Trala, trala, trala!
FROSCH.   Our throats are now on pitch.
(*Singing.*)   Our Holy Roman Empire, lads,   2090
           what holds it still together?
BRANDER. A nasty song! For shame—political,
 disgusting! Thank the Lord each time you wake
 that the Empire is none of your affair.
 I, at least, think myself better off   2095
 not being emperor or chancellor.
 But we must have our leader too,
 so let's elect ourselves a pope—
 you know capacity is the main factor
 for deciding who'll be elevated.   2100
FROSCH (*singing*).
           O nightingale, soar on above,
             and bring ten thousand greetings to my love.
SIEBEL. No greetings to that love! I'll have none of that!
FROSCH. Greetings, and kisses too! You're not the one to stop me!
(*Singing.*)   Draw the bolt, the night is clear.   2105
           Draw the bolt, your lover's here.
           Shut the bolt, now dawn draws near.
SIEBEL. Go on and sing, and praise her all you want.
 The time will come when I will have the laugh on you.

She made a fool of me, and you'll get the same treatment.   2110
She ought to have a goblin for her lover!
He could have fun with her at any crossroads,
and some old goat, back from the witches' sabbath,
should bleat good night to her as he goes galloping by!
A decent fellow of real flesh and blood   2115
is far too good for such a slut.
Greetings! the only kind I'd bring her
are those that break her window-panes!

BRANDER (*pounding on the table*).
  Order, order! I demand order, sirs!
  You will admit I know what's proper;   2120
  we have some lovers sitting with us,
  and I must offer them a serenade
  befitting their condition.
  The song's brand-new, so pay attention,
  and join me loudly for the refrain!   2125

(*Singing.*)   A rat in a cellar had built him a nest
           and daily grew fatter and smoother;
           he lined his paunch with butter and lard,
           was as portly as Doctor Luther.
           The cook, she set some poison out;   2130
           and then he felt as helpless as if—
           as if he'd fallen in love.

CHORUS (*with gusto*). As if he'd fallen in love!

BRANDER.   He ran around, and in and out,
           and drank at every puddle,   2135
           he gnawed and scratched, tore up the house,
           but still was in a fuddle;
           he leaped and leaped in frantic pain,
           but soon he knew it was in vain—
           as if he'd fallen in love.   2140

CHORUS.   As if he'd fallen in love!

BRANDER.   In terror then and broad daylight
           he ran into the kitchen,
           flopped on the hearth and, sad to say,
           lay gasping, moaning, twitching.   2145
           The poisoner now only laughed:
           that sounds to me like a last gasp—
           as if he'd fallen in love.

CHORUS.   As if he'd fallen in love!

SIEBEL. The stupid fools find that amusing!   2150
  I do not think it's very nice
  to go and poison some poor rat.

BRANDER. Are rats some special favorites of yours?

ALTMAYER. He's getting fat and growing bald!
  His own misfortunes have made him soft-hearted,   2155
  and what he sees in a bloated rat
  is a spitting image of himself.

Enter FAUST and MEPHISTOPHELES.

MEPHISTOPHELES. I must, to get us started right,
  now introduce you to conviviality
  and let you see how merry life can be.   2160
  Here, for these people, every day's a holiday.
  Without much wit, but with great satisfaction,
  they whirl in narrow, separate rounds
  like kittens chasing their own tails.
  And if they can't complain of headache   2165
  and still have credit with the landlord,
  they're pleased with life and free of cares.
BRANDER. Those two are travelers who've just arrived,
  as you can see from their peculiar manner;
  they haven't been in town an hour.   2170
FROSCH. That's it, of course! That's why I'm all for Leipzig!
  It is a smaller Paris and refines one's manners.
SIEBEL. What do you think these strangers are?
FROSCH. Leave it to me! Before they've drunk a glass of wine
  I'll worm their secrets out of them   2175
  as easily as you pull out a baby-tooth.
  I think that they're aristocrats,
  since they look haughty and dissatisfied.
BRANDER. I'd wager that they're mountebanks.
ALTMAYER. Perhaps!
FROSCH.   Just watch how I bamboozle them!   2180
MEPHISTOPHELES (to FAUST).
  Simple folk never sense the devil's presence,
  not even when his hands are on their throats.
FAUST. Our greetings, gentlemen!
SIEBEL.   And ours to you, with thanks!
    (In a low voice, looking at MEPHISTOPHELES sidewise.)
  Why does the fellow limp with that one foot?
MEPHISTOPHELES. Do we have your permission to sit down with you? 2185
  Instead of a good drink, since that's not to be had,
  we'll have the pleasure of your company.
ALTMAYER. You seem a very fastidious man.
FROSCH. No doubt you got away from Rippach rather late?
  Did you have supper first with Mr. Jack?   2190
MEPHISTOPHELES. We didn't stop and call today;
  on our last trip we had a word with him.

He had a lot to say about his cousins
and sends his best regards to every one of them.
He bows to FROSCH.

ALTMAYER (*sotto voce*). He got you there! He knows the game!
SIEBEL.   The rascal's sly!   2195
FROSCH. Just wait and see, I'll catch him yet!
MEPHISTOPHELES. If I am not mistaken, we could hear
   some well-trained voices doing choral songs?
   I'm sure that with this vaulted ceiling
   all singing has a fine, full resonance.   2200
FROSCH. Are you by any chance a virtuoso?
MEPHISTOPHELES. Oh no! I lack the strength, although I love to sing.
ALTMAYER. Give us a song!
MEPHISTOPHELES.   As many as you may request!
SIEBEL. No old stuff, though! Some piece that's new.
MEPHISTOPHELES. We've only just come back from Spain,   2205
   that lovely land of wine and song.
(*Singing.*)   A king there was they tell of
                  who had a great big flea –
FROSCH. Hear that! A flea! Did you catch what he said?
   A flea's nice company, I'm sure!   2210
MEPH.   A king there was they tell of
                  who had a great big flea
                  and loved him no less dearly
                  than if a son were he.
                  And so he calls his tailor,   2215
                  and in the tailor goes:
                  Measure my squire for breeches
                  and for a suit of clothes!
BRANDER. Don't you forget to have the tailor clearly told
   to take his measurements precisely   2220
   and, if he values his own neck,
   to leave no wrinkles in the breeches!
MEPHISTOPHELES.   In cloth of silk and velvet
                  the squire now was dressed,
                  had ribbons on his jacket,   2225
                  a cross upon his breast,
                  was minister directly
                  and wore a splendid star.
                  At court all his relations
                  were soon advanced quite far.   2230
                    Court life was then a torment
                  for ladies and their knights,
                  both queen and waiting-woman

had many stings and bites,
but no one dared to crack them   2235
or scratch the place that itched.
We're free to crack and crush them
whenever there's a twitch.
CHORUS (*con gusto*). We're free to crack and crush them
whenever there's a twitch.   2240
FROSCH. Bravo! Bravo! That was fine!
SIEBEL. Down with all fleas, now and forever!
BRANDER. Use your nails well, don't let any escape!
ALTMAYER. Hurrah for liberty! Hurrah for wine!
MEPHISTOPHELES. I'd gladly drink a glass to liberty   2245
if only your wines were a trifle better.
SIEBEL. We don't want to hear that complaint again!
MEPHISTOPHELES. Did I not fear the landlord might object,
I would offer these worthy guests
some samples from our private cellar.   2250
SIEBEL. Just bring them on! I'll be responsible.
FROSCH. If you have something good, we'll sing your praises.
But don't pour just a little in the glass;
if I'm to be a proper judge
my mouth must be well filled.   2255
ALTMAYER (*sotto voce*). I see they're from the Rhineland.
MEPHISTOPHELES. An auger, please!
BRANDER.   And what's it for?
You can't have left your casks outside?
ALTMAYER. Back there's a basket with the landlord's tools.
MEPHISTOPHELES (*taking the auger*).
(*To* FROSCH.) Tell me what wine you'd like to taste.   2260
FROSCH. How do you mean your question? Is there so great a choice?
MEPHISTOPHELES. You each can have whatever you prefer.
ALTMAYER (*to* FROSCH).
Ah, you're licking your lips already, I see.
FROSCH. Well, then! if I can choose, I'll have a good Rhine wine.
One's native products are the best.   2265
MEPHISTOPHELES (*boring a hole next to* FROSCH *in the edge of the table*).
Get me some wax, so I'll have stoppers ready.
ALTMAYER. Oh! it is only a magician's trick.
MEPHISTOPHELES (*to* BRANDER). How about you?
BRANDER.   I'll have champagne,
and of the kind that's really bubbly!
While MEPHISTOPHELES *bores, one of the students makes wax stoppers and
plugs the holes.*
BRANDER. Imported goods can't always be avoided—   2270

what's best is often not home-grown.
Your proper German can't abide those Frenchmen,
but he's quite glad to drink their wines.
SIEBEL (*as* MEPHISTOPHELES *approaches his place*).
 To tell the truth, I don't like wine too dry—
 give me a glass of something good and sweet!   2275
MEPHISTOPHELES (*boring*). This tap will soon give you Tokay.
ALTMAYER. Come, sirs, admit what you are doing!
 It's plain to me you're making fools of us.
MEPHISTOPHELES. Hardly that! With such worthy company
 to do so would be just a bit too risky.   2280
 Speak up! Don't beat about the bush!
 What kind of wine do you prefer?
ALTMAYER. Any will do! Don't waste time asking!
   The boring and plugging of the holes is now finished.
MEPHISTOPHELES (*with fantastic gestures*).
            On the vine grapes grow,
            on the he-goat, horns;   2285
            wine is juice, vine is wood,
            wooden tables give wine as good.
            Nature's secret is now revealed!
            Faith provides a miracle!
 Now draw the plugs and drink your fill!   2290
ALL (*as they draw the stoppers and the several wines flow into their
 glasses*). O lovely fountain, all for us!
MEPHISTOPHELES. But I must warn you—do not spill one drop!
            They drink glass after glass.
ALL (*singing*).   We are as happy as cannibals,
            five hundred swine can't beat us!
MEPHISTOPHELES. There's freedom for you—see a happy people!   2295
FAUST. I wish we could go on our way.
MEPHISTOPHELES. First wait and see a demonstration
 of marvelous animal spirits.
SIEBEL (*drinking carelessly and spilling wine which turns to flame as it
 hits the floor*). Help! fire! help! The flames of hell!
MEPHISTOPHELES (*conjuring the flame*).
 Peace, friendly element, be still!   2300
(*To* SIEBEL.) That time it wasn't much—a spark from purgatory.
SIEBEL. What do you mean? You wait! You'll pay for this!
 Do you know whom you're dealing with?
FROSCH. Don't try that trick a second time with us!
ALTMAYER. I think we might tell him to make himself scarce.   2305
SIEBEL. I say, sir, you are impudent
 to practice your hocus-pocus here!

MEPHISTOPHELES. Be still, old wine-tun!

SIEBEL.   Broomstick, you!
  To injury you want to add your insults!

BRANDER. You wait! You're asking for a beating!   2310

ALTMAYER (*pulling a stopper, so that fire shoots out from the table at him*). I'm burning! I'm on fire!

SIEBEL.   It's black magic!
  Stab him! The fellow is outside the law!

            They rush at MEPHISTOPHELES *with drawn knives.*

MEPHISTOPHELES (*with gravity of tone and gesture*).
              Eye, see what's not!
              Charm, change the scene!
              Stay here, but be there!   2315

        Standing still, they look in amazement at each other.

ALTMAYER. Where am I? What a pretty country!

FROSCH. Do I see vineyards!

SIEBEL.   And grapes everywhere!

BRANDER. Look underneath the leaves of this green arbor!
  See the fine vine! See all the grapes!

He grabs SIEBEL'S *nose; the others do the same with each other, raising their knives.*

MEPHISTOPHELES (*as before*).
  Remove your blindfold from them, Error!   2320
  And you! remember well the devil's joke.

        MEPHISTOPHELES *disappears with* FAUST; *the revelers separate.*

SIEBEL. What's going on!

ALTMAYER.   What's this?

FROSCH.   Was that your nose?

BRANDER (*to* SIEBEL). And here I'm holding yours right now!

ALTMAYER. I felt a shock that went all through me.
  I can't stand up, get me a chair!   2325

FROSCH. Just what did happen? Can you tell me?

SIEBEL. Where is that fellow? If I find him,
  he won't get out of here alive!

ALTMAYER. With my own eyes I saw him—riding on a keg
  out through the tavern door. –   2330
  Somehow my feet are as heavy as lead.

                (*Turning toward the table.*)
  I say, could there still be some wine?

SIEBEL. It was all make-believe—deception and illusion.

FROSCH. I really thought that I was drinking wine.

BRANDER. But did we ever see those grapes?   2335

ALTMAYER. And yet some people claim there are no miracles!

WITCH'S KITCHEN

A low hearth with a caldron on the fire; various figures appear in the vapor rising from it. A SHE-APE *sits beside the caldron, skimming it and watching lest it boil over. The* BUCK *and* YOUNG APES *are sitting beside her and warming themselves. Ceiling and walls are decorated with the most grotesque utensils of sorcery. – Enter* FAUST *and* MEPHISTOPHELES.

FAUST. I do not like this sorcery at all!

How can you promise I'll be cured of anything

in such a mad hodgepodge of lunacy?

Am I to seek assistance from some crone?   2340

Can the foul mess that she concocts

take thirty years from my existence?

Poor me, if you don't know a better way!

Now any hope I had is gone.

Is there no natural specific   2345

discovered by a less ignoble mind?

MEPHISTOPHELES. My friend, you're talking sense again.

Nature does have a way to make you young;

but it's recorded in another book,

and in a rather curious chapter.   2350

FAUST. I demand you tell me.

MEPHISTOPHELES.   Very well! A recipe

that takes no money, magic, or physician:

Go out at once into the country

and set to hoeing and to digging;

confine yourself—and your thoughts too—   2355

within the narrowest spheres;

subsist on food that's plain and simple,

live with your cattle as their peer, and don't disdain

to fertilize in person fields that you will reap.

Take my word for it, there's no better way   2360

to remain young until you're eighty.

FAUST. That's work I am not used to, nor can I bear the thought

of having to do labor with a shovel.

A life so much constricted would never do for me.

MEPHISTO. Since that's the case, your crone will have to help us.   2365

FAUST. Why does it have to be a witch?

Can't you yourself concoct the potion?

MEPHISTOPHELES. A fine way, that, for me to spend my time!

I could construct a thousand bridges quicker.

Knowledge and skill are not enough;   2370

a job like this requires patience.

A calm, still spirit must toil for many years,

only time gives the subtle ferment potency.

And the ingredients are very special!   2375

Of course the devil taught her how to do it,
  but he can't do the work himself.
(*Seeing the* APES.) Look, aren't these people elegant—
  that is the maid, and he is the flunkey!
(*To the* APES.) Your mistress, I infer, is not at home?   2380
THE APES.   Dining out!
                             Off she went
                             by the chimney vent!
MEPHISTOPHELES. How long do her sprees normally last?
THE APES. As long as we rest and warm our paws.   2385
MEPHISTOPHELES (*to* FAUST).
  What do you think of these mannerly beasts?
FAUST. I've never seen any less attractive.
MEPHISTOPHELES. I can't agree—their conversation
  is just the kind that I like best.
(*To the* APES.) But tell me, my little jackanapes!   2390
  why are you stirring that sickening mush?
THE APES. We are cooking a watery soup for the needy.
MEPHISTOPHELES. Make it truly insipid, and many others will want it.
BUCK APE (*sidling up to* MEPHISTOPHELES).
                             Come, sir, play dice!
                             To be rich is so nice—   2395
                             just let me win!
                             Brains I'm not strong in,
                             but if I had pence
                             they'd say I had sense.
MEPHISTOPHELES. This ape would think it was a privilege   2400
  to be allowed to play the lottery!
The YOUNG APES, *who have been playing with a large sphere, now roll it
                             forward.*
BUCK APE.   This is your world:
                             rising and falling,
                             constantly whirling;
                             it tinkles like glass,   2405
                             which breaks so fast,
                             and it's hollow, alas!
                             Here's a bright spot,
                             and here one still brighter—
                             here I'm alive!   2410
                             Son, if you love me,
                             have nothing to do with it
                             or it will kill you—
                             the clay that it's made of
                             turns into sharp splinters.   2415
MEPHISTOPHELES. What is the sieve for?

BUCK APE (*taking it down*).
>   If you're a thief
>   I'd know it at once.

(*Running to the* SHE-APE *and having her look through it.*)
>   Look through the sieve!
>   You know the thief well,   2420
>   but his name you won't tell!

MEPHISTOPHELES (*approaching the hearth*). And what is this pot?

BUCK AND SHE-APE.   Poor idiot he!
>   He's not heard of the pot,
>   not heard of the caldron!   2425

MEPHISTOPHELES. Beasts with no manners!

BUCK APE.   Hold on to this hearth-brush
>   and sit down in a chair!

The APE *forces* MEPHISTOPHELES *into an armchair.*

FAUST (*who meanwhile has been standing before a mirror, sometimes
        approaching and sometimes moving away from it*).
>   What am I seeing in this magic mirror?
>   A form whose beauty is divine!   2430
>   O lend me, Love, your fleetest wings
>   and lead me to Elysium!
>   Alas, that when I leave this point
>   and venture any closer to her,
>   I see her only in a sort of haze! –   2435
>   A picture of a woman of surpassing beauty!
>   Can any woman be so lovely?
>   Am I allowed to see, in this recumbent form,
>   the essence of all paradises?
>   Does earth contain its counterpart?   2440

MEPHISTOPHELES. It's obvious that if a god works six hard days
>   and, when he's done, himself cries bravo,
>   something is bound to turn out right.
>   While you are at it, look your fill!
>   I can easily find you a girl just like that,   2445
>   and the man will be happy whom fate allows
>   to take her as his lawful wife!

While FAUST *continues to look into the mirror,* MEPHISTOPHELES *lounges
        in the armchair, toying with the hearth-brush.*

MEPHISTOPHELES. Here I sit like a king on his throne,
>   holding a scepter, lacking only my crown.

THE APES, *who have been jostling each other and making various strange
    movements, now shout loudly and bring* MEPHISTOPHELES *a crown.*

THE APES.   Be ever so kind   2450
>   and patch up this crown
>   with sweat and with blood!

*(They handle the crown clumsily, breaking it into two pieces, with which
they dance about.)*

   Now we have done it! –

   We've speech and we've sight,

   we listen and write –   2455

FAUST *(looking into the mirror)*. Can this be driving me to madness!

MEPHISTOPHELES *(pointing to the* APES*)*.

 Even my head begins to reel and pound.

THE APES.   And if it's our luck

       to make some bit of sense,

       our writing's profound!   2460

FAUST *(as before)*. A fire has been kindled in my heart!

 Let's get away from here, and quickly!

MEPHISTOPHELES *(still pointing)*.

 Well, there's one thing you must admit:

 these poets are completely honest.

The caldron, which the SHE-APE *has meanwhile neglected, begins to boil
over; there is great flame, which flares up the chimney.*

THE WITCH *(descending through the flame and screaming horribly)*.

 Ouch! Ow! Ouch! Ow!   2465

 You stupid beast! You filthy sow,

 forgetting the kettle and scorching your mistress!

 Confounded beast!

     She sees FAUST *and* MEPHISTOPHELES.

WITCH.   What's going on here?

      Why are you two here?   2470

      What do you want here?

      How did you get here?

      Here is some fire

      to torment your bones!

*She plunges the skimming ladle into the caldron and splashes flames
towards* FAUST, MEPHISTOPHELES, *and the* APES; *the latter whimper.*

MEPHISTOPHELES *(reversing the brush he has been holding, and smashing
glassware and pottery)*.

     To pieces! to pieces!   2475

     See the brew run,

     see the glass break!

     It's jolly good fun

     to be beating the time

     to the song of a slut.   2480

   The WITCH *recoils in rage and horror.*

MEPHISTOPHELES. You horrid bag of bones! Do you know who I am?

 Do you not recognize your lord and master?

 I see no reason not to punish you,

 to dash you and your spirit-apes to pieces.

Have you lost all respect for my red doublet?
Is this cock's-feather now unknown to you?
Have I concealed my countenance?
Am I supposed to introduce myself?
WITCH. Pardon, my lord, the rude reception—
    it's all because I miss your cloven hoof!   2490
    And where on earth are your two ravens?
MEPHISTOPHELES. This one time your excuse will do;
    it has indeed been quite a while
    since we two saw each other last.
    Refinement's making everybody slick,   2495
    and so the devil too has been affected;
    the Northern phantom's gone and vanished,
    you see I have no horns or tail or claws;
    as for the foot I cannot do without,
    it would impair my social chances,   2500
    and so, like many a young man,
    I wear false calves, and long have done so.
WITCH (*dancing*). It's more than my poor mind can grasp,
    seeing here Squire Satan again!
MEPHISTOPHELES. Woman, I will not tolerate that title!   2305
WITCH. Why not? What harm is there in it?
MEPHISTOPHELES. It is now only mythological;
    yet mankind is no better off: the Evil One
    they may be rid of, evil ones have still not vanished.
    If you just call me Baron, that is fine;   2510
    like other gentry, I'm a cavalier.
    You cannot doubt my noble blood—
    look at the coat of arms I wear!
              He makes an indecent gesture.
WITCH (*laughing immoderately*).
    Ha, ha! I recognize your style!
    You always were a rogue, you rascal!   2515
MEPHISTOPHELES (*to* FAUST).
    Observe, my friend, and learn a lesson
    on how you have to deal with witches.
WITCH. Now tell me, gentlemen, what is your pleasure?
MEPHISTO. We'll have one good-sized glass of your well-known elixir,
    but only of the oldest brewage, please,   2520
    since every year the potency is doubled!
WITCH. I am most happy to oblige! Here is a bottle
    from which I sometimes take a nip myself
    and which, besides, no longer stinks at all;
    I hope you'll let me offer you a serving.   2525
(*Sotto voce.*) Of course you know that if he drinks it
    without due preparation, he won't live an hour.

MEPHISTOPHELES. He's a good friend—we can't have any bad effects;
    we'll let him have all benefits your kitchen offers.
    So draw your circle, speak your spells,   2530
    and then give him the well-filled cup!
The WITCH, *making fantastic gestures, draws a circle and places curious objects in it; simultaneously, glasses begin to ring and caldrons to vibrate, providing a musical accompaniment. Next, she fetches a great book and stations the* APES *in a circle, where they are made to serve her as reading-desk and torch-holders, and then beckons to* FAUST *to join her.*
FAUST (*to* MEPHISTOPHELES).
    Don't tell me anything will come of this!
    The silly apparatus, the demented gestures—
    I've seen enough of such jejune deceptions
    to know that I cannot abide them.   2535
MEPHISTOPHELES. Of course it's nonsense! You're supposed to laugh;
    don't be a sober-sided prig!
    This hocus-pocus is her privilege as doctor,
    a guarantee the drink will take effect.
MEPHISTOPHELES *shoves* FAUST *into the circle.*
WITCH (*declaiming bombastically from the book*).
                See how it's done!   2540
                Make ten of one,
                and let two be,
                make even three,
                then you'll be rich.
                Cast out the four!   2545
                Now heed the witch:
                from five and six
                make seven and eight,
                and now you're done:
                Then nine is one,   2550
                and ten is none. –
    That is the witches' one-times-one.
FAUST. I think she sounds delirious.
MEPHISTOPHELES. She's far from being finished yet.
    The book is all like that, as I well know;   2555
    it made me waste a lot of time:
    self-contradiction, when complete, is to the wise
    as much a mystery as to the fool.
    Her art is ancient, friend, as well as modern.
    In every age it's been the fashion,   2560
    with three-and-one and one-and-three
    instead of truth, to propagate confusion.
    That's how they get away with teaching silliness—
    who cares to waste his time on idiots!
    When people hear some words, they normally believe   2565

that there's some thought behind them.
WITCH (*continuing*).   And so our lore
    has wondrous power,
    although completely hidden!
    Who takes no thought,   2570
    will have no cares
    because it's at his bidding.
FAUST. What is this nonsense she's reciting?
    If this goes on my head will split.
    I seem to hear the voices of   2575
    a hundred thousand fools in chorus.
MEPHISTOPHELES. Enough, enough, o excellent sibyl!
    Now let us have your beverage!
    Be quick and fill the goblet to the brim—
    the draught will do my friend no harm,   2580
    for he is certainly no novice
    and has drunk plenty in his day.
  The WITCH, *with much ceremonial, pours the drink into a cup; as* FAUST
       sets it to his lips, there rises from it a slight flame.
MEPHISTOPHELES. Down with it quickly! Don't stop now!
    It is a cordial that works promptly.
    As thick as you are with the devil,   2585
    can you be frightened by a flame?
The WITCH *breaks the circle, and* FAUST *steps forth.*
MEPHISTOPHELES. And now, away! You must keep moving!
WITCH. I hope the dose will do you good!
MEPHISTOPHELES (*to the* WITCH).
    And if there's any favor I can do for you,
    be sure to tell me on Walpurgis Night.   2590
WITCH. Here, take this song, and sing it now and then;
    you'll find it adds a lot to the effect.
MEPHISTOPHELES (*to* FAUST).
    Come quickly now, and follow my instructions!
    It is essential that your body sweat
    if it's to benefit inside as well as out.   2595
    I'll teach you later to enjoy your well-earned leisure,
    and soon you'll feel, to your profound delight,
    young Cupid stir and then race to and fro.
FAUST. Please let me take a last quick look into the mirror—
    that woman was so beautiful!   2600
MEPHISTOPHELES. No, no! It won't be long before you see
    the paragon of womankind in person.
(*Sotto voce.*). With this drink in you, you'll soon see
    in every woman a Helen of Troy.   [*Exeunt.*

A STREET

Enter FAUST *and* MARGARETE, *who walks past him.*

FAUST. My lovely young lady, may I perhaps venture   2605
   to give you my arm and be your escort?

MARGARETE. I'm not a young lady, or lovely either,
   and need no escort to get home.
                           Freeing her arm, she leaves.

FAUST. By God, that girl is a real beauty!
   I've never seen one quite like her.   2610
   She is all modesty and virtue,
   yet there's a bit of pertness too.
   As long as I live I won't forget
   those glowing cheeks and ruby lips!
   Even the way she lowered her eyes   2615
   is stamped forever on my heart;
   as for the brusqueness of her manner,
   that was especially delightful!
                           Enter MEPHISTOPHELES.

FAUST. You must get me that girl, I tell you.

MEPHISTOPHELES. Which one?

FAUST.   The one that just went by.   2620

MEPHISTOPHELES. What, her? She is returning from confession;
   the priest absolved her of all sin—
   I crept up close to the confessional.
   She is an innocent, and so much so
   that she had nothing to confess;   2625
   over that girl I have no power.

FAUST. She's over fourteen, isn't she!

MEPHISTOPHELES. You're talking like Jack Reprobate;
   he covets every pretty flower,
   and fancies there's no honest favor   2630
   which can't be plucked if he but tries;
   that isn't always so, however.

FAUST. My dear Professor Dogmatist,
   you may spare me your moral lessons!
   And let me tell you very bluntly,   2635
   unless that sweet young thing is lying
   within my arms this very night,
   at stroke of twelve we part forever.

MEPHISTOPHELES. Consider practicalities!
   I'll need at least a good two weeks   2640
   to ferret out an opportune occasion.

FAUST. If I could have a simple girl like that
   alone for seven hours, to seduce her
   I would not need the devil's help.

MEPHISTOPHELES. You're almost talking like a Frenchman now,   2645
    but please don't think of this as mere frustration!
    What good is pleasure when it's rushed?
    It's much less satisfactory
    than when in various ways before,
    and with all sorts of fuss and bother,   2650
    you've shaped her up a bit and got her ready—
    this can be learned from many foreign novels.
FAUST. I don't need that to whet my appetite.
MEPHISTOPHELES. No more of this tomfoolery!
    I'm telling you once and for all   2655
    that with this pretty child it is no use to hurry.
    You won't take anything by storm;
    we must resort to strategy.
FAUST. Get me some souvenir of her!
    Bring me to where my angel sleeps!   2660
    Get me a kerchief from her breast,
    a garter to excite my passion!
MEPHISTOPHELES. To prove to you that I am eager
    to be of service when you suffer,
    let us not waste another moment—   2665
    I'll take you to her room this very day.
FAUST. And shall I see her, have her?
MEPHISTOPHELES.   No!
    She will be at a neighbor's house.
    You can, while she's away, be there alone
    and, in the aura that her presence sheds,   2670
    anticipate the taste of future joy.
FAUST. Can we go now?
MEPHISTOPHELES.   It's still too soon.
FAUST. Then get a present for me to take her!   [*Exit.*
MEPHISTOPHELES. Presents right off? Good work! He'll have success!
    I know some excellent locations   2675
    with lots of ancient buried treasure.
    I'd better do a little looking.   [*Exit.*

EVENING

A small, neatly kept room.

MARGARETE (*braiding and tying up her hair*).

I'd give a lot if I could know
who was that gentleman today.
He really was quite debonair,   2680
and is no doubt of noble birth;
that I could tell from his eyes and forehead—
and he wouldn't have been so forward otherwise.   [*Exit.*

Enter MEPHISTOPHELES *and* FAUST.

MEPHISTOPHELES. Come in, but don't make noise—don't hesitate!

FAUST (*after a silence*). I beg you, leave me here alone!   2685

MEPHISTOPHELES (*snooping about*).

Not all young women are this neat.   [*Exit.*

FAUST (*looking around carefully*).

How welcome is the gentle twilight glow
that permeates this sanctuary!
Possess my heart, sweet pain of love
that lives and languishes on dews of hope!   2690
How all here breathes a sense of calm,
of order, of contentedness!
What abundance in this poverty,
what blessedness within this prison!

   (*He throws himself into a leather armchair beside the bed.*).

Grant me a welcome, you whose open arms   2695
have held in joy or pain past generations!
To think how many times some group of children
clung to the sides of this ancestral throne!
Perhaps when still a plump-cheeked child, my love,
thanking her grandfather for his Christmas gift,   2700
here kissed his withered hand with dutiful respect.
I feel, dear girl, stirring about me
the spirit of that rich contentment
which daily teaches you maternal virtues,
bidding you place the table-cover neatly,   2705
and even strew the sand upon the floor in patterns.
Your precious hand is godlike in its power
to make this cottage paradise!
And here!

   (*He lifts one of the bed-curtains.*)

   What awesome ecstasy enthralls me!

I wish that I had hours to spend here.   2710
Here Nature brought, in happy dreams,
the innate angel to harmonious perfection!
Here the child lay, her tender breast

overflowing with the warmth of life,
and here upon the sacred loom of purity   2715
was wrought the image of a goddess!
    And you! What drew you here?
How deeply stirred I feel!
What are you seeking here? Why is your heart so heavy?
Unhappy Faust, so changed I do not know you!   2720
    Is there some magic fragrance here?
My impulse was to gain immediate enjoyment;
a dream of love suffuses all my being.
Are we the sport of every change of air?
    And if she suddenly should enter now,   2725
how you would suffer for this profanation!
The gentleman, become a beggar,
would lie and languish at her feet.

                    Enter MEPHISTOPHELES.
MEPHISTOPHELES. Be quick! Down there I see her coming.
FAUST. Yes, go! I'm never coming back!   2730
MEPHISTOPHELES. Here is a little casket, rather heavy,
    that I picked up somewhere or other.
    Just place it in this chest of drawers,
    and, on my word, she won't believe her eyes;
    you'll find that in it I have put   2735
    knickknacks enough to win two girls.
    Still, children will be children, and a toy's a toy.
FAUST. I wonder, should I?
MEPHISTOPHELES.   Is there any question?
    You surely don't intend to hoard my treasure-trove?
    If that's the case, then I'd advise Your Lustfulness   2740
    to put my time to better use
    and spare me further wasted trouble.
    I do hope you're not miserly!
    I've scratched my head and wrung my hands—
        (*He puts the casket in a chest of drawers and relocks it.*)
    Hurry, we must be gone!—   2745
    in my concern to make a sweet young girl
    complaisant to your heart's desires,
    and yet you look as glum
    as if you had to go to class
    and see before you, gray as life,   2750
    Physics and Metaphysics both!
    Away!   [*Exeunt.*

            Enter MARGARETE, *carrying a lamp.*

MARGARETE. It is so sultry here, so close,
                    (*She opens a window.*)
and yet it's not so warm outside.
I have a feeling I can't describe—   2755
if only Mother would come home!
Something is making my whole body tremble—
I really am a silly, timid thing!
             (*She begins to sing as she changes her clothes.*)
                    There was a king in Thule
                    faithful until the grave;   2760
                    his dying mistress gave him
                    a goblet made of gold.

                         He had no greater treasure,
                    used it at solemn feasts;
                    whenever he drank from it,   2765
                    his eyes would fill with tears.

                         And when he saw death coming,
                    he counted all his towns,
                    and left his heirs his kingdom,
                    but not the cup of gold.   2770

                         He held a royal banquet
                    in a castle by the sea,
                    and with his knights was seated
                    in the ancestral hall.

                         Drinking, the old man stood there,   2775
                    and drank his life's last glow,
                    then flung the precious goblet
                    into the flood below.

                         He watched it fall, and drinking
                    sink deep into the sea;   2780
                    his eyes grew heavy, closing,
                    he never drank again.
(*Opening the chest to put away her clothes, she sees the jewel box.*)
What a fine casket! How did it get here?
I'm almost certain that I locked the chest.
This certainly is strange! I wonder what is in it?   2785
Perhaps it is someone's security,
brought for a loan my mother's made.
Here on this ribbon there's a little key,
I've a good mind to open it.
What is all this? Good heavens! Look!   2790
I've never seen the like in all my days!
A set of jewels that any lady
might wear on highest holidays!
How would this necklace look on me?

To whom can all these gorgeous things belong?   2795
(*She puts on various pieces of jewelry, then stands before her mirror.*)
If only I could have these earrings—
I look so very different right away!
What use are looks to us young girls?
That is all very well and good,
but it's just that, and nothing more;   2800
the praise you get is half in pity.
Wealth is what's wanted,
only gold counts.
And if we're poor—too bad!

PROMENADE

FAUST, *preoccupied, is walking back and forth; he is joined by*
MEPHISTOPHELES.

MEPHISTOPHELES. By all love ever scorned! By all the fires of hell!   2805
    I wish I knew things even worse by which to swear!
FAUST. What ails you now? What's given you the gripes?
    I've never seen a face like yours in all my life.
MEPHISTOPHELES. I'd have the devil take me here and now
    if only I were not myself a devil!   2810
FAUST. Is something out of place there in your head?
    You make a splendid raving maniac!
MEPHISTOPHELES. Imagine this! The jewels we got for Gretchen—
    a priest has gone and grabbed the lot! –
    No sooner does the mother see the stuff   2815
    than she begins to have her private horrors.
    That woman has the keenest sense of smell;
    her snout is always in a book of prayers;
    she sniffs all objects to discover
    whether they're sacred or profane;   2820
    and with those jewels her nose knew right away
    that they were hardly any godsend.
    Treasures of wickedness, she cried, ensnare the soul,
    my child, and then consume our blood.
    We'll consecrate them to the Holy Mother,   2825
    and she'll delight our hearts with heaven's manna!
    Our Maggie made a sour face
    and thought, it is a gift-horse, after all,
    and surely he can't be a godless man
    who was so gallant as to bring it.   2830
    The mother then sent for a priest;

as soon as he had heard the curious story,
he looked quite pleased with what he saw.
He spoke: Those are the proper sentiments,
for he that overcometh shall inherit!   2835
The Church is blessed with a good stomach,
has gobbled down whole countries even,
yet never suffered from repletion;
only the Church is able to digest
treasures of wickedness, dear ladies.   2840
FAUST. That isn't any special talent—
  kings and usurers practice it too.
MEPHISTOPHELES. And then he swept brooch, necklace, and the rings
  into his pocket like so many trifles,
  and thanked them neither more nor less   2845
  than if he'd gotten a basket of nuts,
  promising them all sorts of heavenly rewards—
  which left them highly edified.
FAUST. And Gretchen?
MEPHISTOPHELES.   She is restless, and just sits,
  uncertain what she wants or ought to do,   2850
  thinks day and night about the jewels,
  and even more about who may have brought them for her.
FAUST. I hate to hear my love is grieving.
  Get her another set at once!
  The first one didn't look like much to me.   2855
MEPHISTOPHELES. I know you gentlemen think such things bagatelles!
FAUST. Don't waste your time, just follow my instructions—
  and cultivate the woman who's her neighbor!
  Don't dawdle and delay, you devil,
  but go and get me the new set!   2860
MEPHISTOPHELES. As you command, my lord, and gladly. [*Exit* FAUST.
  To entertain their ladies, love-sick fools like this
  would take the sun and moon, the planets and the stars—
  and blow them up as fireworks.   [*Exit.*

THE NEIGHBOR'S HOUSE

DAME MARTHA, *alone.*

MARTHA. My dear husband—may God forgive him!—   2865
  hasn't done very well by me.
  Without a warning he goes away
  and leaves me to grass-widowhood.
  And yet, God knows, I never caused him grief,

and always loved him tenderly.   2870
(*Weeping*). Perhaps he's even dead! – O misery . . .
  If I but had a death certificate!
Enter MARGARETE.

MARGARETE. Dame Martha!
MARTHA.   Gretelchen, what is it?
MARGARETE. My knees are weak, I can barely stand!
  Now I have found another casket,   2875
  this time of ebony, inside the chest,
  with lots of really gorgeous things;
  it's far more splendid than the first.
MARTHA. You mustn't tell your mother this;
  right off she'd take it to confession too.   2880
MARGARETE. Just take a look! Do look and see!
MARTHA (*putting jewelry on* MARGARETE).
  You are indeed a lucky one!
MARGARETE. I can't appear in the streets, alas,
  or in church either, with them on.
MARTHA. Come over here whenever you can   2885
  and dress up in them privately.
  Then you can walk a while before the looking-glass,
  that will afford us both great pleasure;
  and soon there'll be occasions or some holidays
  when you'll display one piece and then another.   2890
  A necklace first, then a pearl earring next—
  your mother may well not notice, but we'll have some story for her.
MARGARETE. Who on earth could have brought those caskets?
  There's something not quite right about it! (*A knock.*)
  Good heavens! Can that be my mother?   2895
MARTHA (*peeping through the curtain*).
  It's a strange gentleman. – Come in!
Enter MEPHISTOPHELES.

MEPHISTOPHELES. I know I'm intruding, unannounced,
  and hope you ladies will pardon me.
(*He steps back respectfully from* MARGARETE.)
  I was looking for Dame Martha Schwerdtlein.
MARTHA. That's me. What is your message, sir?   2900
MEPHISTOPHELES (*to* MARTHA, *in a low voice*).
  It's enough now that I know who you are;
  I see you have a genteel visitor.
  Excuse the liberty I took,
  I'll return in the afternoon.
MARTHA (*aloud*). For heaven's sake! Imagine, child,   2905
  the gentleman believes you are a lady!
MARGARETE. I'm nothing but a poor young girl;

dear me! the gentleman is much too kind;
    the set of jewelry isn't mine.
MEPHISTOPHELES. Oh, it is not the jewels alone: 2910
    you have an air, such piercing eyes.
    I'm much obliged that I may stay.
MARTHA. What is your news, I'm very eager . . .
MEPHISTOPHELES. I wish that it were happier,
    and hope you won't hold it against me: 2915
    your husband's dead and sends regards.
MARTHA. Is dead? That faithful soul! Oh no!
    My husband dead! My end has come!
MARGARETE. Oh don't, dear woman, don't despair!
MEPHISTOPHELES. Let me tell you the mournful story.   2920
MARGARETE. I couldn't bear to be in love, not ever,
    I'd die of grief from such a loss.
MEPHISTOPHELES. There is no joy but has its sorrow.
MARTHA. Tell me about the way he died!
MEPHISTOPHELES. He lies interred in Padua,   2925
    beside the church of San Antonio;
    in duly consecrated ground
    he has his cool and everlasting rest.
MARTHA. And do you bring me nothing else?
MEPHISTOPHELES. Yes, one request of grave importance: 2930
    be sure to have three hundred masses sung for him!
    My pockets otherwise are empty.
MARTHA. What, not one lucky coin? No single piece of jewelry?—
    what any journeyman has deep down in his bag
    and that to keep as souvenir   2935
    he'd rather starve or be a beggar!
MEPHISTOPHELES. Madam, you have my sympathy;
    still, he didn't throw money away, I assure you.
    Besides, he much repented all his faults
    and even more, in fact, bemoaned his wretched luck!   2940
MARGARETE. It's sad that people have so much misfortune!
    Many's the requiem I'll pray for him, that's sure.
MEPHISTOPHELES. A kind, sweet girl like you deserves
    to get a husband right away.
MARGARETE. That isn't possible as yet.   2945
MEPHISTOPHELES. If not a husband, meanwhile then a lover.
    It's one of heaven's greatest blessings
    to have a nice girl to embrace.
MARGARETE. That's not the custom in these parts.
MEPHISTOPHELES. Custom or not, it's still a practice.   2950
MARTHA. Please tell me more!
MEPHISTOPHELES.   I was beside him when he died.

His deathbed was some straw, half-rotten,
though better than a dunghill; yet he died a Christian,
discovering some largish debts to his account.
How I'm compelled to loathe myself, he cried,   2955
forsaking as I did my trade, my wife!
Alack, to think of that is torment.
If only she'd forgive me while I'm still alive . . .
MARTHA (*weeping*). The dear, good man! I have long since forgiven him.
MEPHISTOPHELES. Yet she, God knows! was more to blame than I.   2960
MARTHA. He lies! And at death's door, at that!
MEPHISTOPHELES. In the last throes he was no doubt delirious,
    if I am even half an expert in these matters.
    I never was allowed, he said, to rest and contemplate,
    but had first to get children, then the bread they needed—   2965
    bread in its most extended meaning—
    and couldn't even eat my share in peace and quiet.
MARTHA. Did he forget, then, all my love, all my devotion,
    and how I was his drudge both day and night!
MEPHISTOPHELES. Oh, no! That never left his heart or mind.   2970
    He said, the time that I left Malta
    I prayed with fervor for my wife and children,
    and Heaven duly granted us its favor,
    and let us take a Turkish barque
    that bore a treasure of the Sultan's.   2975
    Then valor got its just reward,
    and I received, as was my right,
    my proper share of booty too.
MARTHA. How then! Can he have buried it somewhere?
MEPHISTOPHELES. Who knows which of the winds now have it!   2980
    A stranger, he was wandering about in Naples
    when a young, pretty lady there befriended him;
    she gave him lots of loving-kindness,
    he felt its consequences till his dying day.
MARTHA. The thief! A villain who steals from his own children!   2985
    Not even all that misery, all that distress,
    deterred him from his life of shame!
MEPHISTOPHELES. How true! But, then, that's why he now is dead.
    If I were in your place, however,
    I'd mourn him chastely for a year,   2990
    and meanwhile set my sights on a new lover.
MARTHA. Ah, God! This side of heaven I won't find
    another like my first so easily!
    There hardly could have been a man more lovable.
    Only he liked to travel much too much,   2995
    was fond of foreign wines and women,

and had a wicked passion for a game of dice.
MEPHISTOPHELES. Well, then, things would have been all right
  if, on his part, he'd been
  about as tolerant of you as you of him.   3000
  Upon my honor, given some such terms,
  I would myself exchange engagement rings with you!
MARTHA. The gentleman is pleased to jest.
MEPHISTOPHELES (*aside*).
  It's now high time for me to leave—
  she'd hold the very devil to his word!   3005
(*To* GRETCHEN.) And what's the state of your own heart?
MARGARETE. Sir, how's your question meant?
MEPHISTOPHELES (*aside*).   You innocent!
(*Aloud.*) Ladies, farewell!
MARGARETE.   Farewell!
MARTHA.   A quick word first!
  I'd like to have some proof to show
  where, how, and when my dear departed died, was buried.   3010
  I've always done things in the proper way,
  and would like, too, to see his death in the newspaper.
MEPHISTOPHELES. Of course, dear lady. As you know, it always takes
  two witnesses' word to establish a truth;
  I have a friend, an excellent fellow,   3015
  with whom I'll go before the judge.
  I'll bring him here.
MARTHA.   By all means, do!
MEPHISTOPHELES. And the young lady, will she too be here? –
  A fine young man! He is well-traveled,
  and treats young ladies with impeccable politeness.   3020
MARGARETE. Before the gentleman I'd be all blushes.
MEPHISTOPHELES. You wouldn't need to blush before a king.
MARTHA. There in the garden, behind my house,
  we will expect you gentlemen this evening.   [*Exeunt.*

A STREET

Enter FAUST *and* MEPHISTOPHELES.
FAUST. How do things stand? Have you progressed? Will it be long?   3025
MEPHISTOPHELES. Bravo! I see you're now all fire!
  It won't be long before you have your Gretchen.
  At neighbor Martha's you'll see her this evening—
  now there's a woman made to order
  for gypsy work and for procuring!   3030
FAUST. So far, so good!
MEPHISTOPHELES.   But we are asked to do a favor.

FAUST. Well, one good turn deserves another.

MEPHISTOPHELES. We simply have to make a proper deposition
   to the effect her husband's limbs have been laid out
   in consecrated ground at Padua.   3035

FAUST. How clever! Now we have to make the trip there first!

MEPHISTOPHELES. *Sancta simplicitas!* There is no need of that;
   just testify without specific knowledge!

FAUST. I must reject the scheme, if that's your best suggestion.

MEPHISTOPHELES. You saint! If this is not just like you!   3040
   Is this the first time in your life
   that you've committed perjury?
   Have you not, with bold impudence, defined,
   and in the most forceful language too,
   God, and the world, and all that moves therein,   3045
   and what goes on in human minds and hearts?
   Yet if you really searched your soul, you would confess
   you knew as much about these matters
   as now you do about one Schwerdtlein's death!

FAUST. You'll always be a liar and a sophist.   3050

MEPHISTOPHELES. But not the only one, if you'll just think some more.
   Tomorrow will you not, with much protested honor,
   attempt to turn poor Gretchen's head
   and swear upon your soul you love her?

FAUST. Yes—and sincerely!

MEPHISTOPHELES.   Well and good!   3055
   And then your talk about devotion evermore,
   about love's one all-overpowering urge—
   will that as well be so sincere?

FAUST. Stop there! It will! – When I am deeply moved
   and for the turbulence I feel   3060
   vainly endeavor to find a name,
   yet range the world with all my senses
   and search for words sublime enough
   and call this ardor that consumes me
   infinite, endless, and eternal,   3065
   is that some diabolical delusion?

MEPHISTOPHELES. And yet I'm right!

FAUST.   Now listen, and remember this,
   and please don't let me waste my breath:
   if someone claims he's right, and simply has a tongue,
   he's certain to be right.   3070
   Now come, I'm sick of all this verbiage;
   and you are right—I have no other choice.   [*Exeunt.*

A GARDEN

Enter MARGARETE, *on* FAUST'S *arm, and* MARTHA *walking back and forth with* MEPHISTOPHELES.

MARGARETE. I'm well aware the gentleman's just being kind
  and condescending so that I won't feel embarrassed.
  You travelers are so accustomed   3075
  to taking anything you get politely.
  I know only too well that my poor conversation
  can't entertain someone with your experience.
FAUST. One look or word from you is far more entertaining
  than all the wisdom of this world.   3080
                    He kisses her hand.
MARG. Oh, don't! You really shouldn't! How can you bear to kiss it?
  My hand's so ugly, it's so rough.
  It's all the work I've had to do—
  my mother's so particular.
              MARGARETE *and* FAUST *walk on.*
MARTHA. And must you, sir, be always traveling like this?   3085
MEPHISTOPHELES. Alas that business obligations force us to!
  With what regret one leaves so many places,
  and yet one simply can't stay on!
MARTHA. It's fine, I'm sure, when one's still energetic,
  to wander anywhere one wants;   3090
  but the hard years will come along,
  and dragging on alone, a bachelor, to the grave
  was never good for anyone.
MEPHISTOPHELES. That prospect fills me with dismay.
MARTHA. That's why, dear sir, you must plan well ahead.   3095
            MARTHA *and* MEPHISTOPHELES *walk on.*
MARGARETE. Yes, out of sight and out of mind!
  It's easy for you to be so polite;
  but you must have a lot of friends,
  and much more sensible than I.
FAUST. Dear girl, believe me! What people call good sense   3100
  is often vain stupidity.
MARGARETE.   How can that be?
FAUST. Alas that artless innocence
  cannot appreciate itself or its own worth!
  that modesty, humility, the highest gifts
  which Nature lovingly bestows –   3105
MARGARETE. Though you but think of me for one short moment,
  I shall have ample time to think of you.
FAUST. You and your mother see few visitors?
MARGARETE. Oh, yes, our household is a modest one,

but still it has to be attended to.   3110
We have no maid; it's up to me to cook and sweep,
to knit and sew, and to be always on my feet;
and Mother is so fussy!
It's not that she needs to be so economical;   3115
more than a lot of people, we could be living well—
my father left a nice estate,
a small house, and, outside the town, a garden-plot.
But now my days are mostly quiet;
my brother is a soldier,   3120
my little sister's dead.
She was a lot of trouble, to be sure,
but I'd be glad to have it all again,
I loved the child so much.
FAUST.   An angel, if like you!
MARGARETE. I had the care of her, she loved me very much.   3125
    When she was born, my father had already died.
    We gave my mother up for lost,
    she lay there in such misery,
    and she got better very slowly, bit by bit.
    That's why it was impossible   3130
    for her to nurse the little mite herself,
    and so, all by myself, I raised her
    on milk and water; she became my child that way.
    Held in my arms, and lying on my lap,
    she smiled and kicked, began to grow.   3135
FAUST. You've truly known the purest form of happiness.
MARGARETE. But many a hard hour, truly, too.
    At night the baby's cradle stood
    beside my bed; no sooner would she stir
    than I'd wake up; sometimes I'd have to feed her,   3140
    sometimes I had to lay her down beside me
    or, if she was not quiet, get up out of bed
    and pace the room to dandle her,
    and be up early in the morning at the washtub;
    then do the marketing and watch the stove,   3145
    and on and on like that day in, day out.
    At times, good sir, you feel discouraged;
    but then you do enjoy your meals, and sleep well too.
                    MARGARETE and FAUST walk on.
MARTHA. It's hard on women, though, you must admit:
    your long-time bachelor can hardly be reformed.   3150
MEPHISTOPHELES. All it would take would be someone like you
    to teach me something better.
MARTHA. Speak plainly, sir! Haven't you yet found anything?

Is there no romantic attachment anywhere?

MEPHISTOPHELES. The proverb says: a home of one's own,   3155
  a virtuous woman, are as precious as gold and pearls.

MARTHA. My question's whether you have ever wanted one.

MEPHISTOPHELES. I've found great kindness everywhere.

MARTHA. I meant your feelings—were they ever serious?

MEPHISTOPHELES. To trifle with a woman's heart is most improper.   3160

MARTHA. You simply will not understand!

MEPHISTOPHELES.   I'm very sorry!
  But I do understand – that you are very kind.

          MARTHA *and* MEPHISTOPHELES *walk on.*

FAUST. My little angel recognized me right away
  when I was entering the garden?

MARGARETE. Didn't you see how I lowered my eyes?   3165

FAUST. And you forgive my liberty the other day—
  it really was presumptuous impudence—
  when you were coming out of the cathedral?

MARGARETE. I was dismayed, I'd never had that happen;
  till then, nobody could speak ill of me.   3170
  Dear me, I thought, can he have seen in your behavior
  something immodest or improper?
  It was as if he felt he had the right
  to treat me as an ordinary girl.
  Yet to be honest, right away inside me   3175
  something began to intercede for you;
  but just the same I was quite angry with myself
  because I couldn't be still angrier with you.

FAUST. Sweet love!

MARGARETE.   Let me do this!
          Picking a daisy, MARGARETE *plucks its petals one by one.*

FAUST.   Is it for a bouquet?

MARGARETE. No, just a game.

FAUST.   How's that?

MARGARETE.   Stay there! You'd only laugh.
          She pulls off petals, murmuring.

FAUST. What are you murmuring?

MARGARETE (*half aloud*).   He loves me – loves me not.

FAUST. That lovely, that angelic face!

MARGARETE (*continuing*).

Loves me – not – loves me – not –
          (*Elated, she plucks the last petal.*)
  He loves me!

FAUST.   Yes, my child! Let what this flower says   3185
  serve you as oracle. He loves you!
  Do you know what that means? He loves you!

FAUST *clasps her hands.*

MARGARETE. I'm trembling!

FAUST.   Don't be afraid! Look in my eyes,
   let them and let these hands that now clasp yours
   express what tongue can never say: 3190
   complete devotion and a sense of bliss
   that must endure eternally!
   Eternally! – Its end would be despair.
   There must not be an end! Not ever!

MARGARETE *presses his hands, frees herself, and runs off.* FAUST *stands*
                 pensive for a moment, then follows her.

MARTHA (*entering*). It's starting to get dark.

MEPHISTOPHELES.   And we must go.   3195

MARTHA. I'd ask you to remain here longer,
   but this is such an evil-minded town.
   It's just as if nobody had a thing to do
   or keep him busy
   except to stare at what his neighbor's up to,   3200
   and you get talked about no matter how you act. –
   Where's our young couple?

MEPHISTOPHELES.   They've flown down the garden path.
   The wanton butterflies!

MARTHA.   I'd say he's taken with her.

MEPHISTOPHELES. And she with him as well. So runs the world its
                                            course. [*Exeunt.*

A SUMMERHOUSE

Enter MARGARETE, *hurriedly; she hides behind the door with her finger to
                 her lips, and peeks through the crack.*

MARGARETE. He's coming!

                    Enter FAUST.

FAUST.   Little minx, you're teasing me!   3205
   I've caught you!

                    He gives her a kiss.

MARGARETE (*embracing him, and returning the kiss*).
             Dear heart, I love you so!

          Enter MEPHISTOPHELES, *knocking on the door.*

FAUST (*stamping his foot*). Who's there?

MEPHISTOPHELES.   A friend!

FAUST.   A beast!

MEPHISTOPHELES.   It's almost time to leave.

                 Enter DAME MARTHA.

MARTHA. Yes, it is late, good sir.
FAUST.   May I see you both home?
MARGARETE. My mother would . . . . Farewell!
FAUST.   Then I must go?
   Farewell!
MARTHA.   Adieu!
MARGARETE.   Until we shall soon meet again!   3210
                    [*Exeunt* FAUST *and* MEPHISTOPHELES.
MARGARETE. It is astonishing the many,
   many ideas a man like that can have!
   I simply stay embarrassed when I'm with him
   and answer all he says with yes.
   I'm such a silly poor young thing,   3215
   I can't think what he sees in me.   [*Exit.*

FOREST AND CAVE

Enter FAUST, *alone.*

FAUST. Spirit sublime, all that for which I prayed,
   all that you now have granted me. In fire
   you showed your face to me, but not in vain.
   You gave me for my realm all Nature's splendor,   3220
   with power to feel and to enjoy it. You grant
   not only awed, aloof acquaintanceship,
   you let me look deep down into her heart
   as if it were the bosom of a friend.
   You lead the ranks of living beings past me,   3225
   and teach me thus to know my fellow creatures
   in air and water and in silent wood.
   And when the storm-swept forest creaks and groans,
   when, as it falls, the giant fir strips down
   and crushes neighboring boughs and trunks, and when   3230
   the hill echoes its fall as muffled thunder,
   you guide me to the safety of a cave,
   reveal my self to me, and then my heart's
   profound and secret wonders are unveiled.
   And when I see the calming moon ascend   3235
   and pass unblemished, into view there float
   from walls of rock and out of dripping glade
   the argent shapes of ancient times that serve
   to temper contemplation's stern delight.
      That nothing perfect ever can be man's,   3240
   I feel that here. Together with this bliss

which brings me ever nearer to the gods,
you gave me the companion I can now
not do without, though, cold and insolent,
he makes me scorn myself and turns your gifts   3245
to nothing with a single whispered word.
Untiringly he fans within my breast
a burning passion for her loveliness.
I reel between desire and enjoyment,
and in enjoyment languish for desire.   3250

Enter MEPHISTOPHELES.

MEPHISTOPHELES. Will it be long before you've had enough of this?
How can this life continue to amuse you?
No doubt it's good to try it once;
but then go on again to something else!

FAUST. I wish you'd other things to do   3255
than plague me when I am content without you.

MEPHISTOPHELES. Come, now! I'm glad to have you resting—
you cannot honestly complain.
Your company is truly no great boon,
you're so abrupt, ungracious, and erratic.   3260
One has his hands full all day long!
You never can tell from the master's expression
what he might like, or what you shouldn't do.

FAUST. That is exactly the right tone—
the servant who's a nuisance then wants gratitude!   3265

MEPHISTOPHELES. You miserable mortal, how on earth
would you have carried on without me?
My treatment's given you some longish intermissions
from the delirium of your delusions;
and if it weren't for me, you'd have long since   3270
sauntered away from this terrestrial sphere.
Why must you waste time here and, owl-like,
perch in these caves and crevices?
What pleasure do you get imbibing, toad-like,
your nourishment from sodden moss and dripping rocks?   3275
A pretty way to pass the time—
there's a professor in you still!

FAUST. Can you not understand what new vitality
I gain from this sojourn in desolate solitude?
Still, if you had some inkling, you would be   3280
devil enough to envy me my happiness.

MEPHISTOPHELES. Superterrestrial delights—
to lie on mountain tops in dew and darkness,
embracing earth and sky ecstatically,

to be puffed up as though you were a god,   3285
to probe the earth with urgent intuitions,
to feel your heart at one with all six days' creation,
enjoying who knows what in your great arrogance
and, now no more an earthbound mortal,
blissfully merging with the All—   3290
and then to let your lofty intuitions
                    (*He makes an expressive gesture.*)
end in a way that I can't mention.
FAUST. For shame!
MEPHISTOPHELES. You find that, then, unpleasant?
    You're a fine one to cry for shame genteelly.
    Before chaste ears one must not name   3295
    what chaste hearts cannot do without.
    But to be brief, I'm glad if you enjoy
    telling youself a lie once in a while,
    even if it won't sustain you long.
    You are already wearing out again;   3300
    if this goes on, your madness or your fears
    will leave you broken down completely.
    Enough of this! Your love is there in town,
    beginning to feel confined in gloom.
    You're never absent from her mind,   3305
    her love for you is overpowering.
    It's not long since the spate of your mad passion
    came like a brook that floods when snows are melting;
    you let it pour into her heart,
    and now your freshet is a shallow brook again.   3310
    It might be well, I think, if our grand gentleman,
    instead of sitting in his forest kingdom,
    left his throne and remunerated
    that poor young thing for her devotion.
    It is a pity how time seems to drag for her;   3315
    she stands at the window and watches the clouds
    moving away above the old town-wall.
    If I had the wings of a bird—that's her song
    day in and day out, and half of every night.
    Sometimes she's cheerful, though mostly sad,   3320
    while sometimes she has no tears left,
    then she'll seem calm again—
    and always she's in love.
FAUST. Serpent! serpent!
MEPHISTOPHELES (*aside*). I'm sure I've got you now!   3325
FAUST. Damnable villain, get you hence!

And make no mention of that lovely girl!
Do not evoke again before these half-crazed senses
desire for the sweetness of her body!

MEPHISTOPHELES. What do you want! She thinks you've run away,   3330
and that is more or less the case.

FAUST. I always will be near her, even far away,
and never can forget or bear to lose her;
I envy, if her lips should touch it in my absence,
the very Body of her Lord.   3335

MEPHISTOPHELES. That's good, my friend! I've often envied you
the twins that feed among the lilies.

FAUST. Flee, you pimp!

MEPHISTOPHELES.   How splendidly you rant, while I can only laugh.
The god who fashioned boys and girls, at once
gave recognition to the noblest of professions   3340
when he himself created opportunity.
Don't dawdle anymore! Why so much misery!
It's not as if you were about to go face death;
you're only summoned to your sweetheart's room.

FAUST. What bliss can being in her arms afford?   3345
Although upon her breast I do find warmth,
shall I still not be feeling her distress
or cease to be unconstant, homeless,
a restive brutal creature with no purpose
that like a cataract has stormed in greedy fury   3350
from rock to rock toward the abyss below?
Close by, a child not yet awakened,
she has her cottage on an alpine meadow,
and that small world encompasses
her whole home-bound existence.   3355
And I, accursed of God,
I have not been content
to seize the rocks
and shatter them,
but have had to destroy her and her peace!   3360
This victim you demanded, Hell!
Help me, devil, shorten the dread of waiting,
and let what must be, be quickly done!
May I be crushed by what will be her doom,
and let her share my ruin with me!   3365

MEPHISTOPHELES. So much seething and ardor again!
Go back and comfort her, you fool.
When certain dainty fellows meet an impasse,
they right away imagine it's the end.

Long life to him who keeps his courage!   3370
In other ways you're fairly far in devilry.
I know of nothing so insipid anywhere
as is a devil driven to despair.   [*Exeunt.*

GRETCHEN'S ROOM

MARGARETE *is alone, sitting at her spinning-wheel.*

GRETCHEN. My heart is heavy,
    all peace is gone,   3375
    I'll never find it,
    never, again.
      Where he is not,
    is like the grave,
    and all my world   3380
    is turned to gall.
      My poor, poor head
    is all upset,
    my wretched mind
    is torn apart.   3385
      My heart is heavy,
    all peace is gone,
    I'll never find it,
    never, again.
      I look from my window   3390
    only for him
    and only to seek him
    do I leave the house.
      His splendid poise,
    his noble figure,   3395
    the smile of his mouth,
    the spell of his eyes,
      the fascinating
    words he utters,
    his hand on mine,   3400
    and, oh! his kiss!
      My heart is heavy,
    all peace is gone,
    I'll never find it,
    never, again.   3405
      My breast is yearning
    to be with him;

could I but clasp
and hold him tight,
and kiss him   3410
as my heart desires,
under his kisses
I'd swoon and die!

MARTHA'S GARDEN

Enter MARGARETE *and* FAUST.

MARGARETE. Heinrich, tell me the truth . . .
FAUST.   As best I can!
MARGARETE. Then say what your religion is.   3415
   You are a sweet good man, and yet
   I think religion doesn't matter much to you.
FAUST. Hush, child! Your feelings tell you that I love you;
   I'd give my life for those who're dear to me,
   I would deprive no one of either faith or church.   3420
MARGARETE. That's wrong! We must believe these things!
FAUST. Must?
MARGARETE. If I only could persuade you to! But you
   don't even venerate the holy sacraments.
FAUST. I pay them due respect.
MARGARETE.   But you don't want them.
   It's long since you have been to mass or to confession.   3425
   Do you believe in God?
FAUST.   My darling, who can say,
   I believe in God?
   To priests or sages you may put your question,
   and what they answer will but seem
   to mock the asker.
MARGARETE.   Then you have no faith?   3430
FAUST. Listen more carefully, my angel!
   Who can name Him
   and dare profess,
   I believe He is!
   Who can feel deeply   3435
   and then presume
   to say, I don't believe!
   Encompassing all,
   sustaining all,
   does He not hold, sustain   3440

you, and me, and Himself?
Is not the vault of heaven there above?
Here below is earth not firm?
And do not everlasting stars
emerge and gently gleam on high?   3445
And when I look into your eyes
does not all being press
upon your heart and mind,
an unseen presence stir,
visibly, beside you?   3450
Imbue your heart with this immensity,
and when you wholly feel beatitude,
then call it what you will—
Happiness! Heart! Love! God!
I have no name to give it!   3455
Feeling is everything,
name is but sound and smoke
that damp celestial ardor.

MARGARETE. That is all very well and good;
    it's much the same as what our priest has said,   3460
    although in slightly different words.

FAUST. It's what all hearts beneath the light of heaven
    are saying everywhere,
    and each in its own language;
    why not I, too, in mine?   3465

MARGARETE. Hearing it put that way, it seems to sound all right,
    but still there is a hitch in it,
    since you don't hold to Christianity.

FAUST. Dear child!

MARGARETE.   I've long been much distressed
    to see the company you keep.   3470

FAUST. What do you mean?

MARGARETE.   The person with you all the time
    is someone I detest with all my soul;
    never in my whole life has anything
    so cut me to the heart
    as has that man's repellent face.   3475

FAUST. Dear poppet, have no fear of him!

MARGARETE. His presence makes my blood run cold.
    There's no one otherwise whom I dislike.
    but much as I may long to see you
    I dread that man in some mysterious way,   3480
    think him a rogue and villain too.
    May God forgive me if I do him wrong!

FAUST. It takes all sorts to make a world.

Margarete. I wouldn't want to live with anyone like him!
 As soon as he steps in the door   3485
 his expression's half one of mockery,
 and half of anger;
 it's obvious that nothing really interests him;
 you see it written in his face
 that he's incapable of loving anyone.   3490
 I'm so contented when I'm in your arms,
 so unconstrained, so warm and yielding,
 and then his presence chokes me up inside.
Faust. You angel, with your intuitions!
Margarete. This is so overwhelming that,   3495
 no matter when or where he joins us,
 I even think that I no longer love you.
 Then too, if he's around, I couldn't say a prayer,
 and that is eating out my heart;
 you, Heinrich, surely feel this too.   3500
Faust. It's just a personal antipathy.
Margarete. I must go now.
Faust.   Oh, can I never stay
 and rest a single hour upon your heart,
 pressing my breast to yours and letting our souls join?
Margarete. Alas! if I but slept alone,   3505
 I'd gladly leave the bolt undrawn tonight;
 but Mother does not sleep too soundly,
 and if she caught us in the act
 I know I'd die right then and there!
Faust. You angel, that presents no problem.   3510
 Here is a vial. Three drops in anything she drinks
 will be enough to put her
 pleasantly into a deep sleep.
Margarete. What is there I won't do for you!
 I trust it will not do her any harm?   3515
Faust. Would I suggest it otherwise, my love!
Margarete. Dearest, I only have to look at you,
 and something makes me do whatever you desire;
 I've done so much for you already
 that there is almost nothing else to do.   [*Exit.*
       Enter Mephistopheles.
Mephisto. The pert young miss has left?
Faust.   You've played the spy again?
Mephistopheles. I listened to the whole proceedings,
 heard the professor catechized,
 and hope that it will do you good.
 The girls are really keen on knowing   3525

if one accepts the good old simple, pious ways.
  They think conformists easiest to rule.
FAUST. You monster, you cannot conceive
  how such a loyal and loving soul,
  imbued completely with a faith   3530
  that is for her
  the one path to salvation, suffers agonies
  to think she must regard her lover a lost soul.
MEPHISTOPHELES. You supersensual sensualist,
  a little girl can lead you by the nose.   3535
FAUST. Monstrosity of filth and fire!
MEPHISTOPHELES. And what a physiognomist she is!
  My presence fills her with the strangest feelings;
  she reads deep meanings in my ugly face
  and senses that I am some sort of radical,   3540
  perhaps, in fact, the very devil.
  Tonight, then . . . ?
FAUST.   What is that to you?
MEPHISTOPHELES. Oh, it is something I can relish!   [*Exeunt.*

AT THE WELL

Enter GRETCHEN *and* LIESCHEN, *with pitchers.*
LIESCHEN. You haven't heard about poor Barbara?
GRETCHEN. No, not a word. I get about so little.   3545
LIESCHEN. It's true, and Sibyl told me so today.
  She too has let herself be taken in, and how!
  So much for her fine airs!
GRETCHEN.   But how?
LIESCHEN.   It stinks to heaven!
  She's feeding two now when she eats and drinks.
GRETCHEN. Oh no!   3550
LIESCHEN. She got what she deserved, all right!
  She kept the fellow to herself for all that time.
  Those walks together,
  those village dances,
  her always having to be first,   3555
  his always treating her to wine and pastry—
  she was stuck-up about her looks,
  but wasn't proud enough to be ashamed
  to take the presents that he gave her.
  With all that cooing, all that kissing,   3560
  the upshot is, the flower's plucked!

GRETCHEN. Poor thing!

LIESCHEN.   How can you pity her!
When the likes of us were busy spinning,
and when at night our mothers kept us all upstairs,
she'd be with her darling lover,   3565
and on the hallway bench, there in the dark,
they never thought about the time.
Well, she can learn now to conform
and do church penance in her sinner's smock.

GRETCHEN. But surely he will marry her.   3570

LIESCHEN. He'd be a fool! A lively fellow
has lots of places where he's welcome.
Besides, he's gone.

GRETCHEN.   That isn't fair!

LIESCHEN. Even if she should catch him, she'll get what's coming to her!
The boys will grab her bridal wreath,   3575
and we'll strew chaff before her door.   [*Exit.*

GRETCHEN (*walking home*).
How readily I once declaimed
when some poor girl did the wrong thing!
Worked up about the sins of others,
I never had words sharp enough.   3580
What seemed so black, I blackened even more,
and yet that wasn't black enough for me;
I'd cross myself, act high and mighty—
and now I'm prey to sin myself!
And yet, o God, what brought me to it,   3585
was all so good, and oh so sweet!   [*Exit.*

BY THE RAMPARTS

In a niche of the wall, a shrine with an image of the Mater Dolorosa before which stand jars of flowers. – Enter GRETCHEN, *who places fresh flowers in the jars.*

GRETCHEN. Deign, o deign,
            you who are sorrow-laden,
            to look down with mercy on my distress!
                With sword-pierced heart   3590
            and racked by pain,
            you raise your eyes to your son's death.
                You look up to his Father
            and to Him on high
            send sighs for His and your distress.   3595

Who but you
can feel the pain
that courses through my frame?
How afraid my poor heart is,
how it trembles, how it's yearning,   3600
only you can know, and you alone!
   No matter where I go,
what sorrow, oh what sorrow
there is within my breast!
No sooner am I left alone   3605
than I must weep and weep and weep—
inside my heart is breaking.
   I watered with bitter tears
the window flower-pots
when in the early morning   3610
I plucked for you these flowers.
   When the bright sun was rising
and shone into my room,
in all my misery
I was sitting awake in bed.   3615
   Help, and save me from shame and death!
O deign,
you who are sorrow laden,
to look down with mercy on my distress!

NIGHT

Street, before the door of Gretchen's house. – Enter her brother VALENTINE,
a soldier.

VALENTINE. It used to be when we all drank together   3620
  and many of my comrades, as they do,
  would start to boast
  and loudly praise the fairest of the fair
  and drain their glasses to wash down the toasts,
  I'd plant my elbow on the table   3625
  and sit relaxed and, unconcerned,
  listen to all their bragging talk,
  and stroke my beard and smile,
  then reach for my full glass and say,
  to each according to his taste!   3630
  but is there anyone in all the land
  who can come up to my dear Gretel,
  who's fit to hold a candle to my sister?

Hear, hear! and clink of glasses went around the table
as there were shouts of "He is right"   3635
and "She's the flower of her sex!"
Then, all those braggarts sat there silent.
And now—it is enough to make me tear my hair
and drive me up a wall!—
I'm going to have to let myself be mocked   3640
by any scoundrel's taunts and sneers,
and sit like a dishonest debtor
and sweat at any chance remark!
And even though I could give them a beating,
I still could not give them the lie.   3645
    But who's that coming—and so furtively?
There's two of them, I'm almost certain;
if he is one, I'll have his hide,
he won't get out of here alive!

                 Enter FAUST *and* MEPHISTOPHELES.

FAUST. See there how from the window of the sacristy   3650
   the everlasting lamp sends up a flickering light
   that fades away to dusk off toward the sides
   as darkness presses in about it!
   In my heart, too, all now is night.
MEPHISTOPHELES. And I too languish, like the cat you see   3655
   there, stealing past the fire ladders,
   and creeping now beside those walls;
   at the same time I feel quite energetic,
   and eager for a bit of theft or lechery—
   I feel already in my bones   3660
   the glories of Walpurgis Night,
   which will be here again two nights from now,
   and that's a time when there's good reason not to sleep.
FAUST. Perhaps by then that treasure will have risen
   whose aura I see gleaming, off back there?   3665
MEPHISTOPHELES. It won't be long before you have the pleasure
   of raising that small pot from out the ground.
   I happened to peep into it the other day
   and saw some fine Bohemian dollars.
FAUST. No piece of jewelry, no ring,   3670
   with which to prettify my mistress?
MEPHISTOPHELES. I think I did see something in it
   that rather looked like strings of pearls.
FAUST. Then all is well! I'm always sorry
   if I arrive without a present.   3675
MEPHISTOPHELES. It really shouldn't bother you,

enjoying something free sometimes.
Now that the sky shines full of stars,
it's time you heard a bit of virtuosity.
I have a moral song to sing her—   3680
it's sure to make her even more infatuated.

(*He sings, accompanying himself on a guitar.*)

Tell me, Kate dear,
why are you here
at lover's door
so early in the morning?   3685
No more of this!
You are a Miss
when you're let in,
but are no Miss at parting.
    Now all take heed!   3690
Once done, the deed
is done for good—
alas for you, poor things!
So when you love
be sure you aren't   3695
too kind to rogues—
without your wedding rings!

VALENTINE (*advancing*).
Hell and damnation! You accursed Pied Piper,
for whom are your enticements meant!
The devil take your instrument,   3700
then take the singer to go with it!
MEPHISTOPHELES. He's broken my guitar, it's useless now!
VALENTINE. And now it's time to break some heads!
MEPHISTOPHELES (*to* FAUST).
Professor, don't retreat! Be bold!
Get close to me, do as I tell you!   3705
Out with your iron! Do not wait,
thrust home! I'll do the parrying.
VALENTINE. Then parry this!
MEPHISTOPHELES.   Why not?
VALENTINE.   And this!
MEPHISTOPHELES. With ease!
VALENTINE.   It is like fighting with the devil!
And what is this? My hand's becoming numb.   3710
MEPHISTO (*to* FAUST). Now strike!
VALENTINE (*falling*).   What pain!
MEPHISTOPHELES.   There, we have tamed that lout!
But now away! We must at once make ourselves scarce—
there are already cries of blood and murder.

I'm an old hand with ordinary magistrates,
but manage far less well in courts with oaths and bans.   [*Exeunt.*

MARTHA (*at a window*). Into the street!
GRETCHEN (*at a window*).   And bring the light!
MARTHA (*as before*). It is a brawl—a fight, a duel.
                    Enter TOWNSPEOPLE.
PEOPLE. Here's one already lying dead!
MARTHA (*coming from her house*).
    The murderers—have they already fled?
GRETCHEN (*coming from her house*).
    Who is that there?
PEOPLE.   Your mother's son.   3720
GRETCHEN. Almighty God! What misery!
VALENTINE. I'm dying—that is quickly said
    and still more quickly done.
    Why must you women stand there wailing?
    Come close, hear what I say!   3725
                    (*All gather around him.*)
    Gretchen, my dear, you really are still immature
    and are not clever enough yet,
    and only botch your business.
    I tell you this, and just in confidence:
    since you have now become a whore,   3730
    make that your occupation!
GRETCHEN. How can you, brother, in God's name! say that to me?
VALENTINE. You leave our Lord God out of this!
    What's done is done, alas! already,
    and what will be, will be as best it can.   3735
    You started with a single secret lover,
    but soon there will be several more,
    and once a dozen men have had you,
    then the whole town will have you too.
        No sooner is Dishonor born   3740
    than where she is is kept a secret,
    and then they draw the veil of night
    about her brow and ears
    and would in fact be glad to kill her.
    But when she grows, gets to be big,   3745
    she even goes unveiled by day,
    yet isn't any prettier.
    The uglier her face becomes,
    the more she seeks the light of day.
        I swear that I foresee the time   3750
    when all the decent folk in town
    will shrink away, you slut, from you

as from a corpse that breeds infection!
And if they look you in the face
you'll feel despair within your heart!   3755
No more allowed to wear gold chains,
or stand in church next to the altar,
or dress yourself in fine lace collars
and have good times at public dances,
you'll hide with beggars and the lame   3760
in some dark nook of misery
and, even if God should forgive you later,
be damned as long as you're on earth!
MARTHA. Commend your soul to the mercy of God!
    Will you add slander to your debts?   3765
VALENTINE. If only I could reach your scrawny body
    and lay my hands on you, vile bawd,
    I'd hope to get abundant pardon
    for all the sins that I've committed!
GRETCHEN. My brother! This is martyrdom!   3770
VALENTINE. Come, now! don't bother to shed tears!
    When you renounced your sense of pride
    you gave my heart the fatal blow.
    Now in the sleep of death I'll go
    to God, a soldier, and an honest soul.   (*Dies.*)   3775

CATHEDRAL

Mass, with organ and CHOIR. GRETCHEN, *surrounded by people; her* EVIL
SPIRIT *behind her.*

SPIRIT. How different were your feelings
    when, still innocent,
    you could approach that altar
    and from your little tattered book
    would lisp your prayers—   3780
    half childhood games,
    and half devotions!
    Gretchen!
    What are your thoughts?
    What crime is buried   3785
    deep within your heart?
    Are you now praying for your mother's soul,
    that by your fault is gone to long, long agonies?
    Whose is the blood before your door?
    – And now beneath your heart   3790
    does life not stir and quicken,

alarming you and itself too
with its foreboding presence?
GRETCHEN. Alas!
  Could I but escape these thoughts   3795
  that come at me from every side,
  do what I will!
CHOIR.   *Dies irae, dies illa*
                solvet saeclum in favilla.
                                  Organ music is heard.
SPIRIT. Feel God's wrath!   3800
  Hear the trumpet sound!
  The graves now tremble!
  And from its rest as ashes
  your heart,
  brought back again   3805
  to burn in torment,
  awakes and trembles!
GRETCHEN. O to be away from here!
  The organ seems
  to take my breath away,   3810
  the singing to undo
  my inmost heart.
CHOIR.   *Judex ergo cum sedebit,*
                quidquid latet adparebit,
                nil inultum remanebit.   3815
GRETCHEN. I feel so stifled!
  The pillars and the walls
  confine me,
  the vaulting
  presses down. – Air!   3820
SPIRIT. Go hide! There is no hiding
  sin and dishonor!
  Air? Light?
  Woe to you!
CHOIR.   *Quid sum miser tunc dicturus,*   3825
                quem patronum rogaturus,
                cum vix justus sit securus?
SPIRIT. All souls now blessed
  avert their faces from you.
  Those who are pure refuse in horror   3830
  to reach out to you.
  Woe!
CHOIR.   *Quid sum miser tunc dicturus?*
GRETCHEN. Good neighbor, please! your salts!   (*She swoons.*)

WALPURGIS NIGHT

In the Harz Mountains, near Schierke and Elend. Enter FAUST *and*
MEPHISTOPHELES.

MEPHISTOPHELES. Do you not wish you had a broomstick?   3835
    I wouldn't mind a sturdy goat myself.
    This way, it's long until we reach our destination.
FAUST. While I feel fresh still, and my legs aren't tired,
    this walking-stick is all I need.
    And what's the point of shortening our path? –   3840
    To wander in a labyrinth of valleys
    and then to climb these rocks from which,
    forever bubbling, water wells and plunges,
    is a delight that lends such walks as this their zest!
    Spring is now stirring in the birches,   3845
    and even firs already feel its presence—
    why should it not affect our limbs as well?
MEPHISTOPHELES. To tell the truth, I've noticed nothing of the kind!
    It feels like winter here inside of me,
    and I'd prefer a road with snow and frost.   3850
    How drearily with its belated glow
    the red moon's crescent now is rising
    and gives us such poor light that every step you take
    you run into a tree or rock!
    Allow me to summon a will-o'-the-wisp!   3855
    I see one there who's burning merrily.
    Hey there, my friend! May I ask you to join us?
    Why blaze away to no good purpose?
    Be kind enough to light us up that slope!
WILL-O'-THE-WISP. I hope that my respect for you   3860
    will let me curb my buoyancy—
    our custom is to go by zigzags only.
MEPHISTOPHELES. Well, well! your aim's to imitate mankind.
    Now, by the devil, just go straight
    or I'll blow out your flicker of life!   3865
WISP. You're lord and master here, that's plain to see,
    and I'll accommodate myself to you with pleasure.
    Remember, though, the mountain's magic-mad tonight,
    and if a will-o'-the-wisp's to be your guide,
    you must not be particular.   3870
FAUST, MEPHISTOPHELES, WISP (*singing by turns*).
        It would seem we've been admitted
        to the sphere of dreams and magic.
        Guide us well, do yourself credit,
        speed us on our travels onward
        in these vast, deserted spaces!   3875

I see trees, and trees behind them,
moving past us in a hurry,
and see cliffs that make obeisance,
and those rocks with their long noses
snoring loudly—hear them blowing!   3880
    Through the stones and turf are flowing
rill and streams that hasten downward.
Are those murmurs, is that singing?
Do I hear love's sweet lamenting,
voices from my days of heaven—   3885
days of love and all we hope for!
Echo, like an ancient legend,
makes reply off in the distance.
    Hoo, hoo-hoo!—the sound comes closer;
have the owl and jay and plover   3890
all remained awake at nighttime?
Are those long legs and fat bellies
in the bushes salamanders?
Roots as well, just like the reptiles,
send strange coils from sand and crevice   3895
to alarm and to entrap us,
or from the gnarled and living timber
reach out with their polyp-tendrils
towards the passer-by. By legions   3900
mice in myriads of colors
scamper through the moss and heather,
and entire swarms of fireflies,
darting past in dense processions,
form an escort that bewilders.   3905
    Tell me whether we have halted
or continue to go forward?
It would seem that all's revolving—
rocks and trees which make grimaces,
and the errant jack-a-lanterns   3910
which are swelling, multiplying.
MEPHISTOPHELES. Get a good hold of my coattails!
  Here's a sort of half-way peak
  that affords a marvelous sight:
  mammon glowing in the rocks.   3915
FAUST. How strangely there glimmers through the dells
  a murky gleam like dawn's first red
  which even casts its flashing light
  into the deepest gorge of the abyss!
  There steam is rising, vapors there are drifting,   3920

a glow of fire shines here in a veil of mist,
now creeping like a slender filament,
now gushing like a fountain-head;
here for a while it forms a hundred veins
that wend their way along the valley,   3925
then at that narrow bend it suddenly
becomes a single strand.
Nearby a burst of sparks
is strewn about like golden sand.
But see how the whole wall of rock   3930
is now aflame from top to bottom!
MEPHISTOPHELES. Lord Mammon has, you must admit, illuminated
his palace lavishly for this occasion!
You're lucky to have seen the spectacle—
I scent the arrival of boisterous guests.   3935
FAUST. What a tremendous storm is raging—
it's raining blows upon my back!
MEPHISTOPHELES. Unless you grab that rock's old ribs,
it's sure to hurl you to the bottom of these gorges.
A mist now makes the darkness denser.   3940
Hear all the tumult in the forest—
the owls are startled into flight!
Hear how, in palaces of evergreen,
the pillars split asunder.
Branches are grating and breaking,   3945
trunks thunder and rumble,
and roots are creaking and cracking!
In dread confusion they fall and crash
and lie each one atop the other,
and through the chasms filled with wreckage   3950
the winds are hissing and howling. –
Do you hear, above us, voices
in the distance, coming closer?
All along the mountain now
torrents of frenzied spells are heard!   3955
                 Enter WITCHES, *singing in chorus.*
WITCHES.   Witches bound for the Brocken are we,
                    the stubble is yellow, the new grain is green.
                    All our number will gather there,
                    and You-Know-Who will take the chair.
                    So we race on over hedges and ditches,   3960
                    the he-goats stink and so do the witches.
A VOICE. There's ancient Baubo coming alone,
she's riding on a mother sow.

WITCHES.   All honor, then, where honor's due!
                  Dame Baubo, come and lead our crew!   3965
                  A good fat sow with dame on her back,
                  and witches will follow all in a pack.
A VOICE. Which way did you come?
A VOICE.   Past the Ilsenstein.
    I peeped into an owl's nest there—
    she opened both eyes wide!
A VOICE.   O go to the devil!   3970
    And why are you racing?
A VOICE. She's flayed me alive—
    just look at my sores!
WITCHES.   The path is broad, the path is long,
                  and yet we are a frantic throng!   3975
                  The pitchfork pricks, the broomstick pokes,
                  the mother bursts, the infant chokes.
                  Enter WARLOCKS. WARLOCKS (*first semichorus*).
                  Like shell-bound snails we drag along,
    the women are all in the van—
    when folk set out for Satan's house   3980
    woman's a thousand steps ahead.
WARLOCKS (*second semichorus*).
                  We don't take that too much to heart:
                  no matter how much haste they make,
                  they need a thousand steps to do
                  what men can do in just one leap.   3985
A VOICE (*above*). Come join us, you down by the tarn!
VOICES (*from below*). We'd like to go on up with you,
    but since we've washed till spick and span,
    sterility remains our fate.
WITCHES AND WARLOCKS.
                  The wind is hushed, the stars take flight,   3990
                  the clouded moon withdraws from sight,
                  but as we roar along, our rout
                  sprays myriad magic-sparks about.
A VOICE (*from below*). Stop! Wait for me!
A VOICE (*above*). Who's calling from the crevice there?   3995
A VOICE (*below*). Take me along! Take me too!
    I slipped three hundred years ago
    and ever since have tried in vain
    to reach my friends at the top again.
WITCHES AND WARLOCKS.
                  A stick or broom will carry you,   4000
                  so will a goat or pitchfork too;

    and if tonight you cannot soar,
    you are disgraced forevermore.
HALF-WITCH (*below*).
  I've lagged behind a long time now,
  the others are so far ahead;   4005
  at home I have no peace and quiet,
  but, then, I don't find any here.
WITCHES.   To give us courage, salves avail,
          a rag can serve us as a sail,
          and any trough as a ship that's tight;   4010
          you'll never fly, if you don't tonight.
WITCHES AND WARLOCKS.
          And when the summit has been reached,
          scurry along upon the ground
          and with your witchdom's multitudes
          cover, then, all the heath around!   4015
           They settle on the ground.
MEPHISTOPHELES. What crowding, pushing, what noisy clatter!
  What hissing, swirling, what lively babble!
  Those sparks and flashes, that stench and fire,
  are truly witchdom's element!
  Hang on to me, or we will soon be parted!   4020
  Now where are you!
FAUST (*in the distance*). I'm here.
MEPHISTOPHELES.   What! dragged so far already?
  I'll have to show who's master here.
  Make way, your Squire's here! Make way, sweet mob, make way!
  Professor, take my hand! Now, in one jump,
  we can escape this press of people—   4025
  this madness is too much for even me!
  A most peculiar light is shining over there,
  I'm curious about what's in those bushes.
  Come, let's slip in and have a look!
FAUST. Spirit of contradictions, have your way! Lead on! 4030
  But, I must say, what we have done is clever—
  we climb the Brocken on Walpurgis Night
  to isolate ourselves now that we're here.
MEPHISTOPHELES. Just take a look! See those bright fires!
  Some lively club's assembled for a meeting.   4035
  You do not need a crowd to have companionship.
FAUST. But I would rather be up there,
  where I glimpse flames and whirling smoke!
  Those crowds are surging on toward Satan;
  the answer to many riddles is surely there.   4040
MEPHISTOPHELES. But many riddles, too, are set.

Great folk may like the noisy life,
we'll be quite cozy in this quiet spot.
Besides, it is an ancient practice
to make your own small worlds inside the great one.   4045
I see some nice young witches over there,
stark naked next to elders wisely veiled.
Be pleasant to them, simply for my sake;
a little effort gets you much amusement.
But hark! there is the twang of instruments,   4050
a curse one simply has to learn to bear.
Come! come along and face the music;
I'll make the overtures and introduce you,
and you'll be much obliged to me again.
You must admit, my friend, that "small" does not describe   4055
a space—just look!—which hardly seems to end.
All in a row a hundred fires blaze;
folk dance, converse, concoct, imbibe, make love;
just tell me where there's anything to beat this!
FAUST. Do you intend, when introducing us,   4060
to play the devil's role, or that of sorcerer?
MEPHISTOPHELES. Although I'm very used to going incognito,
on gala days one wears one's decorations.
I do not have the honor of the Garter,
but here my cloven hoof is much respected.   4065
Do you see there the snail that's crawling toward us?
With eyes that only feel and grope
it has already caught a whiff of me—
here, there's no denying my identity.
Now come, let's walk about from fire to fire;   4070
I'll be the spokesman, you the tongue-tied suitor.
          (*He addresses a group seated around dying embers.*)
Old gentlemen, why must you stay down here?
I'd like it better if you were right in the middle,
surrounded by the revelry of youth;
to be alone, one doesn't need leave home.   4075
A GENERAL. You cannot trust the Government,
no matter what great service you have done it;
the People are no different from women
and grant all favors to the young.
A STATESMAN. They're much too far off course these days,   4080
give me the old reliables;
when we were all-important, though,
that really was a golden age.
A PARVENU. We weren't exactly stupid either,
and got ahead by dubious means;   4085

but nowadays there's nothing stable—
just when we'd like the status quo.
A WRITER. In times like these who cares to read
a work that has a modicum of sense!
As for the younger generation,   4090
it is more impudent than ever.
MEPHISTOPHELES (*suddenly looking very old*).
Folk are, I feel, now ripe for Judgment Day,
since this ascent of Witches' Mountain is my last;
and since my keg is running turbid,
I'm sure the world is giving out as well.   4095
HUCKSTRESS-WITCH.
Good sirs, don't just walk past like that!
Don't miss this opportunity!
Take a good look at what I offer,
I have a great variety.
And yet there's nothing in my stall,   4100
the like which you won't find anywhere,
that hasn't at some time or other done
great harm to persons and society.
There is no dagger here that has not dripped with blood,
no cup that has not poured its hot consuming poison   4105
into some hale and hearty body,
no ornament but has seduced some good sweet woman,
no sword but served that cause of treason
or stabbed an adversary from behind!
MEPHISTOPHELES. You are, good woman, quite behind the times.   4110
What's done, is past! What's past, is done with!
You should go in for novelties,
that's all that customers now want.
FAUST. I hope my mind remains intact!
I've never seen a carnival so lively!   4115
MEPHISTOPHELES. That milling crowd all wants to be up higher;
you think you're pushing, but it's you who's pushed.
FAUST. Now who is that?
MEPHISTOPHELES.   Take a good look!
That's Lilith.
FAUST.   Who?
MEPHISTOPHELES.   Adam's first wife.
Be on your guard against her lovely tresses,   4120
the only ornament she wears!
When she has caught a young man with them,
it's quite a while until she lets him go.
FAUST. Those witches sitting there, one young, the other old,
have clearly done a fair amount of dancing!   4125

MEPHISTOPHELES. There is no rest for anyone tonight.
  Here's a new dance! Come on, we have our pick!
FAUST (*dancing with the pretty Young Witch*).

One day I had a lovely dream,
in which I saw an apple tree
and on it saw two apples gleam;   4130
they tempted me to climb the tree.

YOUNG WITCH.   You men have always craved that fruit
since it first grew in Paradise.
I quiver with delight to know
that in my orchard apples grow.   4135

MEPHISTOPHELES (*with the* OLD WITCH).

One day I had the wildest dream;
in it I saw a cloven tree,
and in the tree a gaping hole;
big though this was, it suited me.

OLD WITCH.   With reverence I here salute   4140
the knight who has the cloven foot!
Be ready with the right-sized stopper
unless big holes intimidate you.

PROCTOVISIONARY.
  Confounded creatures, what new impudence is this?
  Have you not had it proved to you long since   4145
  that proper spirits never stand on their own feet?
  And here you're even dancing like us ordinary mortals!
YOUNG WITCH (*dancing*). What is that fellow doing at our ball?
FAUST (*dancing*). Oh, he's someone who turns up everywhere.
  His job's to criticize how others dance.   4150
  Unless he can discuss a *pas* at length,
  it might as well not have been danced.
  Steps forward are what most annoy him.
  If you just want to go around in circles,
  the way he does in his old factory,   4155
  he'll condescend to rate that passable—
  especially if you have been polite to him.
PROCTOVISIONARY. You are still there? Now that's impossible!
  Please disappear! We have achieved enlightenment.
  Infernal rabble that ignores all rules of logic!   4160
  We're highly rational, despite all ghosts in Tegel.
  How long I've tried to sweep away delusions,
  and yet there's always dirt. Things are impossible!
YOUNG WITCH. Then stop! You do not need to bore us here.
PROCTOVISIONARY. I tell you spirits to your faces: 4165
  my spirit won't put up with despotism—
  it is itself far too despotic.

(The dancing starts again.)

I see I'm having no success today;
still, I've material for another travel book
and hope, before my final journey,   4170
to exorcise all devils and all poets.

MEPHISTOPHELES. He's going off to sit down in a puddle,
which is the way he gets relief from pain;
when leeches feast upon his rump,
he's cured of spirits and of spirit.   4175

     (To FAUST, *who has left the dance.).*

Why have you deserted the pretty young girl
who sang so nicely when you danced?

FAUST. Why, right while she was singing
a small red mouse leaped from her mouth.

MEPHISTOPHELES. Nothing but that? You shouldn't be so fussy.   4180
At least it wasn't just a gray one.
Such things don't bother ardent swains.

FAUST. And then I saw . . .

MEPHISTOPHELES.   Saw what?

FAUST.   Mephisto, do you see
off there, alone, dead-pale, a lovely girl?
Now she is slowly moving away,   4185
dragging her feet as if they were in fetters.
I have to say I can't help thinking
that she looks like my own dear Gretchen.

MEPHISTOPHELES. Leave that alone—it only can do harm!
It is a magic image, a phantom without life.   4190
It's dangerous to meet up with;
its stare congeals a person's blood
and almost turns him into stone—
you've surely heard about Medusa!

FAUST. I know those are the eyes of someone dead,   4195
eyes that no loving hand has closed.
That is the breast which Gretchen let me press,
that the sweet body which gave me joy.

MEPHISTOPHELES. Don't be so gullible, you fool! It's sorcery:
to every man she looks like her he loves.   4200

FAUST. What ecstasy, and yet what pain!
I cannot bear to let this vision go.
How strange that on that lovely neck
there is as ornament a single scarlet thread
no thicker than a knife!   4205

MEPHISTOPHELES. You're right, I see it too.
She also can transport her head beneath her arm,
thanks to the fact that Perseus lopped it off.

I see you never lose your craving for illusions!
Now come along uphill a little more!   4210
Here it's as gay as in the Prater;
unless I've been bewitched myself,
it is a theater that I see.
What's on up there?
OFFICIOUS SPIRIT.   They're just about to start again.
The play is new, the last of seven such;   4215
it is our custom here to have so many.
The author is a dilettant,
and dilettants will be the actors.
Excuse my disappearing, gentlemen,
but I'm the curtain-raising dilettant.   4220
MEPHISTOPHELES. It's good to find you on the Blocksberg,
for that's where all your ilk belong.

WALPURGIS NIGHT'S DREAM

OR, OBERON'S AND TITANIA'S GOLDEN WEDDING

Intermezzo

STAGE MANAGER. All of us can rest today,
                    sturdy sons of Mieding!
                    Ancient mountain, misty vale,   4225
                    that is all our scenery.
HERALD.   If you want a golden wedding,
                    fifty years are needed;
                    "golden" fits a marriage better
                    when all quarrels are ended.   4230
OBERON.   Spirits, if you're here with us,
                    now reveal your presence;
                    fairy king and fairy queen
                    are again united.
PUCK.   If Puck comes and pirouettes   4235
                    and trips the light fantastic,
                    after him a hundred more
                    will come to share the frolic.
ARIEL.   Ariel begins to sing
                    in clear, celestial tones;   4240
                    though his voice can summon monsters,
                    it also summons beauties.
OBERON.   Spouses, if you're seeking concord,
                    learn the art from us!

	To make couples love each other	4245
	you only need to part them.	
TITANIA.	When husbands sulk and wives have whims,	
	grab hold of them at once,	
	and lead her off to southern climes,	
	and him to the North Pole.	4250
ORCHESTRA	(*tutti, fortissimo*).	
	Snout the Fly, Mosquito Bill,	
	together with their kindred,	
	Grassy Cricket, Leaf-Green Frog,	
	make up the musicians.	
(*Solo*.)	There you see the bagpipe come,	4255
	Soap-Bubble is his name;	
	what you hear is an endless drone	
	coming from his pug nose.	

MATERIALIZING SPIRIT.

Give the little wight some winglets,
a toad's belly, spiders' feet—   4260
the result is nothing living,
but it makes poetic verse.

A TINY COUPLE.   Mincing steps and great high leaps
through honey-dew and fragrance—
though your tempo's right for me,   4265
we never will be fliers.

INQUISITIVE TRAVELER [PROCTOVISIONARY].

What's this silly masquerade!
Can my eyes be trusted?
Oberon's here too, tonight,
godlike in his beauty!   4270

ORTHODOX.   He has neither claws nor tail,
but there's no doubt of this:
like the ancient gods of Greece
he also is a devil.

NORTHERN ARTIST.

What I'm undertaking now   4275
are really only sketches—
but I'm making preparations
for an Italian journey.

PURIST.   What misfortune brings me here,
where everything's improper!   4280
Besides, I see but two wigs worn
in all this host of spirits.

YOUNG WITCH.   Your powdered wigs and petticoats
are meant for old, gray women;
that's why I'm naked on my goat   4285
and show my healthy body.

MATRON.   We're too well-bred and too genteel
                           to squabble here with you;
                           still, let me hope you all may rot
                           while you are sweet young things.   4290

CONDUCTOR.   Snout the Fly, Mosquito Bill,
                           don't buzz that naked beauty!
                           Grassy Cricket, Leaf-Green Frog,
                           do try to keep time also!

WEATHERVANE (*toward one side*).
                           What a delightful gathering!   4295
                           The girls all lovely brides-to-be,
                           the bachelors without exception
                           young men of greatest promise!

(*Toward the other side.*)
                           And if the ground beneath them fails
                           to open up and swallow them,   4300
                           then I will take a running leap
                           and go on down to hell myself.

SATIRIC VERSES.   We appear as insects here,
                           with tongues that cut like scissors,
                           and come to offer our respects   4305
                           to Satan, who's our father.

HENNINGS.   See how they come, the merry crowd,
                           and have no inhibitions!
                           Before they're done they'll even claim
                           they really are kind-hearted.   4310

THE SAME, *as* WOULD-BE APOLLO.
                           It might be well for me to join
                           this company of spirits;
                           I certainly could lead them better
                           than I do the Muses.

THE SAME, *as* QUONDAM SPIRIT OF THE AGE.
                           To get ahead, join the right crowd—   4315
                           come, latch on to my coattails!
                           If there's a lot of room atop the Brocken,
                           that's also true of Germany's Parnassus.

INQUISITIVE TRAVELER.
                           "Tell me who's the stiff-necked man
                           that I see strutting there   4320
                           and sticking his nose into everything?"
                           "He's scenting Jesuits."

CRANE.   I like to fish where water's clear,
                           but also where it's troubled,
                           and so this pious clergyman   4325
                           is seen among the devils.

WORLDLING.	Take this on faith from me: for pious folk
	all things are vehicles,
	and so they form conventicles
	here on the Brocken too. 4330
DOGMATIST.	"There surely is a new group coming—
	I hear a distant drumming."
	"You needn't stop! It is the monotone
	of bitterns booming."
BALLET MASTER.	It's shocking how they move their legs 4335
	and just get through the figures!
	The crooked leap, the awkward hop,
	and have no sense of beauty.
MAN OF TOLERANCE.	
	Although the rabble dearly hate
	and want to kill each other, 4340
	they're brought together by the bagpipe
	like beasts by Orpheus' lyre.
DOGMATIST.	I'll not be led astray by cries
	of sceptics or of critics.
	The Devil really must exist, 4345
	since I am seeing devils.
SUBJECTIVE IDEALIST.	
	Tonight the things my mind imagines
	completely overwhelm me.
	Indeed, if they are all my ego,
	then I am idiotic. 4350
REALIST.	These goings on are most distressing
	and irritate me greatly;
	this once I find I cannot firmly
	stand on my own two feet.
SUPERNATURALIST.	I am delighted to be here 4355
	and share these devils' pleasures;
	if they exist, I can infer
	there are good spirits also.
SCEPTIC.	They're all pursuing jack-a-lanterns
	and think the trove is near. 4360
	Since Doubt's the Devil's boon companion,
	I'm right where I belong.
CONDUCTOR.	Snout the Fly, Mosquito Bill,
	confound you dilettantes!
	Grassy Cricket, Leaf-Green Frog, 4365
	do try to be musicians!
THE ADROIT.	Sans-souci's the name to give
	our large and merry company;
	since we've lost our former footing,
	we are walking on our heads. 4370

THE AWKWARD.	We used to sponge a lot of meals in days now gone forever; since we have danced right through our shoes, we're walking here on bare feet.
WILL-O'-THE-WISPS.	
	We have arrived from the morass 4375 where we just now originated, yet here we're dancing at your ball as beaus who are the height of fashion.
SHOOTING STAR.	In a glow of stars and fire I shot down from the sky; 4380 now I'm frustrated in the grass— who'll help me to my feet?
THE MASSIVE.	Room there! Make more room around us! the grass is to be walked on. We are spirits, too, but are 4385 somewhat ungainly creatures.
PUCK.	Don't behave like fattened swine and stump like elephants! Let no one be more rough today than merry Puck himself! 4390
ARIEL.	If your wings are Nature's gift, or those bred by Fancy, follow me on airy path to the Hill of Roses!
ORCHESTRA (*pianissimo*).	
	Drifting cloud and veil of mist 4395 above are growing brighter. Winds are stirring leaf and sedge, and all things here have vanished.

AN EXPANSE OF OPEN COUNTRY

The sky is overcast. Enter FAUST *and* MEPHISTOPHELES.

FAUST. In misery and despair! So long a wretched vagrant, and now a prisoner! That dear, unhappy girl confined to prison as a criminal and prey to fearful torments! Has it come to this, to this! — Perfidious, contemptible spirit, to keep this concealed from me! — Yes, stand there! Stand and roll your diabolic eyes in silent fury! Stand there and spite me with your intolerable presence! A prison! In misery that is irreparable! Delivered up to evil spirits and to the callousness of human judgment! And all this while you lull me with inane diversions, conceal from me her deepening misery, and abandon her to ruin!

MEPHISTOPHELES. She is not the first.

FAUST. You dog, you monster! — Transform him, Spirit Infinite, transform the serpent back into the canine form in which he often liked at night to trot before me and, rolling at the unsuspecting walker's feet, would trip him up and leap upon his shoulders as he fell. Transform him again into his favorite shape, so that as he crawls before me in the sand upon his belly I may kick the profligate dog! — Not the first! — Misery! Misery too great for human soul to grasp, that more than one poor girl has sunk into these depths of wretchedness, that in her writhing agony before the eyes of the Eternal Forgiver, the first could not atone the guilt of all the others! The wretched lot of this one creature gnaws at my very being's core—and you keep on calmly grinning at the fate of thousands!

MEPHISTOPHELES. Here we are again at our wits' end, the point where, with you humans, minds give way. Why have you entered into partnership with us if you cannot keep its terms? Do you want to fly, and know heights make you dizzy? Did we thrust ourselves upon you, or you on us?

FAUST. Don't bare your teeth at me like that! I loathe your ravenous grinning! — August Spirit who deigned to appear to me, you who know my heart and soul, why fetter me to this vile companion who feeds on mischief and rejoices in destruction?

MEPHISTOPHELES. Have you about finished?

FAUST. Save her, or suffer and be cursed for ages!

MEPHISTOPHELES. I cannot loose bonds laid by the avenger of blood, cannot undo his bars. — Save her! — Who plunged her into ruin! I, or you? (FAUST *looks about in a frenzy.*) Are you searching for a thunderbolt? How fortunate you miserable mortals did not receive that weapon! To crush and slay the man who dares reply to him is how a tyrant finds relief when he's embarrassed.

FAUST. Take me to her! She shall be free!

MEPHISTOPHELES. And what about the risk you run? Guilt of blood spilled by your hand, still lies upon the town! Avenging spirits hover where the slain man fell and lie in wait for the returning murderer.

FAUST. This accusation, too—from you! All death and murder be upon your head, you monster! Take me to her, I say, and set her free!

MEPHISTOPHELES. I will take you there. And what I can do, hear! Is all the power in heaven and on earth mine? When I've befogged the jailer's senses, you take possession of his keys and lead her out with your own human hand! I shall stand guard; my magic horses will be waiting, I'll get you both away—this much I can.

FAUST. Come! Away!   [*Exeunt.*

NIGHT: OPEN FIELDS

Enter FAUST *and* MEPHISTOPHELES, *dashing along on black horses.*
FAUST. What are they doing by that stone block?
MEPHISTOPHELES. I've no idea what they're brewing or making.   4400
FAUST. They soar up, and then down; they are bending and bowing.
MEPHISTOPHELES. A witches' coven.
FAUST. They strew and consecrate.
MEPHISTOPHELES. On! Hurry on!   [*Exeunt.*

PRISON

Enter FAUST, *with a bunch of keys and a lamp; he stands before a small
iron door.*
FAUST. A long-forgotten sense of horror makes me tremble,   4405
   all mankind's miseries have hold of me.
   She is lodged here, behind the dankness of this wall,
   and faith in human goodness was her crime!
   You hesitate to enter where she is,
   you are afraid to see her once again!   4410
   Go now! Your hesitation but lets death come ever nearer.
   As FAUST *takes hold of the lock, singing is heard from behind the door.*
MARGARETE (*within*).   It was mother, the whore!
               who put me to death,
               and father, poor knave!
               the one who did eat me.   4415
               The bones that remained,
               little sister then laid
               in a cool, quiet place;
               I'm changed into a little bird
               and fly away in the forest!   4420
FAUST (*unlocking the door*).
   She's unaware her lover's listening,
   can hear the clanking chains, the rustling straw.
              He enters the cell.
MARGARETE (*cowering on her pallet*).
   O woe! They've come! Death is so bitter!
FAUST (*softly*). Be quiet! Hush! I've come to set you free.
MARGARETE (*rolling over toward him*).
   If you are human, pity me in my distress!   4425
FAUST. Your cries will wake the sleeping guards!
         He takes hold of her fetters to unlock them.
MARGARETE (*on her knees*).
   Headsman, who's given you the right

to treat me thus?
It's only midnight, and you've come to take me.
Have mercy on me, let me live!   4430
Is not tomorrow morning soon enough?
                              (*She rises.*)
I'm still so young, so young,
and yet I am to die already!
I once was pretty, that was my undoing.
I had a lover, now he's far away,   4435
they've torn my bridal wreath, its flowers all lie scattered.
Do not take hold of me so brutally!
Spare me! What harm have I done you?
Don't let me plead in vain,
you know I've never seen you in my life!   4440
FAUST. Can I get through this misery?
MARGARETE. I am completely at your mercy now.
First let me just nurse my child again.
All night I have been holding it close to my heart;
to hurt my feelings, they took it from me,   4445
and now they're saying that I killed it.
And I can't ever be happy again.
People are making me their song! It's mean of them!
There's an old story that ends like that,
who gave them the right to say it's mine?   4450
FAUST (*falling at her feet*).
Here at your feet is someone who loves you,
who's come to deliver you from your misery.
MARGARETE (*throwing herself down beside him*).
O let us kneel and ask the saints to aid us!
Look, beneath these stones,
under this sill,   4455
hellfire is seething.
In terrible anger
hear Satan himself
raising an uproar!
FAUST (*loudly*). Gretchen! Gretchen!   4460
MARGARETE (*becoming attentive*).
That was my lover's voice.
            (*She springs to her feet; the fetters drop to the floor.*)
Where is he? I heard him calling.
I am free! No one can stop me.
I want to rush and throw my arms about his neck,
I want to lie upon his breast!   4465
There at the door he called out: Gretchen!
In the howling and clatter of hell,

and the angry jeering of devils,
I could tell the sound of that dear, sweet voice.
FAUST. I'm here!
MARGARETE.   It's you! O say so once again!   4470
                    (*She embraces* FAUST.)
It's he, it's he! Where are my torments now—
the fearful prison and the dreadful chains?
It's you! You've come to rescue me,
and I am saved! –
There is the street again   4475
where I first saw you,
the happy garden where,
with Martha, I'm awaiting you.
FAUST (*urging her toward the door*).
Come! Come along!
MARGARETE.   Don't hurry! Stay!
I so much like to be where you are staying.   4480
                    She caresses FAUST.
FAUST. Make haste!
Unless you hurry,
there'll be a dreadful price to pay.
MARGARETE. Are you no longer able to return a kiss?
So short a time away from me, my love,   4485
and you've forgotten how to kiss?
Why do I feel so frightened in your arms,
when once your words, your eyes,
brought all of heaven down about me,
and you seemed to want to stifle me with kisses.   4490
Give me a kiss,
or I'll kiss you!
                    (*She embraces* FAUST.)
Your lips are terribly cold,
they do not speak.
What has become   4495
of the love you had?
Who's stolen it from me!
                    She turns away from FAUST.
FAUST. Come, follow me! Dear love, have courage!
If you but follow me, I'll hold you to my heart
with all the warmth it has! I beg you only, come!   4500
MARGARETE (*turning toward* FAUST).
And is it you? And is it really you?
FAUST. Yes! Come with me!
MARGARETE.   You have undone my chains,
are taking me again into your arms.

But why do you not shrink from me in fear?
Do you, my love, know whom you're setting free?   4505
FAUST. Come, hurry! Darkness is already waning.
MARGARETE. I am the one who killed my mother,
  I am the one who drowned my child.
  Wasn't the baby given to us both,
  to you as well? – I hardly can believe it's you!   4510
  Give me your hand. Yes, this is not a dream!
  Your dear, dear hand! But oh, it's wet.
  Wipe it off! I can't help thinking
  there's blood on it.
  Oh God, what have you done!   4515
  Put up your sword,
  I beg you.
FAUST. Let what is past, be past,
  or you will be the death of me.
MARGARETE. No, you must go on living!   4520
  I want to tell how the graves should be;
  you must see to them tomorrow
  the very first thing:
  the best place for mother;
  my brother close beside;   4525
  with me a bit off to the side,
  yet not too far away;
  and the little one at my right breast.
  No one else is to be beside me! –
  How lovely it was and what sweet happiness   4530
  to nestle up against you!
  But I can't do so any more—
  it is as if I had to force myself upon you
  and you were pushing me away.
  And still it's you, looking so kind, so good.   4535
FAUST. Come, if you feel sure of who I am!
MARGARETE. Out through there?
FAUST. To freedom.
MARGARETE.   If the grave's out there
  and death lying in wait, yes!
  From here to my bed of eternal rest,   4540
  and not one step beyond –
  Are you now leaving? Heinrich, would that I could too!
FAUST. You can if you but wish! The door is open.
MARGARETE. I cannot leave; for me there is no hope.
  Why run away when they are watching for me?   4545
  It's terrible to be reduced to begging,
  and then with a bad conscience too!

It's terrible to go not knowing where—
and they will catch me anyhow.
FAUST. I'll be with you.   4550
MARGARETE. Hurry! Hurry,
 save your poor child!
 Quick! Keep to the path
 that goes up along the brook,
 then over the bridge   4555
 and into the woods
 to the left, by the fence—
 in the pond!
 Grab hold, don't wait!
 See the effort to rise,   4560
 the stirring of life—
 save it, save it!
FAUST. Be sensible, I beg you!
 One step, just one! and you'll be free.
MARGARETE. If only we were past the hill!   4565
 On a rock there, my mother is sitting—
 I feel a cold hand grab my hair!
 There on a rock my mother is sitting
 and feebly shaking her head;
 she doesn't wave or nod, her head's too heavy;   4570
 she slept too long to waken ever again.
 She slept to let us have our happiness.
 And those were happy times!
FAUST. If pleas and reasons are of no avail,
 I'll carry you away against your will.   4575
MARGARETE. Let go of me! I won't be forced.
 Take your wicked hands off me!
 You know that up to now I've done what you have wanted.
FAUST. The day dawns gray! – O dearest one!
MARGARETE. Day! Yes, the day begins—the day of judgment   4580
 that should have been my wedding-day!
 Let no one know you've been in Gretchen's room.
 Alas, no wreath—
 what's done can't be undone!
 We'll meet again,   4585
 but not at a wedding dance.
 The crowd is gathering in silence;
 the square and streets
 won't hold them all.
 Hear the knell calling, see the white rod break!   4590
 How roughly they tie and handle me,
 how quickly they carry me to the block!

The edge that rushes down at me
is darting now toward every neck.
All is silence—the silence of the grave!   4595
FAUST. O, that I never had been born!

      MEPHISTOPHELES *appears before* MARGARETE'S *cell.*
MEPHISTOPHELES. Come! Away, or both of you are lost!
  Futile faintheartedness! Delaying and prattling!
  My horses are trembling—
  there's a first glimmer of dawn.   4600
MARGARETE. What's that, rising up from below?
  That man! Send him away!
  Why is he here, in this holy place?
  He's come for me!
FAUST. You shall not die!
MARGARETE. Divine justice, in you I placed my trust!   4605
MEPHISTOPHELES (*to* FAUST).
  Come, or I'll abandon both of you.
MARGARETE. I am your child, Father—save me!
  Angels and heavenly hosts,
  compass me about and keep me safe!
  Heinrich! I fear and loathe you.   4610
MEPHISTOPHELES. She is judged!
VOICE (*from above*).   She is saved!
MEPHISTOPHELES (*to* FAUST).   Away, with me!
      He disappears with FAUST.
VOICE (*from within, growing faint*). Heinrich! Heinrich!

PART TWO OF THE TRAGEDY
in Five Acts

ACT I

A PLEASANT LANDSCAPE

FAUST *is couched on grass and flowers, fatigued, restless, and endeavoring to sleep as twilight is about to become darkness; hovering* SPIRITS— *graceful diminutive figures —circle about him.*

ARIEL (*singing to the sound of aeolian harps*).

As the falling springtime blossoms
float above them everywhere
and all mortals see great promise   4615
in the greenness of the fields;
small in size, but large in spirit,
elves are quick to be of help,
pitying the man of sorrow,
whether he be saint or sinner.   4620
You who are circling in the air above this head,
now demonstrate your elfin worth—
compose the angry strife within his heart,
remove the burning barbs of his remorse,
and purge him of all sense of horror!   4625
The watches of the night are four;
start now to make each one agreeable.
First rest his head on cushioning coolness,
then bathe him in the dew of Lethe's waters;
his body will recover quickly from its numbness   4630
if sleep gives him the strength to face the coming day;
perform your noblest elfin duty
and grant him restoration to its sacred light!

SPIRITS (*in chorus; singly, by twos and more, alternately and collectively*).

When about the green-girt meadow
breezes stir with gentle torpor,   4635
twilight falls with fragrant sweetness,
closes in with veils of mist.
Murmur dulcetly of calmness,
cradle this heart in childhood's peace,
and upon his tired eyes   4640
shut the portals of day's light.

    Night has now already fallen,
sacred ranks of stars are forming;
dazzling lights and lesser sparklings

glitter near or gleam afar,   4645
glitter here in the lake's mirror,
gleam above in night's translucence;
the regnant moon in all its glory
seals and confirms the bliss of sleep.
    Hours are obliterated,   4650
pain and joy have vanished now;
be assured, you will recover—
take hope from this day's first gleaming!
Greening valleys and emerging hills
offer bush-filled shadow and repose,   4655
and in pliant, argent waves
new grain billows harvestward.
    To obtain desires' fulfillment,
look and see the radiance there!
You are under no deep spell,   4660
cast away sleep's veil-thin husk!
Do not hesitate, be daring
while the aimless crowd delays:
all is achieved by noble minds
that understand and quickly act!   4665
      A great clangor heralds the approach of the sun.

ARIEL. Hearken! Hear the onrush of the Horae!
  In these sounds we spirits hear
  the new day already born.
  Cavern portals grate and rattle,
  rolling wheels of Phoebus clatter,   4670
  light arrives with deafening din!
  Brasses blare, the trumpets peal,
  eyes are blinking, ears astounded—
  things unheard you must not hear:
  hide away in flowers' petals   4675
  or, to dwell in deeper stillness,
  in the rocks below their leafage;
  you'll be deaf if such sounds reach you.   [*Exeunt.*

FAUST. Life's pulses beat with fresh vitality
  and gently greet the sky's first glimmering;   4680
  you also, Earth, have lasted out this night
  and breathe new-quickened there below,
  compassing me already with inchoate joy.
  You rouse and stir a vigorous resolve
  to strive henceforth towards being's highest form. –   4685
  But now the light of dawn unveils the world:
  the woods resound with myriads of living voices;
  everywhere valleys are filled with streaks of fog,

but still the heavens' brightness penetrates their depths,
and from the misty chasm where they slept   4690
fresh-quickened boughs and branches have burst forth;
muted no more, color on color emerges in the dell
where trembling pearls drench every leaf and flower—
all that surrounds me forms a paradise!
    Look now, above! The mountains' mighty peaks   4695
herald the hour of full solemnity,
by right partaking of the everlasting light
before it veers towards us below;
new radiant clarity extends its boon
to alpine meadows sloping green beneath them   4700
and stage by stage completes its downward journey; –
now it appears!—and, to my sorrow blinded,
I turn my gaze away suffused with pain.
    The same thing happens when our eager hope
believes its highest goal has been obtained   4705
and finds the portals of fulfillment open wide:
then there bursts forth from those eternal depths
excess of flame, and so we halt confounded;
our wish had been to light the torch of life—
instead, a very sea of fire engulfs us.   4710
Do love and hate envelop us in flame,
savagely alternating pain and joy,
so that we look once more towards earth and seek
concealment in its first new lacery?
    I am content to have the sun behind me.   4715
The cataract there storming through the cliff—
the more I watch it, the more is my delight.
From fall to fall it swirls, gushing forth
in streams that soon are many, many more,
into the air all loudly tossing spray and foam.   4720
But see how, rising from this turbulence,
the rainbow forms its changing-unchanged arch,
now clearly drawn, now evanescent,
and casts cool, fragrant showers all about it.
Of human striving it's a perfect symbol—   4725
ponder this well to understand more clearly
that what we have as life is many-hued reflection.

AN IMPERIAL PALACE

THE THRONE ROOM

STATE COUNCIL, *awaiting the Emperor. Trumpets. Enter* COURTIERS *and* RETAINERS, *splendidly attired; the* EMPEROR *ascends his throne, and the* ASTROLOGER *stands at his right.*

EMPEROR. I greet you, dear and loyal subjects,
    assembled here from near and far . . . —
    I see my Sage is at my side,   4730
    but what has happned to my Fool?
A SQUIRE. As you were coming up the stairs
    he suddenly collapsed behind your trailing robe;
    the hulk of fat was lugged away,
    but whether dead or drunk we do not know.   4735
SECOND SQUIRE. At once, and with amazing quickness,
    another fool pushed into his place.
    He is most splendidly accoutered,
    but so grotesque that everyone is leery;
    the guards there at the doorway hold   4740
    their halberds crossed in front of him—
    why here he is, foolhardy fellow!
MEPHISTOPHELES (*kneeling at the throne*).
    What is accursed, yet always welcome,
    what ardently desired, and yet chased away,
    what constantly receives our favor,   4745
    yet is denounced and much reviled?
    Whom can you never summon to you,
    whose name do all delight to hear?
    What seeks a place before your throne
    although it chose self-banishment?   4750
EMPEROR. Spare us your words on this occasion!
    Your riddles here are out of place,
    these gentlemen have brought their own.
    I should be glad if you'd just fill this gap.
    My former fool, I fear, has gone far, far away.   4755
    Be his relief, come stand beside me.
            MEPHISTOPHELES *ascends the steps and places himself at the* EMPEROR'S *left.*
VOICES (*murmuring*).
    Another fool. – And other troubles. –
    Where is he from? – How did he get in here? –
    The old one fell. – His time was up! –
    He was a barrel. – Now we have a stave!   4760
EMPEROR. And so, my dear and loyal subjects,
    I welcome you from far and near!

You gather under a propitious star,
that we shall thrive stands written in the sky.
But tell me why at such a time,   4765
when we would like to banish cares,
put on the masks of carnival,
and only cultivate what's pleasant,
we should torment ourselves by holding council?
But since you think there's no alternative,   4770
we now are met, and so, to the agenda!
CHANCELLOR[-ARCHBISHOP].
The highest virtue, halo-like,
encircles the Imperial head; the Emperor
alone can exercise it validly:
its name is Justice! – Loved by all mankind,   4775
demanded, wished for, hard to live without,
it is what he must grant his people.
Alas! Can reason help the human mind,
goodness our hearts, or willingness our hands,
while fever rages rampant in the state   4780
and brooding evil breeds prolific evils?
If from this lofty vantage point one views below
your far-flung realm, it seems an ugly dream
in which Deformity holds sway among deformities
and Lawlessness prevails by legal means   4785
as Error spreads and fills the world with error.
    One man makes off with flocks, another with a woman,
or with the altar's chalice, cross, and candlesticks,
and then for years they boast unscathed of what they've done
with no attainder of their persons.   4790
Plaintiffs now crowd the halls of justice
where judges sit in cushioned ease,
and all the while in angry flood
sedition's growing turmoil surges higher.
With the support of partners no less guilty   4795
men dare to brag of infamy and heinous crime,
but you will only hear the verdict "Guilty!"
when innocence defends itself.
Society thus strives for its own fragmentation
and to destroy whatever things are seemly—   4800
with this the case, how can the sense develop
that will alone guide us to what is right?
Ultimately the man of good intentions
must bow to sycophants and to suborners,
while judges impotent to mete out punishment   4805
become at last associates of criminals.

I've painted a black picture, even though
I should prefer it veiled in greater darkness still.
                    (*He pauses.*)
There can be no avoiding of decisions;
when all commit and suffer wrongs,   4810
then Majesty itself becomes a victim.

GRAND-MASTER OF THE ARMIES.
What tumult marks these violent times!
Men kill, and then are killed in turn,
and turn deaf ears to any orders.
The citizen behind his walls,   4815
the knight up in his rock-built aerie,
have vowed they will outlast our sieges
and are maintaining all their forces.
Our mercenaries grow impatient
and angrily demand their pay;   4820
and if we didn't owe them money still,
they would by now have all deserted.
If one denies them what all claim is theirs,
he has stirred up a hornets' nest;
the realm they were to have protected   4825
lies plundered now and devastated.
By letting their mad fury work its havoc
we've lost half of our world already;
there still are kings beyond our borders,
but none believes this might somehow affect him.   4830

INTENDANT OF THE TREASURY.
Who'd dare to claim that we have allies—
like water in defective pipes,
their promised subsidies do not arrive!
Moreover, Sire, who now holds property
in every part of all your wide domains?   4835
No matter where you go, some upstart's settled in
and wants to live in independence;
one must watch passively as he goes his own way;
we've given up so many rights
that we no longer have a right to anything.   4840
Then too, as for the parties, as they're called,
there's no relying on them nowadays;
it does not matter if they blame or praise,
since love and hate have ceased to be of consequence.
Both Ghibellines and Guelfs are now in hiding   4845
in order to enjoy some rest;
who cares to help his neighbor now,
when all must care for their own selves!

The portals of access to gold are barricaded;
everyone's scraping, digging, and amassing,   4850
and still our coffers are unfilled.
LORD STEWARD. What disasters I must suffer too!
Every day we try to save,
but every day our needs increase
and day by day my troubles grow.   4855
The cooks are suffering no shortage;
wild boars, and stags and does, and hares,
chickens and turkeys, geese and ducks—
payments in kind—are income we are sure of
and by and large arrive on time.   4860
But wine's beginning to run out.
Although there was a time our cellars were heaped high
with cask on cask of the best years and vintages,
your nobles' never ending drinking bouts
are slushing down the final drops.   4865
Even the city councils have to tap their stocks
as festive wine is drunk from tankards or from bowls
and goes to waste beneath the table.
I'm now supposed to pay the bills and wages,
but can expect no mercy from the money lenders,   4870
who execute agreements that eat up
what future years must yet produce.
Our hogs are not allowed to fatten,
the bolster on our bed's hypothecated,
the bread we're served already's been consumed.   4875
EMPEROR (*after some reflection, to* MEPHISTOPHELES).
Speak, Fool. Do you not know some further cause for woe?
MEPHISTOPHELES. I know of none, and only see the splendor
surrounding you and all your court! – Could confidence
be wanting where the sovereign's word is absolute
and troops stand by to rout all opposition,   4880
where, strengthened by intelligence, good will
and energy of many kinds await your use?
What forces could combine to cause disaster
and to eclipse a world where stars like these are shining?
VOICES (*murmuring*).
The fellow's a rogue. – And clever too. –   4885
Lies gain him favor . . . – at least for a while. –
I see already . . . – what's behind this. –
And then what next? – Some grand-scale scheme!
MEPHISTOPHELES. Where in the world is something not in short supply?
Someone lacks this, another that, but here the lack is money.   4890
Of course you can't just pick it off the floor,

but Wisdom's skill is getting what's most deeply hidden.
In mountain veins and in foundation walls
you'll find both coined and uncoined gold,
and if you ask who will extract it, I reply: 4895
a man that nature has endowed with mighty intellect.

CHANCELLOR. Nature and intellect are not words said to Christians.
Because such language is so dangerous
the atheist is executed at the stake.
Nature is sin, and Intellect the devil;   4900
hermaphroditic Doubt their child
which they together foster.

　　Such words to us! – Time has brought forth but two estates
within the lands that are the emperor's ancient holdings;
they are the clergy and the knights,   4905
the proper pillars of his throne,
who are our shield against tempestuous violence
and as reward are granted Church and State.

　　Sedition starts with intellects
bemuddled by plebeian sentiments: 4910
they are the heretics and sorcerers,
corrupting countryside and town!
Now, with your brazen jests, you try
to smuggle them into these highest circles;
you and your kind thrive on corrupted hearts   4915
whose folly makes them closely kin to you.

MEPHISTOPHELES. Your words reveal to me what makes a man of learning!
What you can't touch, for you is leagues away,
what you can't grasp does not exist at all,
what you can't count, you don't believe is true,   4920
what you can't weigh is of no weight to you,
and what you do not coin, you think of no account.

EMPEROR. All this does not supply a thing we lack—
why offer us a Lenten sermon now?
I've had my fill of these eternal ifs and buts;   4925
money is short; well, go and get it then!

MEPHISTOPHELES. I'll get you what you want, and more besides;
it's easy, to be sure, but easy tasks take effort;
the gold's already there, but getting at it
is the great trick, and who knows how to do so?   4930
Still, bear in mind how often in those days of terror,
when human tides submerged entire nations,
people, despite all fear and trembling,
would hide what they most prized somewhere or other.
The custom, old when Rome was the great power,   4935
has since prevailed till yesterday—yes, till today.

These buried things all rest in peace within the earth,
the subsoil is the Emperor's, they're his to have.
TREASURER. He doesn't speak so badly, for a fool:
that is indeed an old imperial right.   4940
CHANCELLOR. Satan is laying golden snares for you:
there's something here that's neither right nor pious.
LORD STEWARD. If he'd but get our court the payments due it,
I would not mind if something weren't exactly right.
GRAND-MASTER. The Fool's no fool, he promises what's needed;   4945
a soldier least of all will ask about its source.
MEPHISTOPHELES. And if perhaps you think that I'm deceiving you,
here's the Astrologer for you to question,
who knows in every sphere the mansions and the hours.
Well, tell us, sir, what aspects now prevail!   4950
VOICES (murmuring).
They both are rogues . . . – and hand in glove. –
The visionary and the fool . . . – so near the throne!
An old, old song . . . – heard much too often. –
Folly is prompting . . . – as the sage speaks.
ASTROLOGER (with MEPHISTOPHELES prompting).
The Sun himself is gold without alloy,   4955
his herald, Mercury, will serve if kindly paid;
Dame Venus has already cast her spell upon you,
who see her lovely face at dawn and dusk;
chaste Luna, who's erratic, does have whims;
Mars' power threatens you, although he does not smite.   4960
And Jupiter is still the brightest star,
while giant Saturn seems remote and small.
The latter is, as metal, not much venerated
and has, despite its density, but little value.
What's certain is that skies will shine   4965
when Sol and Luna, gold and silver, are conjoined;
all other things are then obtainable,
palace and park and rosy cheek and pretty breast,
and they will be provided by the erudition
of one with power none of us possesses.   4970
EMPEROR. I hear each word he utters twice
but don't find what he says convincing.
VOICES (murmuring).
What is the sense of this? – The joke's jejune. –
Astrology . . . – or alchemy! –
I've heard it all before . . . – and had false hopes. –   4975
And even if this great man comes . . . – he'll be a quack.
MEPHISTOPHELES. I see both general amazement
and lack of confidence in this great plan,

hear silly talk of mandrake roots
and of black dogs deaf to their cries.   4980
It does not matter that the sceptics sneer
or that the credulous cry sorcery,
for in the end their soles will itch
and in full stride their feet will stumble.

    You can all sense the hidden operations   4985
of Nature's never-ceasing power,
and from her ultrasubterranean regions
there slowly now emerge its vital signs.
As soon as all your limbs start twitching
or if some spot gives you uncanny feelings,   4990
be not afraid, but start at once to scrape and dig,
for where you stumble, is where treasure lies!

VOICES (*murmuring*).
My foot feels like a lump of lead. –
My arm has cramps. – You have the gout. –
There is an itch on my big toe. –   4995
My spine is one great mass of aches. –
If all these symptoms meant a thing,
this hall would be a treasure island.

EMPEROR. Now hurry up—you shall not slip away—
and demonstrate your blather's truth   5000
by showing us at once these precious vaults.
I'll put aside my sword and scepter,
and will, if you're not lying, execute
the project with my own imperial hands—
or send you, if you lie, to hell.   5005

MEPHISTOPHELES (*aside*).
That's one place I know how to find!
(*Aloud.*) I feel, however, that I must say more
about the unowned wealth that's waiting everywhere.
The peasant, as he plows his furrow,
will turn up with the soil a pot of gold;   5010
he hopes to scrape saltpeter from its clay
and finds, to his amazement and delight,
in his impoverished hand a roll of yellow gold.
What vaults will have to be blown up,
and through what crevices and shafts,   5015
that border on the underworld,
the knowing treasure hunter needs must press!
In spacious cellars, long intact.
he'll see row after row
of golden tankards, bowls, and plates;   5020
there will be goblets made of rubies,
and if he wants to drink from them,

he'll find nearby an ancient vintage.
But—take the expert's word for this—
the staves decayed completely long ago, 5025
and tartar formed a cask to hold the wine.
These essences of precious wines,
not merely jewels and gold,
lie veiled in horrid darkness.
The sage is eager to explore this world; 5030
a child can recognize what's seen in day's clear light,
the home of mysteries is darkness.

EMPEROR. Those I shall leave to you! What good can come of gloom?
Whatever is of value must stand the light of day.
You cannot tell the thief when it's so dark 5035
that every cow is black and all the cats are gray.
Those pots down there, so heavy with their gold—
go draw your plow, bring them to light.

MEPHISTOPHELES. Take hoe and spade, and dig yourself,
this peasant labor will augment your greatness, 5040
and from the soil you'll liberate
a herd of golden calves. And then you can
with no delay, and to your great delight,
adorn yourself, and then your mistress;
a lustrous, iridescent jewel 5045
enhances majesty and beauty.

EMPEROR. Quick, let us start at once! How long must this drag out!

ASTROLOGER (as before).
Sire, moderate this eagerness
until the merriment of carnival is past;
we'll not achieve our end if we're distracted. 5050
We first must, with composure, win our peace of soul
and earn what is below with help from what's above.
Who wants what's good must first be good;
who wishes happiness must calm his blood;
he who desires wine must press ripe grapes; 5055
who hopes for miracles must fortify his faith.

EMPEROR. Then let us pass the time in gaiety
until Ash Wednesday comes, most opportunely!
Meanwhile we'll celebrate—of this I'm sure—
all the more merrily the madness of our carnival. 5060

Trumpets. Exeunt all except MEPHISTOPHELES.

MEPHISTOPHELES. That merit and good fortune are connected
is something that these idiots will never see;
the philosopher's stone could be in their possession,
but there'd be no philosopher to use it. [*Exit.*

A GREAT HALL

The hall and rooms into which it opens are decorated as described
in the Masquerade.

HERALD. Imagine that you're not in Germany—   5065
    instead of Dance of Death or dancing fools and demons
    expect a cheerful entertainment.
    When in your interest and his own
    our Emperor traversed the lofty Alps
    and traveled down to Rome,   5070
    he found a cheerful land and took possession of it.
    He first obtained, prostrate at holy feet,
    the confirmation of his sovereign powers,
    but if he went to get himself his crown,
    he brought us back the domino as well.   5075
    Thus we are all regenerated now,
    and men of great urbanity are nothing loath
    to draw its hood about their head and ears;
    they may then look like idiots
    but underneath are still as wise as ever. –   5080
    I now see the people start to gather,
    the hesitant desert, the confident pair off,
    and groups crowd into place for the procession.
    Don't wait to make your entrances and exits—
    mankind, with all its myriad antics   5085
    has always been and always will remain
    the single great embodiment of Folly!
FLOWER GIRLS (*singing to the accompaniment of mandolins*).
    So that we may win your favor,
    we've adorned ourselves tonight
    as young girls who've come from Florence   5090
    to this splendid German court;
      in brown hair you see us wearing
    a profusion of gay flowers
    in which silken threads and pieces
    play no unimportant role.   5095
      And we think it meritorious,
    even highly laudatory,
    that our artificial flowers
    bloom resplendent all year long.
      Bits of cloth dyed many colors   5100
    are arranged in symmetry;
    you may ridicule components,
    but will find the whole attractive.
      We are pretty things to look at,
    flower girls with easy manners,   5105

    since what's natural for women
    is so similar to art.
HERALD. Show the treasures of the baskets
    which you bear upon your heads
    and which fill your arms with color,   5110
    so that all may take their choice.
    Hurry, now, so that these arbors
    can appear to be a garden!
    What is sold and those who sell it
    well are worth your crowding closer.   5115
FLOWER GIRLS.
    Hawk your wares where we are welcome—
    but allow no haggling here!—
    and announce what you can offer
    in a few well-chosen words.
AN OLIVE BRANCH, BEARING FRUIT.
    There's no flower that I envy,   5120
    I avoid all forms of conflict,
    staying true to my own nature;
    many nations' major resource,
    I am also everywhere
    sign and surety of peace.   5125
    May it be my luck today
    to adorn a pretty head!
A WREATH OF GOLDEN GRAIN.
    Ceres' gifts, as finery,
    will supplement your loveliness;
    may what men most prize as useful   5130
    serve as ornament of beauty.
A WREATH OF FANCIFUL FLOWERS.
    Mallow-like, and many-colored,
    flower-marvels rise from moss;
    we are not a mode of Nature,
    but what Fashion can produce.   5135
A BOUQUET OF FANCIFUL FLOWERS.
    Theophrastus couldn't tell you
    any name that might describe us;
    nonetheless I hope we'll please,
    if not all, at least some ladies,
    whom I think we would suit nicely   5140
    if they'd braid us in their hair
    or decided they might grant us
    resting places on their bosoms.
CHALLENGE [OF ROSEBUDS].
    Let these motley fancies blossom   5145

for the sake of passing fashion
and assume strange, curious shapes
unlike any Nature shows!
Golden cups on stems of green,
peep forth from luxuriant tresses! –
We prefer to stay in hiding,   5150
happy to be found while fresh.
    Who, when summer is proclaimed
and the rosebud glows with flame,
would forgo that happiness?
Everywhere in Flora's realm   5155
promise and fulfillment hold
sight, mind, heart beneath one spell.

The FLOWER GIRLS *arrange their wares neatly under arcades of greenery.*

GARDENERS (*singing to the accompaniment of archlutes*).
    By all means watch flowers grow,
see them grace your charming heads,
but though fruits are less seductive   5160
they can please your sense of taste.
    If bronzed faces offer you
cherries, peaches, or greengages,
buy them, but not for their looks:
the best judge is tongue and palate.   5165
    Come and eat fruit fully ripened—
you'll enjoy its scent and flavor!
You may write an ode on roses,
apples must be bitten into.
    You who have abundant youth,   5170
let us join you and form couples;
as your neighbors we'll heap high
and display ripe wares we offer.
    Then, beneath these gay festoons,
in the alcoves of these arbors,   5175
you will find at the same time
bud, and leaf, and flower, and fruit.

Singing separately and together to the accompaniment of the guitars and lutes,
the GARDENERS *and* FLOWER GIRLS *continue to set up the displays of their*
wares in gradually rising tiers and to offer them for sale. –
Enter a MOTHER *and* DAUGHTER.

MOTHER. When you were my baby girl,
    dressed in pretty bonnets,
    what a lovely face you had,   5180
    what a dainty figure!
    Right away I could imagine
    you betrothed to someone rich,

then a bride, a matron.
   Now so many fleeting years   5185
have, alas! been wasted,
a variety of beaus
gone their way so quickly,
though you promptly danced with some
or your elbow sometimes gave   5190
gentle hints to others.
   Every party that we planned
proved to be a failure;
games of forfeit, odd-man-out,
were a waste of effort.   5195
Fools are on the loose today:
if you spread your lap, my dear,
surely you can catch one.

They are joined by FRIENDS *and* ACQUAINTANCES, *all young and pretty girls; sounds of intimate conversation are heard. — Enter* FISHERMEN *and* BIRDCATCHERS, *with nets, rods, limed sticks, and other gear, who mingle with the girls. A general snatching, grabbing, twisting away, and being caught affords occasion for an exchange of pleasantries.*

WOODCUTTERS (*entering with boorish boisterousness*).
   Make room, a clearing!
We need great spaces   5200
to fell our timber,
which lands with thunder
and which, when carried,
can knock you over.
But to our credit   5205
do not forget this:
Unless coarse fellows
did heavy labor,
how would fine folk,
smart though they be,   5210
ever exist?
Learn well this lesson,
for you'd be frozen
if we'd not sweated!

PULCINELLI (*awkward, almost dunce-like*).
   You are born foolish   5215
who stoop and carry.
We who are clever
were never burdened;
our dunce's caps
and our flimsy jackets   5220
are not great burdens,

and we enjoy
being always idle
and free to saunter
in slippered feet   5225
through the crowded market,
to stop and gape
and crow at our friends,
then, at their crowing,
to glide like eels   5230
through the crowds of people
and dance together
in wild disorder.
You may commend,
or you may condemn,—   5235
but you can't upset us.

PARASITES (*greedily fawning*).

You worthy porters
and your relations,
the charcoal burners,
serve us as models.   5240
What, by themselves, would be the use
of scraping and bowing,
affirmative noddings,
tortuous phrases,
and blowing so that what we say   5245
is hot or cold
according to who hears it?
What use would be
the mightiest fire
sent men from heaven,   5250
if we lacked wood
and charcoal, brought
so that their hearths
may glow with flame?
There's where pots boil and bubble,   5255
where roasts and stews are made.
The true gourmets—
the parasites who lick each plate—
inspired by a roast's aroma
or intuition that there's fish,   5260
perform great deeds
at patrons' tables.

A DRUNKARD (*in a stupor*).

Nothing can go wrong today!
I have never felt so fine!

I've produced my own high spirits   5265
and the jolly songs I sing.
So I'm drinking! Have a drink!
Let's clink glasses! Hear them clink!
You back there, come over here!
After clinking, you'll be finished.   5270
   How the little woman screeched,
ridiculed my nice bright costume,
and although I swaggered bravely
called me just a mannequin.
I can drink though! Have a drink!   5275
Clink your glasses! Hear them clink!
Mannequins, let's clink our glasses—
that's the sound that says we've finished.
   Don't you tell me that I'm lost,
I am where I like to be.   5280
If the landlord won't give credit,
then his wife will or their maid.
I'll keep drinking! Have a drink!
On your feet! Let's hear that clink!
Let's keep drinking to each other,   5285
though I think we're nearly finished.
   I don't care where I am happy
just as long as it is somewhere;
let me lie here where I'm lying,
I don't feel like standing up.'   5290

CHORUS.   Brothers, let us all have drinks!
Raise a lively toast and clink!
Don't fall off your bench or keg—
he who's on the floor is finished.

The HERALD *announces various* POETS: *Nature Poets, Court Singers, Chivalric Minstrels, Sweet Singers, and Rhapsodists; in the press of rivals competing for attention, none will allow another to declaim, although one manages to say a few words as he passes.*

SATIRIC POET.   Perhaps you'd like to know   5295
what most would please this poet?
To be allowed to say
what no one wants to hear.

Poets of Night Thoughts and Graveyard Poets beg to be excused, since they have just become involved in a most interesting discussion with a Vampire visibly fresh from his grave, which might possibly permit the development of a new poetic genre. The HERALD *cannot gainsay them, and so he summons figures from Greek mythology, which loses neither its charm nor its character when its figures appear in costumes adapted to later tastes.*

Enter the GRACES.

AGLAIA.   We bring grace into your lives;
               when you give, be gracious too.   5300

HEGEMONE.   When receiving, show good grace:
               to fulfill a wish is kindness.

EUPHROSYNE.   And when quiet years are reached,
               learn to thank with gracefulness.

Enter the FATES.

ATROPOS.   I, who am the oldest sister,   5305
               have been asked to spin today;
               care and thought are greatly needed
               when the thread of life is fragile.

               To make sure it's soft and supple,
               I have sleyed the finest flax;   5310
               to make sure it's smooth and even,
               I shall dress it with deft hands.

               If you're prone to be too carefree
               in a time of revelry,
               don't forget this thread has limits,   5315
               and beware lest it should break!

CLOTHO.   I must explain that recently
               these shears were given to my care
               because there was dissatisfaction
               with how our oldest sister acted.   5320

               She draws forth and keeps extending
               threads that have no worth whatever;
               cutting those of greatest promise,
               off she lugs them to the grave.

               Still, when I was young and active   5325
               I made hundreds of mistakes;
               so, as curb upon myself,
               now the shears are in their case.

               And I welcome this constraint,
               liking as I do this place;   5330
               as for you, enjoy yourselves
               while you have immunity.

LACHESIS.   I, alone endowed with judgment,
               keep my task of sorting threads;
               though my reel is always moving,   5335
               it has never turned too fast.

               Strands arrive and then are twisted,
               each one guided by my hand;
               none may overlap another,
               each must stay where it belongs.   5340

Should I ever be forgetful,
I'd despair for humankind;
years and hours both are measured,
and the Weaver holds the skein.

HERALD. You will not recognize the figures coming now,   5345
however many classic books you've read;
judging these trouble-makers by their looks,
you'd be inclined to call them welcome guests.
   They are the Furies—this you won't believe—
endowed with beauty, grace, with friendliness and youth!   5350
Yet once involved with them, you soon find out
how doves like these can wound with serpents' tongues.
   Although they are malicious, on this day
when every boasting fool admits his faults
they too won't pose as angels—they'll confess   5355
that in both town and country they're a plague.

Enter the FURIES.

ALECTO. Forewarned is not forearmed! You will believe us
because we're young and pretty
and if there's one among you with a sweetheart,
we'll tickle his ears with blandishments   5360
   until the time has come to tell him privately
that *she* is also ogling *him* and *him,*
that she's dull-witted and misshapen, limps,
and, though his financée, a worthless minx.
   We know the way to make her wretched too: 5365
"It was your friend himself who, a few weeks ago,
said slighting things about you to Miss So and So!"
They may make up, but doubts will still remain.

MEGAERA. Those are but petty matters! When they're wed
it is my turn, and then I never fail   5370
to spoil connubial bliss with galling quirks.
Mortals are not consistent—every hour differs—
   and no one has in his embrace his heart's desire
who is not fool enough to hope he'll get
from Fortune something more desirable—   5375
he flees his sun and tries to melt new ice.
   I am an expert at this sort of thing
and bring along my faithful Asmodeus
to sow, when it's the season, seeds of discord—
I thus corrupt mankind two units at a time.   5380

TISIPHONE. Instead of using slander, I mix poison,
      sharpen steel, for faithless lovers!
      Late or soon, if you love others,
      you'll suffer in a vital organ.

    Love will prove to be a bubble,   5385
    ecstasy will turn to gall!
    Compromise is not allowed,
    circumstances won't excuse him.
       Sing no song to me of pardon!
    Rocks hear the charges I recite,   5390
    and echo—hark!—replies ''Requite!''
    Death to all inconstant lovers!
HERALD. Please be so good as to withdraw to either side,
    for what is coming now is strange and different.
    You see a mountain pushing toward us   5395
    whose flanks are proudly hung with brilliant tapestries,
    and from whose head long tusks and snakelike trunk extend;
    this seems a mystery, yet I'll give you its key.
    The woman seated on its neck is delicate,
    but with that slender wand she makes it do her will;   5400
    while she who stands in majesty beside her
    is bathed in dazzling radiance;
    beside it, wearing chains, there walk two noble ladies,
    one with a worried air, the other looking cheerful:
    the former pines for freedom, the latter thinks she's free.   5405
    Let each now tell us who she is.
FEAR.   Reeking torches, lamps, and candles
    dimly light this festive turmoil;
    here amid deceitful faces
    I, alas! am bound in chains.   5410
       Don't come near me, foolish scoffers,
    smiles like yours cannot be trusted;
    all my enemies are crowding
    in about me here tonight.
       Here's a friend who's now a foe,   5415
    but I see through the disguise;
    there's someone who meant to kill me
    but sneaks off when recognized.
       Oh, how I would like to flee
    to any place far, far away,   5420
    but the threat of death out there
    confines me to this dark, dread place.
HOPE. Ladies, I greet you as sisters!
    Even though, these past two days,
    you've enjoyed these masks and costumes,   5425
    I'm aware that you intend
    to unmask yourselves tomorrow.
    And although we feel uneasy
    here amid these flickering torches,

sunlit days, we know, are coming   5430
when we shall, as suits our fancy,
walk with friends or by ourselves
through the lovely countryside,
free to rest or to be active,
and enjoy a carefree life,   5435
never lacking what we want.
Confident we're always welcome,
we are pleased to join you here:
the best things in life, I'm certain,
can be found wherever one is.   5440

PRUDENCE. Two of mankind's greatest scourges,
       Fear and Hope, stand here in fetters,
       kept away from you by me;
       you're all safe, but please stand back!
          I am guiding, as you see,   5445
       this live, turreted colossus
       which, despite its heavy burden,
       steepest passes would not daunt.
          There, upon its tower's top,
       is a goddess with swift pinions,   5450
       poised for flight to any point
       where advantage may await her,
       enveloped in a cloud of light
       whose brilliance reaches far and wide;
       her name is Victory,   5455
       the goddess of all undertakings.

ZOILO-THERSITES.
This is too much! I see I'm just in time
to tell you what a tawdry lot you are!
My special butt, however, is
Dame Victory up there.   5460
With those white wings she doubtless thinks
that she's an eagle
and that wherever she may choose to look
all peoples and all lands belong to her;
I, on the other hand, am quick to wrath   5465
when I see any deed of glory done.
When I exalt what's base, degrade what's grand,
put crooked straight, what's straight askew,
then, and then only, do I feel elated,
for that is how I want things here on earth.   5470

HERALD. In that case, cur, feel how my sacred staff
can deal a might blow!
Now you will writhe and twist! –

How quickly does the double dwarf
become a loathesome, shapeless mass! –   5475
But what strange thing is this?
The mass becomes an egg that swells and bursts,
and from it twins emerge,
an adder and a bat;
one crawls off through the dust,   5480
the other, black, flies upward to the roof.
They're hurrying outside for a reunion
in which I would prefer to have no part.

VOICES (*murmuring*).
    Come! back there they are already dancing. –
    Well! this place is not for me. –   5485
    Do you feel those ghastly things
    pressing in about us? –
    Something hissed right past my hair. –
    I glimpsed something at my feet. –
    No one's suffered any harm –   5490
    but we all have had a scare. –
    What was fun is spoiled completely –
    that's what the nasty creatures wanted.

HERALD. Ever since I undertook
    to be herald at your pageants,   5495
I have solemnly stood guard,
never yielding, always firm,
to insure that nothing harmful
should get in and spoil your revels.
But I fear that air-born spirits   5500
are now coming through the windows,
and I'm helpless to protect you
from such ghostly sorcery.
If that dwarf was somewhat doubtful,
look back there, see what's now coming!   5505
I would like to do my duty
and expound these figures' meaning,
but what can't be comprehended,
I am helpless to explain
and must ask for your assistance. –   5510
See what's swerving through the crowd!
A magnificent quadriga
borne along past one and all,
opening no lane or passage,
causing none to push aside!   5515
From afar its colors shimmer,
all about it stars are flashing
such as magic lanterns cast,

as it storms and snorts along.
Clear the way! I find this awesome! 5520
YOUNG CHARIOTEER.
Horses, halt! No longer use your wings,
heed the customary bridle,
curb yourselves if I now curb you,
when I urge you, speed away –
for we must respect these halls! 5525
See the circles growing larger
as admirers gather round us.
Herald, come! continue custom
and, before we rush away,
draw our picture, tell our names— 5530
after all, we're allegories,
and you therefore ought to know us.
HERALD. I can't guess what your name is,
though I might be able to describe you.
CHARIOTEER. Try to do so then.
HERALD.   To start, 5535
I'll concede you're young and handsome.
You are an adolescent still; a woman, though,
would rather have you fully grown.
I see in you a future ladies' man,
and of the kind that breaks a lot of hearts. 5540
CHARIOTEER. All well and good! Go on like that,
and formulate some more of this amusing riddle.
HERALD. I see black lightning in your eyes, and night-dark hair
enlivened by a ribbon set with jewels.
And what a graceful robe cascades 5545
with purple hem and glittering baubles
down from your shoulders to your slippers!
You might be called effeminate,
but if, for better or for worse,
you tried your luck with girls right now, 5550
they'd help you learn the A B C.
CHARIOTEER. And what about this splendid figure
so proudly seated on my chariot's throne?
HERALD. He seems to be a rich and kindly king
whose favor would ensure prosperity. 5555
He looks not for new realms to conquer,
but to discover where there's want,
and the pure joy he takes in giving
outweighs all the delights of ownership.
CHARIOTEER. It will not do to stop with these remarks, 5560
you must describe him properly.

HERALD. There's no describing innate worth.
    But I'll go on: a face that glows with health,
    an ample mouth, well-rounded cheeks,
    show proudly forth beneath a jeweled turban;   5565
    his pleated gown is rich, noɩ gaudy,
    worn with decorum that I hardly need describe.
    I recognize in him one born to rule.
CHARIOTEER. His name is Plutus! He, the god of wealth,
    is here arrived in regal state,   5570
    a guest your noble Emperor has wanted.
HERALD. But tell us, also, what you are and do!
CHARIOTEER. I am that spendthrift, poetry;
    as poet, I augment my worth
    by squandering my very substance.   5575
    I, too, am rich beyond all measures
    and count myself the peer of Plutus,
    add life and beauty to his revels,
    and give you what he can't bestow.
HERALD. You brag quite gracefully,   5580
    but we would like a demonstration of your skill.
CHARIOTEER. Watch! I but snap my fingers, and at once
    bright, glittering lights surround our chariot.
    Now see a string of pearls appear!
        (*He continues to snap his fingers in various directions.*)
    Accept these golden clasps for neck and ear,   5585
    these flawless combs and coronets,
    these rings set with the rarest jewels;
    I also, now and then, distribute tiny flames
    in hope that some of them may start a blaze, a fire.
HERALD. How these good people reach and grab—   5590
    the giver's almost helpless in this crowd!
    He flips gems with fantastic skill,
    and the whole crowd is grabbing for them.
    But now I see there are new tricks:
    no matter what a person clutches,   5595
    it proves to be a sorry prize—
    his gift takes wing and flies away;
    the string of pearls breaks in his hand
    and he's left holding wriggling beetles,
    and when, poor dupe, he shakes them off,   5600
    they start to buzz about his head;
    others, instead of things with worth,
    catch only wanton butterflies.
    For all his promises, the rogue
    bestows as gold what merely glitters.   5605

CHARIOTEER. I see that you describe all costumes well,
    but it is not a herald's courtly duty
    to fathom what may lie beneath their surface—
    for that a keener eye is needed.
    But I have no desire for disputes,   5610
    and will address, my lord, to you my questions.
                      (*He turns to* PLUTUS.)
    Did you not put into my charge
    this wind-swift team of four?
    Do I not guide them as you wish?
    Am I not always where you want me?   5615
    Have I not boldly soared aloft
    to win you palms of victory?
    Whenever I have fought on your behalf,
    success has always crowned my striving,
    and if your brows are graced with laurels,   5620
    were they not woven by my thoughtful hand?
PLUTUS. If you need a good character from me,
    I gladly say, you are the essence of my spirit.
    You always act the way I'd wish to act,
    your treasury contains more gold than mine.   5625
    Of all the crowns I can bestow,
    I value most the laurels that your service merits.
    To all I testify as gospel truth:
    with you, dear son, I am well pleased.
CHARIOTEER (*addressing the assemblage*).
    See how I've scattered all about   5630
    the greatest gifts I can bestow.
    Above the heads of some among you
    there glows a spark that I ignited;
    it skips along from head to head,
    pausing on some, but not at all on others,   5635
    and only now and then, as short-lived flame,
    rapidly bursting into incandescence;
    but even before most people know of its existence,
    the feeble spark, alas, has been extinguished.
WOMEN (*chattering*).
    That fellow on the chariot   5640
    is certainly some charlatan,
    for, perched behind there sits the Fool,
    who's even more emaciated
    than he has ever looked before—
    so fleshless he'd not feel a pinch, I think.   5645
THE STARVELING.
    Don't lay your hands on me, disgusting females!

I know you never like to see me. –
When women managed their own homes,
my name was still Dame Avarice;
our households throve while the rule held: 5650
acquire much, let nothing be discarded!
I strove to keep our chests and cupboards filled,
a virtue some then called a vice.
But now that women, some years since,
became unused to penny-pinching   5655
and, like delinquent debtors anywhere,
have far more wants than they have money,
their husbands have a lot to suffer
and see debts everywhere they look.
Whatever they can earn by spinning   5660
goes on their backs or to their lovers,
and with their armies of admirers
they eat and drink more lavishly as well.
This makes me fonder still of gold,
so now I am Sir Greed, and masculine.   5665

LEADER OF THE WOMEN.
  Let's leave this stingy devil to the stingy!
  In any case, he's nothing but a liar
  who wants to get our husbands all worked up,
  although they're troublesome enough already.

THE WOMEN (all together).
  The scarecrow! Slap his mouth! How can a servant,   5670
  and just a drudge at that, dare threaten us?
  As if his ugly face could scare us!
  Those dragon-steeds are only wood and paper;
  come on, let's up and at him!

HERALD. Now, by my staff, be quiet! –   5675
  But there is hardly any need of my assistance:
  see how those fearful monsters come to life
  and, spreading double pairs of wings,
  quickly force people to draw back.
  Enraged, the dragons shake their scaly jaws   5680
  and spew forth fire; the crowd now flies,
  there is an open space.
                    (PLUTUS alights from the chariot.)
  Now he steps down with regal ease.
  He gives a sign; the dragons get to work,
  lift from their chariot the chest of gold,   5685
  bear it with Greed still crouching on it,
  and set it down there at his feet—
  a miracle has been performed!

PLUTUS (*to his* CHARIOTEER).

   Now that you're rid of what encumbered you,

   are wholly free, be off to your own realm!   5690

   It is not here, amid this wild confusion

   of motley and grotesque inventions.

   Away to clarity perceived with clarity,

   to where you owe allegiance to yourself,

   where beauty and goodness alone afford delight—   5695

   to solitude! Create your own world there.

CHARIOTEER. I shall regard myself as your proud emissary,

   still love you as my next of kin.

   Where you abide, there is abundance,

   and where I am, all men feel rich,   5700

   although, perplexed by life, they often wonder

   if they should consecrate themselves to you, or me.

   Your votaries may live in idleness,

   but those who follow me can never rest.

   My deeds are not performed in secrecy—   5705

   if I but breathe a thought, I am betrayed.

   And so, farewell! I know you wish me happiness,

   yet I'll return at once if you but whisper for me.

                              [*Exit, with chariot.*

PLUTUS. It's time to free our treasures from their fetters!

   I take the Herald's staff and smite the locks.   5710

   The chest flies open. Look! See how, blood-red,

   in brazen pots, gold surges up,

   beside it choicest chains and rings and crowns,

   and threatens to engulf and melt them.

THE CROWD (*exclaiming in turn*).

   Look and see how it's running over,   5715

   filling the chest up to the rim. –

   Vessels of gold are being melted,

   golden rouleaus are tossed about. –

   As if just minted, ducats dance

   and make my heart begin to leap –   5720

   to see all I have ever wanted

   rolling now along the floor! –

   They are a gift, accept it promptly,

   by stooping down you'll soon be rich. –

   Let us be nimble and make off,   5725

   lightning-quick, with the chest itself!

HERALD. What is the meaning of this madness?

   These things are only make-believe.

   No more such greediness tonight!

   Do you believe it's gold you're getting?   5730

For you, and at a masquerade,
tin counters would be far too good.
You louts who right off want a pretty show
to be the truth of coarse reality!
What's truth to you who try to grab   5735
hollow illusions randomly? –
Masked Plutus, hero of this masque,
I beg you, put this mob to rout!

PLUTUS. Your staff, I think, can serve as weapon;
lend it to me for a short time. –   5740
I quickly dip it in the seething flames. –
Now, masqueraders, on your guard!
See it flash, explode, and sparkle—
the staff is now a thing of fire!
If anyone should crowd too close   5745
he'll suffer cruel burns at once. –
I'll start my circuit now.

THE CROWD (pushing and exclaiming).
What pain! We're done for now. –
Escape if you are able to! –
Move back, move back, you in the rear! –   5750
Hot sparks are spurting in my face. –
I'm crushed beneath the burning staff–
we're lost and done for, one and all. –
Don't crowd us so, you masqueraders,
move back, move back, you senseless mob! –   5755
If I had wings, I'd leave by air.—

PLUTUS. The circle now has been pushed back,
with no one scorched, I do believe.
The crowd retreats,
fear did the job. –   5760
To guarantee this order is maintained,
I'll draw a ring that none can see.

HERALD. What you have done is marvelous—
I'm much obliged to your sagacity!

PLUTUS. More patience will be needed, noble friend,   5765
for more disorder's still to come.

SIR GREED. At last one can, if he so wishes,
survey with pleasure this assemblage,
since women always are out front
when there is something good to see or eat.   5770
I'm not so far gone yet as not to find
a pretty woman beautiful,
and since the entertainment's free today,

there's nothing to prevent my picking up a girl.
Still, in a place so overcrowded,   5775
my words cannot be heard by all,
I'll take a prudent course, and hope I can succeed
in being pantomimically explicit.
My purpose can't be served by gesture, hand, or foot,
so I shall have to try a prank.   5780
Gold can be converted into anything,
and so I'll use this metal just like clay.
HERALD. What is our thin fool up to now!
Can he be both a hunger artist and a comic?
He's kneading all the gold into a dough   5785
that in his hands becomes quite slack
and stays a shapeless mass
no matter how he molds or pummels it.
He's turning toward those women there,
who scream and try to get away   5790
and act as if they all were much disgusted;
our clown turns out to be a mischief-maker,
and one of those, I fear, who think it fun
to cause offense to decency.
I cannot countenance such conduct—   5795
give me my staff, and I'll expel him.
PLUTUS. You need not interrupt his nonsense!
He's unaware there is a menace in the offing
that won't leave space for his buffoonery—
compulsion has more force than preachment.   5800
VOICES (noisily singing).
          What now arrives is the Wild Hunt,
          advancing irresistibly
          from mountain height and wooded vale:
          all celebrate their great god Pan.
          In on a secret none here shares,   5805
          they'll throng into this empty ring.
PLUTUS. I know you well, and Great Pan too—
together you are undertaking something daring!
Knowing the secret only some few share,
with due respect I open this closed circle.   5810
[Aside.] May a propitious fate attend them!
What is to come could well seem strange;
they do not know for what they're headed,
they've not thought to prepare for what might happen.
WILD MEN (singing).
          O you bedizened tinsel crowd,   5815

see coarse and savage people come
who leaping high and running fast
now enter with a vigorous stride.

FAUNS. We are the fauns
of carefree dance   5820
and oakleaf wreaths
in tousled hair!
Delicate ears with pointed tips
protrude from every curly head;
though nose be flat and face be broad,   5825
the ladies won't take that amiss:
when dancing fauns put out their paws,
even the fairest won't say no.

SATYR. A satyr dances in behind
with foot of goat and fleshless leg   5830
that must be thin and sinewy—
perched chamois-like on mountain peaks,
he's entertained by looking round about.
Invigorated in the air of freedom,
he jeers at woman, child, and man   5835
who down below in smoggy valleys
fondly believe they too exist,
and knows that he alone possesses
the world so calm and pure up there.

GNOMES. These little people take short steps   5840
and do not like to march by pairs;
in moss-green smock, with lighted lamp,
each busy with his own concerns,
they hurry helter-skelter past
like teeming swarms of fireflies   5845
and scurry back and forth like ants
who're busy everywhere at once.
    Near relatives of the kind brownies,
we're barber-surgeons to the rocks;
we bleed high mountains,   5850
tap their full veins,
and, confident our luck will hold,
accumulate a store of metals.
We do this with the best intentions—
we like to help men of good will.   5855
Although the gold we bring to light
is used for pandering and theft
and to provide the steel the arrogant require
who have invented universal killing,
and though whoever breaks these three Commandments 5860

will pay no heed to all the rest,
we aren't responsible for that;
therefore remain, like us, forebearing.
MEN OF GREAT STATURE.
Wild Men is what they call these figures
who, in the Harz, have local fame;   5865
naked and strong, as nature made them,
they come, gigantic one and all,
with a pine club in their right hand
and wear as padded belt about their loins
an apron coarsely made of leafy boughs—   5870
guardsmen quite different from the Pope's!
NYMPHS (*in chorus, encircling* PAN).
Now he arrives,
the great god Pan
who represents
the cosmic All!   5875
Let all who dance about him here
be light of foot and blithe of heart;
although he's dour, he's also kind,
and so he wants us to be merry.
Outdoors beneath a vault of blue   5880
he also tries to be alert,
but when he hears the murmuring brooks
he's lulled to sleep by gentle breezes.
And when his sleep comes at high noon,
no leaf will stir on any branch;   5885
the silent air, now motionless,
grows heavy with the scent of herbs;
and nymphs no longer may be lively,
but fall asleep right where they've stood.
Yet when with violent suddenness   5890
Pan's voice is heard, a cry as loud
as thunder-roll and ocean roar,
uncertainty reigns everywhere:
brave battle lines become a rout
amid which even heroes tremble.   5895
All honor, then, where honor's due,
and hail to him who's brought us here!
DEPUTATION OF GNOMES (*addressing* PAN).
While metallic strands of wealth
glitter in their rocky fissures
and divining rods alone   5900
trace their labyrinthine courses,
we, as troglodytes, shall build

vaulted homes in somber caverns,
and, where bright pure breezes blow,
you'll bestow largesse of treasure.   5905
 Now, however, here beside us
we have found a wondrous fountain
which should provide with little effort
wealth hardly to be had before.
        Its perfecting needs your help;   5910
Sire, be its guardian:
any treasure you control
serves the welfare of mankind.

PLUTUS (*to the* HERALD).

We must maintain complete composure
and, come what may, not intervene.   5915
I know you've always shown the greatest courage,
but what's about to happen will seem utter horror;
since chroniclers will stubbornly deny its truth,
record it faithfully in your report.

HERALD (*laying hold of his staff, which* PLUTUS *does not relinquish*).

Slowly, the gnomes conduct Great Pan   5920
towards the fountainhead of fire;
it surges up from its abyss,
then sinks again down to the bottom,
and only gaping darkness shows;
again it wells up, glowing, seething,   5925
Great Pan stands dauntless and enjoys
the strange and wondrous sight,
and iridescent bubbles spray about.
How can he trust such goings-on—
he's bending low to look inside! –   5930
Why, now his beard is falling off! –
To whom can the smooth-shaven chin belong
that's hidden by his hand?
A great disaster now ensues:
his beard bursts into flame and, flying back,   5935
sets fire to his crown, his hair, his torso,
and merriment turns into agony. –
The members of his crew rush to his aid,
but none of them escapes the flames,
and efforts to beat down the fire   5940
only ignite still further flames;
trapped in this sea of fire,
all of this group of masqueraders burn to death.
    But what is this I hear reported
and spread by mouth from ear to ear!   5945

O evermore ill-fated night,
what hurt and grief you've caused us!
Tomorrow will proclaim abroad
tidings no one will want to hear;
but what I hear cried everywhere,   5950
is that the Emperor's a victim too.
If only something else were true!
The Emperor and all with him on fire!
A curse on them who led him so astray,
who strapped themselves in boughs of resin   5955
to bellow songs and in their frenzy
produce this universal ruin!
O youth, when will you ever learn
to moderate exuberance?
O princes, will you never be   5960
as sensible as you are sovereign?
    Our forest has caught fire now,
and tongues of pointed flame
strive toward the rafters of the coffered ceiling
and threaten us with conflagration.   5965
Our cup of misery is overflowing,
I can't imagine who might save us.
Tomorrow this imperial magnificence
will be the ash-heap of one night.
PLUTUS. There has been sufficient panic;   5970
let relief now be provided! –
Sacred staff, smite with such might
that this floor will shake and echo!
Airy spaces of this room,
quickly fill with fragrant coolness!   5975
Wisps of fog, rain-bearing mists,
come and hover all about,
hide this fiery confusion!
Cloudlets, trickle, murmur, whirl,
billow softly, gently dampen,   5980
fight the flames, put out all fires,
and as soothing rain and moisture
change the futile glow of fire
into harmless summer lightning! –
When demonic forces threaten,   5985
magic must come to our aid.

A Garden

Morning sunlight. The Emperor, *with* Courtiers; *before him kneel* Faust
   and Mephistopheles, *both soberly dressed in proper court costumes.*

Faust. Do you forgive our fiery illusion, Sire?

Emperor (*gesturing to him and* Mephistopheles *to rise*).

   I'll welcome many more such entertainments. –

   There I was suddenly inside a realm of fire—

   almost like Pluto, was what came to mind—   5990

   and saw a floor of coal-black rock

   that glowed with tiny flares. From various abysses

   myriads of savage flames swirled up

   and merged as one to form a vault of fire

   whose lofty cupola, the tongues of all these flames,   5995

   was always taking shapes that never stayed the same.

   In this vast space I saw my peoples, in long lines,

   move past its twisted fiery pillars;

   from every compass point they crowded toward me

   to do me homage in their usual ways.   6000

   I recognized some members of my court among them,

   and fancied I was lord of countless salamanders.

Mephistopheles. You are that, Sire, for every element

   acknowledges imperial supremacy.

   You now have proof that fire is your servant;   6005

   but should you plunge into the wildest sea,

   the moment that you tread its pearl-strewn floor

   its billows will enclose you in a splendid sphere,

   and you'll see waves, light green and purple-edged,

   unite to build a glorious mansion   6010

   whose center you will be. Move where you will,

   these halls will follow step by step.

   Their very walls will teem with life

   that darts about and surges to and fro.

   Sea monsters will crowd toward the new, soft light,   6015

   lunge at your sphere, but never enter it.

   Gold-scaled and colorful, sea dragons frolic here,

   and though the shark may gape, its jaws will make you laugh.

   However proud your present court may be,

   you've never seen such crowds as these.   6020

   Nor will you lack what's always loveliest:

   their curiosity will bring the Nereids—

   the youngest shy yet, eager to be baited,

   their elders shrewd—to see the sumptuous dwelling here

   in this eternal freshness. Thetis hears the news   6025

   and grants her person to a second Peleus. –

   If, next, you choose to sit on Mount Olympus . . .

EMPEROR. You need not bother with ethereal regions—
the throne up there is all too soon ascended.
MEPHISTO. As for this earth, you are its sovereign now!   6030
EMPEROR. What happy chance has brought you straight to us
from the Arabian Nights?
If you can match Scheherazade's fertile mind,
I promise you the highest favors I can grant.
Always be ready when, as often happens,   6035
I find this routine world unbearable.
Enter LORD STEWARD, *hastily.*
STEWARD. Your Highness, never in my life
did I expect I would announce
this splendid news, which fills me with such great delight
that, in your presence, I am still in transports: 6040
all our accounts are settled,
the claws of usury have been appeased,
I'm rid of those infernal torments;
in paradise things can't be looking brighter.
GRAND-MASTER (*following quickly*).
We've started to pay off what's owed the mercenaries,   6045
our troops have all signed up again,
the lansquenets feel like new men,
and wench and landlord prosper.
EMPEROR. How easily you breathe today!
How cheerful have become your furrowed faces!   6050
How briskly you approach the throne!
INTENDANT (*entering as the* EMPEROR *speaks, and indicating* FAUST *and*
MEPHISTOPHELES). Ask these, who did it, how this came about.
FAUST. Rightly, the Chancellor should give the explanation.
CHANCELLOR (*arriving slowly*).
Who, in old age, can be carefree at last. –
Now hear, and see, the fateful document   6055
that has transformed all grief into contentment.
(*Reading.*) "To whom it may concern, be by these presents known,
this note is legal tender for one thousand crowns
and is secured by the immense reserves of wealth
safely stored underground in our Imperial States.   6060
It is provided that, as soon as it be raised,
said treasure shall redeem this note."
EMPEROR. There's been some great and criminal fraud, I fear.
Who forged the Emperor's signature to this?
Does this crime still remain unpunished?   6065
INTENDANT. Don't you recall, only last night
you signed your name yourself? You were Great Pan;
the Chancellor came up with us to you, and said:

"Allow yourself the culminating festive pleasure—
salvation for your peoples—with a few strokes of the pen."   6070
You signed, and then before the night was over
quick conjurors made copies by the thousands.
To guarantee that all may share this blessing,
at the same time we placed your name on a whole series;
thus tens and thirties, fifties, hundreds too are ready.   6075
You can't imagine how this pleased your subjects.
See how the town, so long half-dead and mildewed,
is full of life and teems with pleasure seekers!
Although your name has long been much beloved,
never before has it been viewed with such affection.   6080
The alphabet is really now superfluous,
for in this sign all men can find salvation.

EMPEROR. And people value this the same as honest gold?
    The court and army take it as full pay?
    Much as I find it strange, I see I must accept it.   6085

LORD STEWARD. There is no way these bills can be recaptured;
    they fled with lightning speed and are dispersed.
    The money changers' shops are all wide open;
    there every note is honored and exchanged—
    at discount, to be sure—for gold and silver coin   6090
    which soon gets to the butcher's, baker's, and the dramshop;
    half the world seems obsessed with eating well,
    the other half with showing off new clothes.
    The drapers cut their cloth, the tailors sew.
    Wine flows in taverns where your Majesty is toasted   6095
    as food is boiled and fried, and dishes make a clatter.

MEPHISTOPHELES. If you should walk about these grounds all by yourself,
    you'd soon espy a lovely lady, dressed to kill
    and peeking from behind a splendid peacock fan;
    she'll smile at you and look to see if you've these notes,   6100
    which will procure love's richest favors
    far quicker than can wit or eloquence.
    You do not need to fuss with pouch or purse;
    a note tucked in your bosom is no burden
    and fits together nicely with a billet doux.   6105
    The pious priest can put one in his breviary,
    and so that they can move more swiftly,
    soldiers will hasten to reduce the weight around their waists.
    I hope your Majesty will pardon if I seem
    to minimize the value of this vast achievement.   6110

FAUST. The overplus of wealth that lies, lethargic,
    deep in the soil beneath your territories,

still waits to be exploited. But no mind
is vast enough to grasp these treasures' full extent;
imagination in its loftiest flight may strain,   6115
but cannot ever do them feeble justice.
Yet minds that can look deep will have
the vast assurance that vast undertakings need.
MEPHISTOPHELES. These notes, when used in lieu of gold and pearls,
are handy, too; you know right off how much you own   6120
and can, without first bargaining or haggling,
enjoy the full delights of love and wine.
If metal's wanted, there are money-changers,
and if they're short, you go and dig a while;
the golden cups and chains can then be sold at auction,   6125
and prompt redemption of these shares
confounds all sceptics who might mock us.
Once used to this, no one will want another system,
and from now on all your imperial states
will thus be well supplied with jewels, gold, and paper.   6130
EMPEROR [*addressing* FAUST *and the* INTENDANT OF THE TREASURY].
Our nation owes its great prosperity to you;
your services deserve commensurate reward.
To you we now entrust the subsoil of our empire,
who most deserve to be its treasurers' guardians.
You know their full extent and where they're safely kept,   6135
and any digging shall be done as you direct.
Collaborate, you masters of our treasury,
enjoy the honors of your office,
that joins together in one happy union
the upper and the nether worlds.   6140
INTENDANT. Between us there shall never be the slightest discord;
I welcome the magician as my colleague.   [*Exit, with* FAUST.
EMPEROR. I'll now distribute gifts to all my suite,
but each must say what use you'll put it to.
FIRST PAGE (*eagerly*). High spirits and a merry life for me!   6145
SECOND PAGE (*likewise*). I'll buy my girl a necklace and some rings.
FIRST CHAMBERLAIN (*politely*).
The wines I drink will now be twice as good
SECOND CHAMBERLAIN (*likewise*).
The dice have started dancing in my purse.
FIRST BANNERET (*thoughtfully*).
My lands and castle shall be freed of debt.
SECOND BANNERET (*likewise*).
It's wealth to place with other things of value.   6150
EMPEROR. I hoped you'd be inspired to new ventures,

but you are no surprise to one who knows you.
This marvelous prosperity, I see,
leaves you exactly what you were before.
COURT FOOL (*entering*).
Since you're dispensing presents, don't exclude me!   6155
EMPEROR. If you've come back to life, they'll only go for drink.
FOOL. I don't quite understand these printed charms.
EMPEROR. I don't doubt that! You'll never grasp their proper use.
FOOL. Some dropped; should I do anything about them?
EMPEROR. They fell your way, so you may take them.   (*Exit*.)
FOOL. Five thousand crowns! Is that what I am holding?
MEPHISTOPHELES. Wineskin on legs, have you been resurrected?
FOOL. Many a time, but never with such profit.
MEPHISTOPHELES. You're sweating with excited happiness!
FOOL. Is what I'm showing you the same as money?   6165
MEPHISTOPHELES. It will supply your gut's and gullet's wants.
FOOL. And can I buy some land, a house, and cattle?
MEPHISTOPHELES. Of course! Offer enough and they'll be yours.
FOOL. A castle, too, with woods, a chase, and fishing?
MEPHISTOPHELES. I'd give a lot to see you as a country squire!   6170
FOOL. Tonight I'll dream of my estates.   (*Exit.*)
MEPHISTOPHELES (*solus*). Who still can doubt our Fool has wit!

A DARK GALLERY

Enter FAUST *and* MEPHISTOPHELES.

MEPHISTOPHELES. Why have you dragged me to this dreary hallway?
Isn't it lively enough for you in there?
Doesn't the brilliant, crowded court provide   6175
plenty of scope for entertaining tricks of magic?
FAUST. Spare me such talk! In the old days
you used to wear your shoes out in my service,
but now you only rush about
in order to evade my orders.   6180
But I'm now under pressure to perform,
urged by the Steward and the Chamberlain.
The Emperor wants to see, and will brook no delay,
Helen of Troy and Paris here before him,
and gaze upon clear counterfeits   6185
of those two paragons of male and female beauty.
Quick, get to work! I must not break my word.
MEPHISTOPHELES. You were a fool to make a thoughtless promise.

FAUST. You are the one, my friend, who didn't think
   to what your cleverness would bring us;   6190
   now that we've made him rich,
   we are expected to amuse him.
MEPHISTOPHELES. You think such things can be arranged offhand;
   we're here confronted with a steeper flight of stairs,
   and you are meddling in an alien sphere;   6195
   you'll end up with worse debts than ever,
   if you believe that Helen can be conjured up
   as easily as phantom money. –
   At any time I can supply an ugly witch,
   a spectral ghost, a changeling dwarf,   6200
   but devils' goodwives, though they have their merits,
   can't be palmed off as heroines.
FAUST. Now you are grinding out that same old tune!
   With you one always finds that nothing's certain.
   You are the father of all stumbling blocks   6205
   and want a new reward for any means you offer.
   Some murmured words, I know, will do the trick,
   and you'll have brought them here before I've turned to look.
MEPHISTOPHELES. Pagans are none of my affair—
   they live in their own special hell.   6210
   Yet there's a means . . .
FAUST.   Then tell me, and be quick!
MEPHISTOPHELES. You force me to reveal a higher mystery. –
   Majestic goddesses enthroned in solitude
   apart from space, outside of time—
   to speak of them I find embarrassing—   6215
   these are the Mothers!
FAUST (startled).   Mothers!
MEPHISTOPHELES.   What? Afraid?
FAUST. The Mothers! "Mothers" sounds so strange!
MEPHISTO. And strange they are. No mortal knows these goddesses,
   whom even we are loath to name.
   You'll have to plumb the lowest depths to find their home,   6220
   but it's your fault we need their help.
FAUST. And what way must I go?
MEPHISTOPHELES.   No way at all!
   To where no one has trod, where none may ever tread,
   and where no prayer is heard or answered. Are you willing? –
   Although you won't have locks or bolts to open,   6225
   you'll have to bear the buffetings of solitude.
   Is dreary solitude a thought that you can grasp?
FAUST. You might, I think, be less verbose!

All this recalls the Witch's kitchen
and smacks of times now long since past. –   6230
Was I not forced to live among mankind,
to study empty nothings and to teach them too?
If I spoke sense and what seemed sense to me,
the voice of contradiction shouted twice as loud;
indeed, it was to get away from my opponents' blows   6235
that I withdrew to dreary solitude
and, not to live neglected and alone,
then put myself into the devil's hands.
MEPHISTOPHELES. Although you swam across the ocean
and there beheld what's limitless,   6240
you still would see wave follow wave
even as death inspired you with terror;
you'd still see something—dolphins darting
in the green spaces of the quiet deep,
or scudding clouds, or sun and moon and stars.   6245
In ever empty distance you'll see nothing,
you will not hear the sound of your own step,
will find no solid spot on which to rest.
FAUST. You are the father of all mystagogues
who ever cheated docile neophytes,   6250
but you reverse their method—send me to a void
for higher wisdom and for greater powers.
You're making me the cat whose task it is
to pull your chestnuts from the fire.
But do not stop! Let's probe the matter fully,   6255
since in your Nothingness I hope to find my All.
MEPHISTOPHELES. Before we part, I'll say this to your credit:
you know your devil very well.
Here, take this key!
FAUST.   That tiny thing!
MEPHISTOPHELES. Just grasp it, and remember what it's worth! 6260
FAUST. It's growing in my hand—it shines and flashes!
MEPHISTOPHELES. You're quick to see that it has special properties!
It has an instinct for the place one wants to be;
follow its lead down to the Mothers.
FAUST (shuddering).
The Mothers! It's a shock each time I hear their name!   6265
What is this word I so dislike to hear?
MEPHISTOPHELES. Have you some prejudice against new words?
Must you hear only what you've heard before?
Nothing you are about to hear should cause dismay
to one so long inured to all that's strange.   6270

FAUST. I do not seek salvation in mere apathy—
    awe is the greatest boon we humans are allotted,
    and though our world would have us stifle feeling,
    if we are stirred profoundly, we sense the Infinite.
MEPHISTOPHELES. Well then, descend! Or, if you wish, ascend—   6275
    it makes no difference which I say. From finitude
    escape to realms where forms exist detached,
    where what has ceased to be can still afford delight.
    There shapes will crowd and swirl like clouds—
    brandish your key and keep them at a distance!   6280
FAUST (with enthusiasm).
    I hold it tight and feel new strength, new courage.
    Let the great enterprise begin!
MEPHISTOPHELES. A glowing tripod, finally, will let you know
    that you have reached the deepest depth of all,
    and in the light it sheds you'll see the Mothers.   6285
    Some will be seated, some will stand or walk—
    there is no rule—for all is form in transformation,
    Eternal Mind's eternal entertainment.
    About them hover images of all that's been created,
    but you they will not see, for they see only phantoms.   6290
    Now summon up your courage—there's great danger—
    and go directly to the tripod,
    and touch it with your key!
    (FAUST, with the key, strikes an imperious pose as MEPHISTOPHELES
                    watches.)
                    Yes, that's the way! –
    It then will be your faithful follower;
    sustained by your success, you can ascend at leisure,   6295
    be back before they know it's gone.
    As soon as you have brought it here, call forth
    your hero and your heroine from darkness—
    a feat no man has ever dared attempt
    has been performed, and you're the one who's done it.   6300
    Henceforth, if you so will, by magic art
    this cloud of incense can be changed to gods.
FAUST. What happens now?
MEPHISTOPHELES.   Direct your strivings downward;
    to sink you stamp your foot, to rise you stamp again.
          (FAUST stamps his foot and sinks out of sight.)
    The key, I hope, will serve him well—   6305
    I'm curious to see if he'll return!

BRIGHTLY LIT ROOMS

EMPEROR *and* PRINCES, *with* COURTIERS; *there is much coming and going.*
A CHAMBERLAIN (*to* MEPHISTOPHELES).
　We still are waiting for the phantom scene you owe us;
　our master is impatient, so get started!
LORD STEWARD.
　His Highness asked just now about it;
　do not embarrass him by more delays.   6310
MEPHISTOPHELES. That's why my friend has disappeared,
　he is the expert in these matters;
　in undisturbed seclusion, he is working hard
　at what demands his total concentration;
　the man who would reveal the treasure Beauty   6315
　must use that highest art, the magic of the sages.
STEWARD. What arts are used is immaterial—
　the Emperor wants you to be ready now.
A BLONDE (*to* MEPHISTOPHELES).
　A word, kind sir! You see my clear complexion,
　but summertime does nasty things to it;   6320
　that's when a hundred red-brown blemishes appear
　and cover this white skin and vex me.
　I'd like a remedy!
MEPHISTOPHELES.　It's sad that beauty so translucent
　should, when May comes, be spotted like a panther cub!
　Take spawn of frogs and tongues of toads, mix well,   6325
　distill this carefully in full-moon light;
　apply, where needed only, as the moon is waning,
　and when spring comes your spots will all be gone.
A BRUNETTE. The crowd that seeks your favors is increasing.
　I beg you for a cure. A chilblained foot   6330
　impairs my walking and my dancing;
　it even makes it hard for me to curtsy.
MEPHISTOPHELES. You'll have to let me press your foot with mine.
BRUNETTE. Why, that's the sort of thing that lovers do!
MEPHISTO. A kick from me, my child, means something more important.
　Similia similibus applies to all disorders;
　as foot cures foot, so does each other member.
　Come close! And mind you don't reciprocate!
BRUNETTE (*screaming*). That hurts! My foot's on fire! It was as if
　a horse's hoof had kicked me hard.
MEPHISTOPHELES.　　　　　　　　　But you are cured.   6340
　Now you can have your fill of dancing
　and press your lover's foot beneath the banquet table.
A LADY (*pushing forward*). Let me get through! I cannot bear
　the burning pains that rack my being; till yesterday

he searched my eyes in quest of happiness,   6345
but now he's turned his back and only talks to *her*.
MEPHISTOPHELES. Your case is serious, but follow this advice:
  you must steal softly up to him
  and, with this charcoal, draw a line somewhere
  on his sleeve, cloak, or shoulder;   6350
  his heart will suffer pricks of sweet remorse.
  You must, however, promptly swallow the charcoal,
  letting no wine or water touch your lips,
  and he'll be sighing at your door this very night.
LADY. This isn't harmful?
MEPHISTOPHELES (*indignantly*). Please! You owe me more respect!   6355
  To find its like you'd have to go some distance;
  it comes from where we once, when zeal was greater,
  eagerly fanned the flames around the stake.
A PAGE. Though I'm in love, they tell me I am too young.
MEPHISTOPHELES (*aside*).
  I hardly know to whom to listen next.   6360
(*To the Page.*). Don't set your heart on someone very young;
  elderly women will appreciate you best.
          (*More people crowd in about him.*)
  More yet! This gets to be a struggle.
  I may end up by having recourse to the truth;
  my plight's so bad, I'll take the worst expedient. –   6365
  O Mothers, Mothers, free Faust from your spell!
(*Looking about.*) In the great hall the candles are now dimmer,
  and suddenly the whole Court starts to move.
  I see the decorous procession go
  through corridors and distant galleries.   6370
  Good! They're assembling in the old Knights' Hall
  that, though it's large, can hardly hold them.
  Its spacious walls are richly hung with tapestries,
  its nooks and corners filled with armor.
  In such a place, I think, spells are not needed;   6375
  ghosts will come here without an invitation.

KNIGHTS' HALL

    Dim lighting. The EMPEROR *and* COURT *have already entered.*
HERALD. Mysterious forces of the spirit world prevent
  my usual announcing of the play;
  there's no point trying to explain
  all the confusion in some rational way.   6380

The chairs have been arranged already;
the Emperor is placed so that he'll face the wall,
so close that he can contemplate in perfect comfort
tapestried battles fought in days of glory.
He now is seated, with his court around him   6385
and crowded benches in the background;
but even at this time of somber apparitions
love provides room for lovers side by side.
And now that all have found their proper places,
our work is finished. Let the ghosts appear!   (*Trumpets.*)   6390
ASTROLOGER. By royal command the play shall start at once.
    Become an opening, what now is wall!
    When magic operates, all things are easy;
    like jetsam swept by tides, the arras vanishes;
    the wall divides and is reversed,   6395
    creating the effect of a deep stage
    as we seem bathed in some mysterious glow;
    I'll now climb up to its proscenium.
MEPHISTOPHELES (*popping up in the prompter's box*).
    I trust my being here will be approved by all:
    the devil's eloquence is always *sotto voce*.   6400
(*To the* ASTROLOGER.)
    As one who knows the tempi of the stars,
    you'll understand my prompting perfectly.
ASTROLOGER. By dint of magic there is here revealed
    the massive structure of an ancient temple.
    Like Atlas, formerly the skies' support,   6405
    its serried rows of columns stand, no doubt sufficient
    to hold the weight of stone they stand beneath,
    since two could well support a mighty edifice.
AN ARCHITECT. They call this Classical! I can't see much to praise;
    awkward and cumbersome would be more apt.   6410
    What's crude is labeled noble, and what's clumsy, grand.
    Give me slim pillars striving toward infinity,
    ogival zeniths that exalt the spirit;
    these make our edifices uniquely edifying.
ASTROLOGER. Welcome with awe this well-starred hour;   6415
    let Reason be the thrall of Magic,
    and let bold Phantasy appear
    in all her freedom, all her glory.
    See now before your eyes what you have dared to ask for:
    what is impossible, and hence is surely truth!   6420
        (FAUST *climbs on to the proscenium at the opposite side.*)
    Behold the thaumaturge, in priestly robe and wreath,
    who'll now complete his daring enterprise.

A tripod rises with him from a cavernous hole;
I think I now smell incense from its bowl.
He is prepared to consecrate his mighty feat;   6425
only good fortune can attend him now.

FAUST (*grandiosely*).
In your name, Mothers, who in boundless space
dwell enthroned in eternal solitude,
yet sociably. About your heads there hover,
moving but lifeless, images of living things.   6430
Resplendent glories, now no more,
are stirring still, for they would be eternal.
And you, in your omnipotence, assign them
to light's pavillion or the vault of darkness.
Some are caught up in life's propitious course;   6435
others, the dauntless sorcerer seeks out,
who generously displays for all to see
the marvels that their hearts desire.

ASTROLOGER. His glowing key's no sooner touched the bowl
than smokelike haze obscures the stage,   6440
first creeping in, then billowing like clouds
that swell, condense, entwine, divide, and join.
Heed how the master now controls the spirit-world—
as the shapes move, the air is filled with music.
Aerial tones produce a strange effect   6445
and, as they flow, all is melodious.
Each column with its triglyphs resonates,
and the whole temple seems to me to sing.
The mist subsides; from the thin haze,
in time with the music, a comely youth steps forth.   6450
Here I may pause, for there's no need to name him—
who would not know that this was lovely Paris!

A LADY. He glows with adolescent vigor!
SECOND LADY. As fresh and juicy as a peach!
A THIRD. What finely chiseled, sweetly swollen lips!   6455
A FOURTH. That is a cup you'd surely like to sip from.
A FIFTH. He's quite good-looking, but a bit coarse too.
A SIXTH. He might be just a bit less stiff.
A KNIGHT. I think that I detect the shepherd in him;
nothing suggests a prince or courtier.   6460
SECOND KNIGHT. Half-naked he's no doubt a handsome boy,
but we would need to see him wearing armor!
LADY. He's sitting down with almost feminine langour.
KNIGHT. Perhaps you'd feel at home there on his knees?
SECOND LADY. How gracefully he rests his arm upon his head!   6465
CHAMBERLAIN. I think such boorishness cannot be pardoned.

LADY. You gentlemen are always finding fault.
CHAMBERLAIN. To think of lolling in the Emperor's presence!
LADY. He's only acting as if he were all alone.
CHAMBERLAIN. Here, even in a play, we want decorum.   6470
LADY. Now the dear boy is sleeping gently.
CHAMBERLAIN. You'll have full truth to nature when he starts to snore!
YOUNG LADY (*ecstatically*).
    What perfume's mingling with the incense
    and bringing cool refreshment to my heart?
AN OLDER LADY. There really emanates from him a gentle breath   6475
    that deeply stirs my soul!
THE OLDEST LADY.   It's youth's ambrosial bloom
    that in the adolescent is distilled
    and permeates the air about us.
                  Enter HELEN.
MEPHISTOPHELES. So that is she! She won't make me lose sleep;
    no doubt she's pretty, but she's not my style.   6480
ASTROLOGER. I see that at this point I am superfluous,
    and as a man of honor say so frankly.
    Had I but tongues of fire to sing this beauty,
    whose loveliness has long been praised!
    To see her is to lose all sense of self,   6485
    to have possessed her, undeserved good fortune.
FAUST. Does some more inward sense than sight perceive
    the overflowing fountainhead of beauty?
    My dread ordeal is gloriously rewarded.
    How circumscribed and empty was my world before!   6490
    Now, with this priesthood, it at last becomes
    desirable and has a lasting basis.
    May I no longer have the power to breathe
    if I should ever want to live without you! –
    The lovely form that in the magic mirror   6495
    once ravished me with such delight
    was but this beauty's feeble counterfeit. –
    To you I offer as my homage
    all my vitality, and passion's essence:
    devotion, love, idolization, madness.   6500
MEPHISTOPHELES (*from the prompter's box*).
    Control yourself, and don't forget your part!
AN OLDER LADY.
    The head's too small for her good height and figure.
A YOUNGER LADY. Those feet! They hardly could be more ungainly.
A DIPLOMAT. She has a quality I've seen in princesses;
    I find her beautiful from head to toe.   6505
A COURTIER. She's stealing closer to the sleeping figure.

LADY. Beside unsullied youth how odious she looks!

POET. Her beauty casts a radiance upon him.

LADY. A picture of Diana and Endymion!

POET. That's it! The goddess seems about to kneel,   6510
    but then bends forward to drink in his breath;
    enviable fate—a kiss! – His cup is full!

A GOVERNESS. In front of people! Really, that's too much!

FAUST. How awful she should favor such a boy!

MEPHISTOPHELES.   Be quiet!
    Don't interfere in what the phantom's doing.   6515

COURTIER. She now tiptoes away as he wakes up.

LADY. Just as I thought she would, she's looking back!

COURTIER. He is surprised by the miraculous!

LADY. She's not the least surprised by his reaction.

COURTIER. She turns back toward him with great dignity.   6520

LADY. I see that she intends to be his tutor;
    all men are stupid in such situations,
    and he no doubt thinks too that he's the first.

KNIGHT. Don't carp at elegance and queenly bearing!

LADY. The wanton thing! I call such conduct vulgar.   6525

A PAGE. I wouldn't mind if I could take his place!

COURTIER. Who would object to being in her toils?

LADY. That piece of jewelry's more than second-hand
    and quite a lot of gilt has been worn off it.

SECOND LADY. Since she was ten she's been a good-for-nothing.   6530

KNIGHT. Sometimes you take the best that is available;
    I'd not refuse what's left of such great beauty.

A PEDANT. Although I see her clearly, I'll point out
    that there may be some doubt if she's authentic.
    We're apt to be misled by what's before us,   6535
    and I prefer to trust what's written down.
    There I have read as fact that she found special favor
    with all the elders of the Trojans;
    that fits the case here perfectly, I think;
    I find her pleasing, though I am a graybeard.   6540

ASTROLOGER. No longer boy, a man and hero now,
    he boldly seizes her, scarce able to resist.
    On strengthened arm he lifts her high above him—
    is he perhaps abducting her?

FAUST.   Rash fool!
    How can you dare! Do you not hear? Desist! Enough!   6545

MEPHISTOPHELES. But you're the author of this spectral masque!

ASTROLOGER. One last word! Now that the piece has been performed,
    I can entitle it: *The Rape of Helen*.

FAUST. A rape indeed! Am I of no importance here?

Does not my hand still hold this key   6550
that brought me back to this firm shore
through dismal solitudes of rock and sea?
I won't give way! This is reality, and here
the human spirit can contend with spirit beings
to win itself a double kingdom.   6555
She was so far away, but now could not be nearer.
Once I have rescued her, she will be doubly mine.
I'll venture all! – This, Mothers, you must grant me!
He who discerns her worth can never live without her.

ASTROLOGER. What are you doing, Faust? – With violent hands   6560
he seizes her; her figure is already less distinct.
His key is pointed toward the young man now,
it touches him! – Woe to us all! In just a moment . . . !

Explosion. FAUST *is seen lying on the floor; the phantom figures dissolve
as vapors.*

MEPHISTOPHELES (*hoisting* FAUST *on his shoulder*).
That's life for you! To be encumbered with a fool
can't even help the devil in the end.   6565

Darkness and noisy confusion as the curtain falls.

ACT II

A HIGH-VAULTED, NARROW GOTHIC ROOM

Faust's former study is unchanged. – Enter MEPHISTOPHELES *from behind a curtain; as he holds it up and looks back,* FAUST *is seen lying on an old-fashioned bed.*

MEPHISTOPHELES. Lie there, unhappy victim of a love
   whose bonds it will be hard to break!
   One who is paralyzed by Helen
   won't easily regain his senses.
(He looks about.)

   Nothing, no matter where I look,   6570
   has changed or suffered harm; perhaps
   the colored window-panes are more opaque,
   the cobwebs certainly have multiplied;
   the ink has thickened and the paper yellowed,
   but everything is where it was before;   6575
   even the pen's still lying here
   with which Faust signed his contract with the devil.
   In fact, down here inside the quill there's stuck
   a drop of blood like that I wheedled out of him;
   I would congratulate the connoisseur   6580
   who laid his hands on such a piece as this.
   The fur-trimmed gown still hangs on its same hook,
   reminding me of all the nonsense
   I told the student I once counseled;
   a young man now, he may still find it food for thought;   6585
   I really have an urge, old friend,
   to wrap myself again in your moth-eaten warmth
   and strut about as a professor
   completely confident he's right—
   a habit scholars easily acquire,   6590
   but one the devil's long since lost.
Taking down Faust's gown, he shakes it; moths, balm crickets, and beetles fly out of its fur.

INSECTS (*in chorus*).
     We welcome and greet you,
     old master of ours.
     We buzz and we hover,
     we know who you are.   6595
     You planted us singly,
     in silence, long since;
     as thousands of dancers now,
     father, we're here.

The rogue in one's bosom
remains out of sight—   6600
the lice in a furpiece
come sooner to light.

MEPHISTOPHELES. What a pleasant surprise these children are!
You only have to sow, and some day you will reap.   6605
I'll give the old coat another shake;
here and there a few more fluttering things emerge. –
Up and about, you darling creatures! Hurry,
conceal yourselves in all these countless corners—
in those old boxes standing there,   6610
here in this browning manuscript,
in dusty shards of ancient vessels,
and in those deathheads' empty eyes.
Such musty chaos always will be rife
with real and imaginary maggots.   6615

(He puts on the gown.)

Come, cloak my shoulders one more time!
Today I'll be the Principal again.
But what's the use of such a title
when no one's here to pay me due respect?

*He pulls a bell cord; there is a shrill, penetrating sound that causes the
halls to tremble and the door to fly open. – Enter* FAMULUS, *staggering
out of a long, dark corridor.*

FAMULUS. What an awesome sound this is!   6620
Stairways sway, the walls are shaking;
through the trembling colored panes
I see flashing streaks of lightning.
Floors have cracks, and from above
dislocated plaster trickles.   6625
And this door, securely locked,
by some magic is unbolted. –
There—o horror!—stands a giant
wearing Faust's old woolen gown!
He now sees and beckons me,   6630
and my knees seem to give way.
Should I flee? Should I remain?
Oh, what will become of me!

MEPHISTOPHELES *(beckoning).*
Approach, my friend! – Your name is Nicodemus?

FAMULUS. That is my name, your Reverence—*Oremus.*   6635

MEPHISTOPHELES. We'll skip the prayer!

FAMULUS.   I'm pleased you recognize me.

MEPHISTOPHELES. I know the type—the student who keeps on
until he's middle-aged! But even learned men
continue studying because of some compulsion.

That's how a shabby house of cards is often started   6640
which even the best mind cannot complete.
Your master, though, knows all the tricks;
who has not heard the fame of Doctor Wagner,
the world of learning's leading luminary now!
He, all alone, keeps it in proper order,   6645
and constantly extends the realm of wisdom.
Eager for universal knowledge, crowds
of students and disciples gather round him.
He is by far the lectern's brightest star
and, like St. Peter, holds the keys   6650
that open earth's and heaven's locks.
His ardor and brilliance have long since obscured
all others' fame and reputation;
even Faust's name has been eclipsed,
and Wagner is your sole inventor.   6655

FAMULUS. Your Reverence will, I hope, forgive me
  if I now dare to contradict you:
that's not the way things are at all.
He is a very modest person,
and never has been reconciled   6660
to that great man's unfathomed disappearance,
for whose return he prays in hope of solace.
This room, exactly as it was when Doctor Faust was here,
and never changed while he has been away,
awaits its former master;   6665
I hardly dare to venture in.
What stars must now prevail in heaven,
when walls, I think, do quake with fear?
Yet doorposts did tremble and locks were sprung,
or you would not be here yourself.   6670

MEPHISTOPHELES. Where has your master sought seclusion?
  Lead me to him!—bring him to me!

FAMULUS. Oh, sir! his prohibition is so strict;
  I do not know if I should take the risk.
For many months, to further his great project,   6675
he's worked in deepest secrecy.
This frailest of all men of learning
looks like a charcoal burner;
with blackened cheeks,
eyes red from blowing up the fire,   6680
he's always breathless with anticipation;
the clattering tongs seem music to his ears.

MEPHISTOPHELES. I doubt that he'll refuse to see me;
  I am the man to hasten his success.   [*Exit* FAMULUS.

      MEPHISTOPHELES *seats himself in a dignified pose.*

MEPHISTOPHELES. I scarcely have entrenched myself   6685
  when a familiar guest is under way back there.
  This time he comes with a diploma,
  and so his arrogance will know no limits.
BACCALAUREATE (*storming up the corridor*).
    Here, I see, the door's wide open!
    At long last, then, there is hope   6690
    that the occupant no further
    will remain, as up to now,
    in this mildew like a corpse,
    atrophying, self-destroying,
    dying of the life he's leading.
    All these walls, all these partitions,   6695
    lean and sag, about to fall,
    and unless we soon retreat,
    we'll be victims of disaster.
    I'm as bold as anybody,
    yet no one will drag me farther.   6700
    But what's this that I've discovered!
    It was surely here that I,
    timid then and ill at ease,
    came naively years ago,
    still a freshman trusting graybeards,   6705
    edified still by their prattle.
    Lies they found in ancient volumes
    they passed on to me as knowledge
    not believing it themselves,
    wasting their own lives and mine.   6710
    But what's this? Here's one still sitting
    in his chiaroscuro cell!
    Getting closer, I'm amazed;
    he's still sitting as I left him,
    in the same drab fur-trimmed gown;   6715
    I would swear I see no change!
    When I didn't understand him yet,
    he of course seemed rather clever.
    That won't work with me today—
    I shall tackle him at once!   6720
  If, ancient sir, your sidewise-bent and hairless head
  has not already swum through Lethe's turgid waters,
  behold a grateful student here
  who has outgrown the canes of academe.
  I find you still as I last saw you,   6725
  but I've returned completely changed.
MEPHISTOPHELES. I'm glad my ringing's brought you here.

Even back then I saw you had a great potential;
the grub, or even the cocoon, presages
that there's some gorgeous butterfly to come.   6730
Your head of curls and your lace collar
afforded you a childlike satisfaction—
I don't believe you even wore a queue?—
But now I see your hair's cropped short.
This makes you look quite resolute and gallant;   6735
just don't go home with nothing left up there!
BACCALAUREATE. My dear old chap! The place may be the same,
but don't forget that times have changed,
and spare us double meanings;
we're now aware of things we weren't before.   6740
You bantered a naive young fellow,
and got away quite easily with something
that nowadays no one would risk.
MEPHISTOPHELES. If you tell callow youth what they dislike to hear,
unvarnished truth which afterwards   6745
they learn from years of hard experience
applies to their own persons, in their conceit
they then believe it sprang from their own heads
and still assert their teacher was dull-witted.
BACCALAUREATE. Better, perhaps: dishonest—since what teacher   6750
tells us the truth without evasions?
Solemn or animated, as his prudence prompts him,
he knows what to omit or add for docile children.
MEPHISTOPHELES. There is a time to learn, I think we must admit,
but you, I see, are now prepared to teach.   6755
Several suns and still more moons will have sufficed,
I'm sure, for you to gain experience.
BACCALAUREATE. Experience! Mere froth and fluff—
no peer of thought, of mind, of spirit!
Admit that what has up to now been knowledge   6760
does not deserve that name at all.
MEPHISTOPHELES (after a pause).
I've long suspected that I was a simple soul,
but now I see how dull a fool I am.
BACCALAUREATE. I'm very pleased to hear so much good sense;
at last I've found a sensible old man!   6765
MEPHISTOPHELES. I hoped to find some secret store of gold
and brought back only horrid cinders.
BACCALAUREATE. Be honest, and admit that your bald head
is worth no more than those skulls over there!
MEPHISTOPHELES (indulgently).
May I assume my friend is unaware he's rude?   6770

BACCALAUREATE. To be polite in German is to lie.
MEPHISTOPHELES (*continually rolling his chair closer to the proscenium and addressing the audience*).

Up here I'm not allowed to see or breathe —
have you perhaps a place for me down there?
BACCALAUREATE. I think it arrogance, when time gets short
    and you no longer count, to claim that you exist.   6775
    Our lives lie in our blood, and where is circulation
    better than in the blood of those still young?
    Their blood's alive, is fresh and vigorous,
    and from its life creates life that is new.
    Then things begin to move, then things get done;   6780
    weakness succumbs, and fitness takes its place. –
    While we have conquered half the universe,
    what have you done but nod and ponder,
    dream and deliberate? Plans, always plans!
    Age is indeed an ague much augmented   6785
    by the capricious frost of impotence.
    One who has passed the thirtieth year
    already is as good as dead—
    it would be best to kill you off by then.
MEPHISTOPHELES. To this, the devil can but say amen!   6790
BACCALAUREATE. Unless I will it, devils don't exist.
MEPHISTOPHELES (*aside*).
    It won't be long before some devil trips you up.
BACCALAUREATE. The noblest mission is reserved for youth!
    There was no world before I bade it be;
    out of the sea I summoned forth the sun;   6795
    with me the moon's inconstant course began;
    then, as I passed, the day put on its finery
    and earth saluted me with greenery and flowers.
    At my command, in primal night the stars
    and planets shone in all their splendor.   6800
    Who, if not I, delivered you
    from the confinement of Philistine thought?
    But I am free! And as the spirit moves me,
    I happily pursue the inward light
    and, in an ecstasy of joy, speed on,   6805
    brightness before me, darkness at my back.   [*Exit.*
MEPHISTOPHELES. Farewell, you pompous ass! – How greatly would
    you be offended if you heard me ask:
    can anyone have wise or stupid thoughts
    that ages past have not already thought? –   6810
    In any case, we're in no danger here,
    and in a few more years all will have changed;

the juice may foam absurdly in the barrel;
but in the end it yields some kind of wine.
 (*To the younger members of the audience, who fail to applaud.*)
My dear young friends, I do not take it ill   6815
that you're left cold by what I say;
but please remember that the devil's old—
you must grow old, and then you'll understand him!

LABORATORY

A medieval alchemist's chamber filled with cumbersome apparatus designed
for various fantastic purposes.

WAGNER (*at the hearth*).
The terrifying bell reverberates
and sends a tremor through these soot-black walls.   6820
The end has come of the uncertainties
attendant on my solemn hopes.
The shadows have begun to be less dark,
and in the inmost vial
something is glowing like a living ember   6825
and, like a glorious carbuncle,
irradiates the darkness with red lightning flashes.
A clear, white light can now be seen!
If only, this time, I don't lose it! –
Oh Lord! what is that clatter at the door?   6830
     Enter MEPHISTOPHELES.
MEPHISTO. Say "Welcome!" since I've come to be of help.
WAGNER (*apprehensively*).
By the prevailing star, be welcome!
(*In a low voice.*) Don't breathe, don't say a word!
Something tremendous is just about completed.
MEPHISTOPHELES (*in an even lower voice*).
What's going on?
WAGNER (*in a still lower voice*). A human being's being made. 6835
MEPHISTOPHELES. A human being? And what amorous pair
have you imprisoned in your flue?
WAGNER. None, God forbid! Old-fashioned procreation
is something we reject as folly.
The feeble force that was life's starting point,   6840
like the compelling strength that from it sprang
and took and gave, ordained to shape its own design,
assimilating first like elements, and then unlike,

that force is now divested of all rights and privileges;
the beasts may still enjoy that sort of thing,　　6845
but human beings, with their splendid talents,
must henceforth have a higher, nobler source.
(He turns to the hearth.)
Look there, a flash! – We now can really hope:
if we compound the human substance
by mixing many hundred substances　　6850
—the mixture is what matters—carefully
and seal it tight with clay in a retort,
then re-distill it properly,
our secret labors will be finished.
(As before.)
It works! The moving mass grows clearer,　　6855
and my conviction the more certain:
what's been extolled as Nature's mystery
can be investigated, if but Reason dare,
and what she used to let be just organic
we can produce by crystallizing.　　6860
MEPHISTOPHELES. One who lives long will have seen much,
and nothing here on earth is ever new for him.
When I was still a journeyman
I met some mortals who seemed crystallized.
WAGNER *(who has continued to watch the vial attentively).*
It's rising, flashing, piling up—　　6865
another moment and it's done!
A grand design may seem insane at first;
but in the future chance will seem absurd,
and such a brain as this, intended for great thoughts,
will in its turn create a thinker too.　　6870
(He contemplates the vial delightedly.)
I hear a strong but pleasing sound; the glass vibrates,
clouds up, then clears—success is certain!
I see a pretty mannikin
who's making dainty gestures.
What more can we or can the world demand　　6875
now that the mystery has been revealed?
Listen! The sound we hear is changing—
that is a voice, now I hear speech.
HOMUNCULUS *(in the vial, to* WAGNER*).*
Is daddikins all right? A serious business, that!
Come and give me a nice affectionate hug,　　6880
but gently, so the glass won't break!
It is a curious property of things
that what is natural takes almost endless space,
while what is not, requires a container.

(*To* MEPHISTOPHELES.)

Cousin, are you here too, you rogue?   6885
You chose the proper moment, and I owe you thanks.
It is a lucky chance that you should join us—
Since I am now alive, I also must be active.
I'd like to gird myself right now for work;
and I can count on you to know the best procedures.   6890
WAGNER. Please, one more word! I've been harassed by young and old
  with problems that, till now, have put me in a quandary.
  For instance, no one's ever understood
  how soul and body fit so well together,
  clinging to one another as if they'd never part,   6895
  and yet torment each other all the livelong day.
  Nor how . . .
MEPHISTOPHELES. Stop there! I'd rather learn
  why man and wife must get along so badly.
  These matters, friend, you never will clear up.
  This little chap wants action, we have work to do.   6900
HOMUNCULUS. What needs be done?
MEPHISTOPHELES (*pointing to a door at the side*).
                    There! Demonstrate your talent!
WAGNER (*still gazing into the vial*).
  You really are the loveliest of boys!
        The side door opens and FAUST *is seen lying on a couch.*
HOMUNCULUS (*in an astonished voice*).
  An omen! –
(*The vial slips out of* WAGNER'S *hands, hovers over* FAUST, *and casts its
                    light upon him.*)
                Beauty everywhere! In a dense grove
  clear streams! And, taking off their clothes,
  the loveliest of women! – The picture is improving. –   6905
  Yet one, issued from hero-kings or even gods,
  is more resplendent than the others.
  She sets her foot into the bright transparence;
  the flawless body's precious living flame
  finds coolness in the water's pliant crystal! –   6910
  But what's this sound of whirring wings,
  this noisy splashing that disturbs the polished mirror?
  Her maidens flee, alarmed, while only she,
  the queen, remains composed and watches;
  with proud and womanly delight she sees   6915
  the leader of swans, importunate yet gentle,
  press against her knees. He seems to grow familiar. –
  A mist, however, suddenly arises
  and with its closely woven veil conceals
  the scene that's loveliest of all.   6920

MEPHISTOPHELES. That's quite a story you have told us—
  you may be small, but you've a great imagination!
  I don't see anything . . .
HOMUNCULUS.   And I can well believe it!
  Born in a later, fog-bound age,
  in a chaotic world of monkery and knighthood,   6925
  how can your northern eyes be anything but blinkered—
  you only feel at home where gloom prevails:
                (He surveys the surroundings.)
  Stonework with pointed arches, florid carvings,
  all mouldy, ugly, drab, and vulgar!
  If *he* wakes up, there'll be new trouble: 6930
  in such a place he would be dead at once.
  He has been dreaming hopefully
  of sylvan springs, of swans and naked beauties,
  so how could he put up with this?
  I'm most adaptable, yet I can hardly stand it.   6935
  Let's get him out of here.
MEPHISTOPHELES.   I'm all for that!
HOMUNCULUS. Order a hero into battle
  or ask a girl to join the dance,
  and there will be no long objections.
  Right now, as I've remembered quickly,   6940
  is Classical Walpurgisnight,
  which is, for him, most opportune.
  Transport him to his proper element!
MEPHISTOPHELES. I've never heard of anything like that.
HOMUNCULUS. And how could it have come to your attention?   6945
  Romantic spectres are the only ones you know,
  but any proper ghost has to be classical.
MEPHISTOPHELES. But what's the destination of our journey?
  I know I'll find my ancient colleagues odious.
HOMUNCULUS. Your favorite quarter, Satan, lies northwest of here, 6950
  but we must sail southeast on this occasion. –
  Through thickets, groves, and quiet humid reaches
  the free Peneus flows across a mighty plain
  extending to the mountains' gorges,
  and up above lies Old and New Pharsalus.   6955
MEPHISTOPHELES. Horrors! No more! And spare me your account
  of all those fights of slaves with despotism!
  They bore me, for no sooner are they over
  than the combatants start again
  and fail to see that they're egged on   6960
  by Asmodeus, who's behind it all.
  They claim it is a fight for independence,
  but all it really is, is slaves against each other.

HOMUNCULUS. Let mankind have its measure of contention!
   From childhood on, as best it can, the self must fight   6965
   to stay intact, and so adulthood is at last attained. –
   The only issue here is, how he can get well.
   If you have a specific, here's the place to test it;
   but if you're helpless, leave the job to me!
MEPHISTOPHELES. There's many a Brocken cure that I could try,   6970
   but pagan bars confront me here.
   Those Greeks were really never good for much,
   although they charm your senses with external show
   and lure the human heart to sinful pleasures;
   with us, however, sin will always be thought gloomy. –   6975
   Now what is on your mind?
HOMUNCULUS.   You never have been bashful,
   and so I think it quite sufficient
   if I just say: Thessalian witches.
MEPHISTO (*lecherously*). Thessalian witches! Good! They're persons
   I long have had an interest in.   6980
   To be with them night after night
   might not be restful, I suspect;
   but a trial visit . . .
HOMUNCULUS.   Take your cloak
   and in it wrap our sleeping cavalier!
   That bit of cloth will, as before,   6985
   carry the two of you together;
   I'll go ahead and light the way.
WAGNER (*apprehensively*).   And I?
HOMUNCULUS. Why, you'll stay home and do what's most important.
   Peruse your ancient manuscripts,
   collect life's elements as they direct;   6990
   then put the parts together—cautiously—
   and think about the What and, even more, the How! –
   Meanwhile I shall explore the world a bit
   and so perhaps discover how to dot the i's.
   Then your great purpose will have been achieved,   6995
   and the rewards your striving merits:
   gold, honor, fame, a long and healthy life,
   and maybe knowledge too and virtue.
   Farewell!
WAGNER (*sadly*). Farewell! – The word weighs on my heart.
   I fear, already, that I'll not see you again.   7000
MEPHISTOPHELES. Let's down at once to the Peneus!
   My cousin isn't one to be ignored.
(*Ad spectatores.*) The fact is, we remain dependent on
   the creatures we ourselves have made.   [*Exit.*

CLASSICAL WALPURGISNIGHT

The Pharsalian Fields. Darkness.

ERICHTHO. How often to this night's dread celebration   7005
 have I thus come, Erichtho I, all somberness,
 yet not so frightful—they exaggerate and set
 no limits to their praise or blame—as hateful poets
 slanderously say! I see the outstretched plain
 now wanly lightened by the gray of surging tents,   7010
 the after-image of that anxious, fearful night.
 How often it has been repeated! And it must
 recur eternally. Each wants to rule alone
 and, holding power gained through power, neither yields
 it to the other. – Those not competent to rule   7015
 their own unruly selves, with eager arrogance
 seek to impose their will upon their neighbor's will. –
 Here a battle was fought that grandly illustrates
 how power always meets some power greater still,
 how fragile is the many-flowered wreath of freedom,   7020
 how the stiff laurel, on the tyrant's head, is pliant.
 Great Pompey, here, had dreams of burgeoning hopes fulfilled,
 there wakeful Caesar watched each movement of fate's scales!
 They are well matched—who wins, the world already knows.
  Watch fires glow and lavish redness all about,   7025
 the ground exudes a semblance of shed blood,
 and lured by the night's strange and magic radiance
 the legions of Greek legend gather.
 Around the fires are fabled shapes of olden times—
 some hover timidly, some sit at ease.   7030
 Although not full, the rising moon is bright and clear,
 and as it spreads its mellow brightness everywhere
 the ghost tents vanish and the fires' glow turns blue. –
  Up there! What is that unexpected meteor?
 Its shining light reveals a solid sphere in which,   7035
 so instinct tells me, something lives. Destructive as I am
 to life, I would be ill-advised to get too close—
 my good name would be harmed and I would gain no profit.
 It now descends, and with due prudence I withdraw.   [*Exit.*

Enter, above, the AËRONAUTS.

HOMUNCULUS. Since the valley down below us   7040
     looks so very weird and spectral,
     I am flying one more circle
     over all these horrid fires.

MEPHISTOPHELES. Since these ghosts are just as horrid
     as those seen through ancient casements   7045

in the wild and dismal North,
I'm as much at home as ever.
HOMUNCULUS.   Look! In front! A thin tall woman
walks away with lengthy stride.
MEPHISTOPHELES.   Probably she has been frightened   7050
by our passage through the sky.
HOMUNCULUS.   Let her go! – Your cavalier,
once you set him on the ground,
will come promptly back to life,
since he seeks his Life in lands of myth.   7055
FAUST (*as he touches the earth*). And where is She?
HOMUNCULUS.   That's something we don't know,
    but, like as not, can here be learned by asking.
    If you hurry while it still is dark
    you can pursue the trail from flame to flame—
    the man who dared approach the Mothers   7060
    will find no obstacles before him.
MEPHISTOPHELES. I have my interests here as well;
    perhaps it would be best if we,
    each singly, went from fire to fire
    seeking adventures of our own.   7065
    And when it's time to reunite, our little friend
    must let his lamp shine bright and resonate.
HOMUNCULUS. This is the way it will flash and ring.
            (*The vial resounds and emits a strong light.*)
    Now off without delay to find new marvels!   [*Exit.*
FAUST (*solus*). Where is she? That no longer needs be asked! –   7070
    Although this may not be her native soil,
    nor these the waves that touched her feet,
    this is the air that spoke her tongue.
    Here, by a miracle, in Greece!
    I knew at once the land on which I stood;   7075
    as, when I slept, I gained new inspiration,
    so now, when I stand here, Antaeus' strength is mine.
    However strange the things I may encounter,
    I'll zealously explore this labyrinth of flame.
            FAUST *moves away from center stage.*
MEPHISTOPHELES (*investigating*).
    Wandering through these rather modest fires   7080
    I really feel I'm in a foreign land—
    nakedness everywhere, with now and then a shift:
    the Sphinxes shameless, Griffins unembarrassed,
    all sorts of hairy or befeathered creatures
    offering us both rear and frontal views.   7085
    At heart, of course, we also are indecent,

but classical antiquity, I find, is too realistic;
this kind of thing is handled best in modern fashion
by pasting leaves and such on various places.
A hideous lot! Newcomer that I am, however,   7090
I must be willing to address them nicely. –
My compliments, fair ladies! Sage graybeards, greetings!
GRIFFIN (*with guttural r's*).
    Not graybeards! Griffins! – no one likes to hear
    himself called gray. The sound of words reflects
    the origins from which their sense derives;   7095
    gray, grieving, grumpy, gruesome, graves, and groaning,
    that have one etymology,
    all put us out of sorts.
MEPHISTOPHELES.   More to the point is this:
    in Griffin, *gri* is nicely honorific.
GRIFFIN (*as before, and so henceforth*).
    Of course! There is one tried and true connection   7100
    that's often faulted, yet more often praised:
    get a good grip on gold, a girl, a government,
    and Lady Fortune seldom frowns.
GIANT ANTS. You mention gold—we had amassed a great amount
    and crammed it into secret crevises;   7105
    those Arimasps located it, and now they laugh,
    knowing how far from here it's been transported.
GRIFFINS. Count on our getting an avowal from them.
ARIMASPS. But not tonight—this is a general holiday!
(*Aside.*) We'll get it all away before tomorrow,   7110
    and so this time our venture should succeed.
MEPHISTOPHELES (*who has seated himself between the Sphinxes*).
    It's easy here to feel at home—
    I understand these fellows, one and all, so well!
A SPHINX. We spirits whisper what we have to say,
    and then you turn it into your own substance. –   7115
    Your name will do until we know you better.
MEPHISTOPHELES. There's a belief that I have many names.
    Are any British here? They're usually great travelers,
    looking for battlefields and waterfalls,
    dilapidated walls and dreary ancient sites;   7120
    this is an ideal place for them to visit.
    My name's attested in their ancient drama,
    where I appeared as Old Iniquity.
A SPHINX. And why that name?
MEPHISTOPHELES.   I cannot even guess.
A SPHINX. Perhaps! – Have you some knowledge of the stars?   7125
    What aspects would you say prevail right now?

MEPHISTOPHELES (*looking up*).
    Stars scoot across the sky, the waning moon is bright,
    and, keeping warm beside your lion skin,
    I feel quite snug and cozy here.
    It doesn't pay to go beyond one's depth;   7130
    so let's have riddles, or at least charades!
A SPHINX. Say what you are, and that will be a riddle.
    Now try to solve your true identity:
    "The pious and the wicked man each need you—
    a breastplate for the first's ascetic fencing,   7135
    a partner for the second's foolish actions,
    and, as both, a source of Zeus' amusement."
FIRST GRIFFIN (*gruffly*). I can't abide him!
SECOND GRIFFIN (*more gruffly*).   What can he want of us?
BOTH GRIFFINS. No one so nasty should be here!
MEPHISTOPHELES (*brutally*).
    Perhaps you think your guest lacks nails   7140
    that scratch as well as your sharp claws?
    Try me and see!
A SPHINX (*gently*). No one will make you go away;
    you'll be impelled, yourself, to leave us;
    at home you feel yourself important,
    but here, unless I'm wrong, you're ill at ease.   7145
MEPHISTOPHELES. Above, you look quite appetizing;
    the beast stretched out below is horrifying.
A SPHINX. You double-dealer, you will rue that bitterly—
    our claws are in the best condition;
    you, with your shriveled horse's hoof,   7150
    cannot get pleasure from our company.
        SIRENS, *above, play introductory notes on their harps.*
MEPHISTOPHELES. What are those birds, swaying back and forth,
    on poplar boughs beside the river?
A SPHINX. Be on your guard! The best of men
    have been the victims of their singing.   7155
SIRENS.   Why must you debase your taste
        with what's ugly and fantastic!
        Listen to us come as choirs
        singing in well-tempered voices
        music that is right for Sirens.   7160
SPHINXES (*to the same tune, mocking them*).
        Force them to come down from there!
        They are hiding in those branches
        their repulsive, hawk-like claws
        that are waiting to destroy you
        if you heed their siren song.   7165

SIRENS.   Hence, all hate! All envy, hence!
           Let us gather the pure essence
           of joys everywhere abounding
           and, on water or on land,
           greet each welcome passer-by   7170
           with inviting cheer and grace!
MEPHISTOPHELES. It is, I see, the latest fashion
    that throat and strings should be obliged
    to interweave the sounds they make.
    This trilling's wasted in my case;   7175
    although it titillates my ears,
    it does not penetrate my heart.
A SPHINX. Don't brag about your heart to us—
    a shrunken leather pouch
    would better match your face!   7180
FAUST (*returning to center stage*).
    How strange that contemplation satisfies me thus—
    even in ugliness there's strength and grandeur!
    Transported by this solemn spectacle,
    I sense already that the future is auspicious.
        (*He now refers successively to the* SPHINXES, SIRENS, GIANT ANTS, *and*
                          GRIFFINS.)
    Long ago Oedipus stood facing one of these;   7185
    these saw Ulysses writhe in hempen cords;
    these gathered stores of treasure never equalled,
    of which these were the faithful guardians.
    I feel sustained by new vitality—
    the forms are grand, and grand what they recall.   7190
MEPHISTOPHELES. Time was you'd have abominated shapes like these,
    yet now you seem to thrive on them;
    if one is looking for his lady-love,
    even monsters, I see, are welcome.
FAUST (*addressing the Sphinxes*).
    As females you can surely answer this: 7195
    Has any one of you seen Helen?
A SPHINX. Our line died out before her time—
    the last of us were slain by Hercules.
    Chiron could give you information;
    on this occasion he'll be galloping about,   7200
    and if he'll stop and answer you, that's a good start.
SIRENS. You'll succeed somehow or other! . . .
           When Ulysses graciously
           stayed a while as guest with us,
           he proved quite a story-teller;   7205
           we will tell you all he told us
           if you'll visit our domain

by the green Aegean's shores.

THE SPHINX. Don't be duped by them, your worship!
  Ulysses had himself restrained by ropes—   7210
  let our good counsel serve you as restraint instead;
  if you can find the noble Chiron,
  you'll have the answer that I promised.

              FAUST *withdraws from center stage.*

MEPHISTOPHELES (*ill-temperedly*).
  Now what is croaking past with beating wings,
  this endless file that moves so fast   7215
  that it remains invisible?
  They'd soon wear any hunter out!

THE SPHINX. These creatures storming like swift winter winds,
  that with his arrows Hercules himself
  could barely hit, are the Stymphalian birds,   7220
  with feet of geese and beaks of vultures,
  whose croaks are meant as friendly greeting.
  They like to point out that they are our kin
  whenever they are in our neighborhood.

MEPHISTOPHELES (*as if intimidated*).
  But there's another hissing sound, as well.   7225

THE SPHINX. It's nothing you need be afraid of!
  Those are the heads of the Lernaean Hydra;
  though severed from its trunk, they think they're still important. –
  But tell us, what's the matter now?
  What is the meaning of these signs of restlessness?   7230
  Where are you heading? Well, go on your way! . . .
  It's the group over there that has, I see,
  made you a wryneck. Do not be inhibited!
  Go, compliment them on their pretty faces!
  They are the Lamiae, refined cocottes   7235
  with smiling mouths and brazen eyes,
  who are the satyrs' favorites;
  your cloven hoof insures you'll have full freedom there.

MEPHISTOPHELES. You'll still be here, I hope, should I return?

SPHINXES. Oh, yes. Go join your flighty rabble.   7240
  We, being of Egyptian origin,
  do not mind sitting for millennia enthroned
  and will, so long as we are not disturbed,
  govern the lunar and the solar day.

    Placed before the Pyramids,   7245
    as the nations' highest court,
    we see flood, and war, and peace,
    never changing our expressions.   [*Exit* MEPHISTOPHELES.

The River God PENEUS, *surrounded by* TRIBUTARY STREAMS *and* NYMPHS.

PENEUS. Stir and whisper, sedgy rushes,
    ease my interrupted dreams! 7205
    Sister-reeds, breathe gently, softly!
    slender willow-bushes, murmur!
    trembling poplar branches, rustle! –
    An uncanny sound of thunder,
    some mysterious general tremor, 7255
    wakes me from my watery rest.

FAUST (*advancing to the river's edge*).
    If my ears do not deceive me,
    I can hear behind this screen
    of interwoven boughs and bushes
    sounds resembling human voices. 7260
    It's as if the waters prattled
    or the breezes played and jested.

NYMPHS (*to* FAUST). You would do well
        to lie down and rest;
        here in our coolness 7265
        fatigue does not last,
        and you would enjoy
        the peace that eludes you.
        We lull and we murmur,
        we whisper to you. 7270

FAUST. This is not sleep! O may they never vanish,
    these forms beyond compare
    that I envision in a miracle
    of all-pervasive feeling!
    Can they be dreams? Or are they memories?— 7275
    I have already, once before, been so enchanted.
      The quiet waters glide through cool
    and gently stirring thickets,
    and scarcely make the slightest murmur;
    a hundred rills from every side 7280
    converge in clear bright shallows
    that form a perfect place for bathing.
      Young women of unblemished beauty—
    forms that, to delight the eye,
    the mirroring wave reduplicates! 7285
    Soon all are playing in the pool,
    the timid wade, the bolder swim;
    and then, to shouts, join water-battle.
      These forms afford the eye such pleasure
    that I should be content with them, 7290
    but my senses still desire more.

And so I turn my probing gaze
towards the rich veil of leafy green
by which the noble queen is hidden.
    But how strange! Now swans come swimming,   7295
all pure majesty of motion,
out of inlets and draw near.
They float gently side by side,
yet are proud and self-complacent
as they move their heads and bills.   7300
    One, however, bolder than the others
ahead of whom he quickly sails,
seems to swell his breast in pride;
with his plumes and feathers raised,
himself a wave on waving waters,   7305
he pushes toward the sanctuary. . . .
    With shining plumage undisturbed,
the rest swim back and forth; they soon
engage in lively show of battle
and so divert the timid girls   7310
that these think only of their safety
and forget their proper duties.

NYMPHS.   Sisters, come and put an ear
                to the river's green embankment—
                I believe that what I hear   7315
                is the sound of horse's hoofs.
                Who, I wonder, can have brought
                urgent messages this night!

FAUST. It's as if the earth vibrated
with the sound of a horse in a hurry.   7320
        Look there!
        Is some special good fortune
        to be mine so soon?
        This marvel is unique!
Upon a horse of dazzling whiteness   7325
a rider is approaching at a trot;
he seems endowed with a courageous spirit. . . .
There is no doubt! I know him now—
the famous son of Philyra! –
Halt, Chiron! Stay! I need to talk to you. . . .   7330

CHIRON. What's this about?

FAUST.   Slow down a bit!

CHIRON. I never pause.

FAUST.   Then take me with you, please!

CHIRON. Mount! Once you're on my back there's time to ask
    what way you want to go. You're standing on the shore;

I'm willing to transport you through the water.   7335
Faust (*mounting*).
  Go anywhere you wish. I'll be forever grateful
  to the great man and noble teacher
  who, to his glory, reared a race of heroes:
  the Argonauts, that splendid company,
  and all the rest who helped create the poet's world.   7340
Chiron. Let's not pursue that further!
  Pallas herself, as Mentor, doesn't do so well;
  and, in the end, as if they'd not been taught,
  men keep on doing what they please.
Faust. I here and now embrace, in body and in spirit,   7345
  the doctor to whom every plant is known,
  who understands the virtues of each root,
  who heals the sick and eases painful wounds!
Chiron. If at my side some hero suffered hurt,
  I did know how to give assistance,   7350
  but finally surrendered all my skills
  to priests and simple-gathering women.
Faust. Yours is the greatness of the truly great,
  who cannot bear a word of praise,
  who modestly give precedence to others   7355
  and act as if they were quite ordinary.
Chiron. I think you have the skills to be a sycophant,
  flatter both the ruler and the ruled.
Faust. Yet surely you will not deny
  that you did see your great contemporaries,   7360
  did emulate, in deed, the noblest of them,
  lived out your days a never frivolous demigod.
  But which of those heroic figures
  did you consider worthiest?
Chiron. Among the glorious Argonauts   7365
  each had his own particular merit
  and could, according to the virtue he possessed,
  do what was needed when the others lacked his skill.
  Castor and Pollux always came out first
  when looks and youthfulness were most important.   7370
  The happy talent of the Boreiads
  was quick, decisive action for the sake of others.
  As ruler, Jason, whom the ladies liked,
  was wary, clever, firm, and easy to consult.
  Next, Orpheus: a gentle, quiet, always prudent man   7375
  who, when he played his lyre, was mightiest of all.
  Then keen-eyed Lynceus, who steered their sacred ship
  past rocky shores by day and night. . . .

Danger is best endured in company with others:
what one achieves obtains the praise of all.   7380
Faust. And aren't you going to mention Hercules?
Chiron. Ah, me! Do not arouse nostalgia! –
　As yet I had not seen Apollo,
　or Mars, or Hermes—all those gods—
　when with these eyes I saw before me   7385
　what all men worship as divine.
　He was born to be a king,
　this youth magnificent to see,
　though subject to his elder brother—
　and to the charms of lovely ladies too.   7390
　Earth never will bring forth his like again,
　nor Hebe raise a second Hercules to heaven.
　In vain the lyre labors to evoke him,
　in vain the sculptors martyr stone.
Faust. They may take pride in how they have portrayed him,   7395
　but you have made his greatness far more vivid.
　Now, having talked about the handsomest man,
　say something too, about the greatest beauty.
Chiron. It's meaningless to speak of women's beauty,
　which far too often is mere lifeless show;   7400
　my praise I save for those who have
　a buoyant, optimistic zest for life.
　Beauty's blessing is its own existence;
　add grace to it, and it becomes invincible—
　like Helen when I carried her.   7405
Faust. You carried her?
Chiron. 　　　　　　　Upon my back, of course.
Faust. As if I weren't confused enough already—
　and now the joy of sitting here!
Chiron. She held on by my hair,
　just as you do.
Faust. 　　　　I'm now beside myself completely!   7410
　Please tell me all about it—
　she is the one and only thing I want!
　From where, to where, was it you carried her?
Chiron. It's easy to provide the answer to that question.
　It happened when the Dioscuri   7415
　had freed their little sister from abductors' clutches.
　The brigands, unaccustomed to defeat,
　regained their courage and came storming in pursuit.
　But then the marshes near Eleusis checked
　the brothers' and their sister's speed;   7420
　Castor and Pollux waded—I paddled—across;

then she dismounted, stroked my dripping mane,
made flattering remarks, and, self-assured,
expressed her thanks with gracious gravity.
A charming child—though young, an old man's joy!   7425
FAUST. And only ten years old!
CHIRON.   Philologists, I see,
have led you, as they have themselves, astray.
A woman, in mythology, is an exception
whom poets introduce in any way they want:
she never comes of age or ever ages;   7430
a form that always whets the appetite,
when young she is abducted, in age she still is courted—
in fine, poets ignore constraints of time.
FAUST. Then time shall not constrain her either!
Himself no longer in the realm of time,   7435
Achilles made her his at Pherae. What rare bliss,
to win one's love by besting death and fate!
And shall not I, sustained by poignant longing,
endow this perfect form with life—
this timeless being, the true peer of gods,   7440
tender but grand, august yet gracious too?
You saw her long ago, but I this very day—
the dream of beauty, charm, and loveliness.
My whole existence now is held in bondage,
and I shall die unless I make her mine.   7445
CHIRON. Strange man! In mortal realms you may just be exalted,
but in the spirit world the way you act seems madness.
Our meeting is a fortunate coincidence!
It is my custom once a year to pay,
for a few moments, my respects to Manto,   7450
Aesculapius' daughter, who in silent prayer
implores her father, for his good name's sake,
to bring some light at last into physicians' minds
and so convert them from their reckless slaughter.
Of all the sibyl guild I like her best;   7455
she doesn't writhe grotesquely, is really kind and helpful.
With healing herbs, if you'll but stay a while,
she will, I have no doubt, cure you completely.
FAUST. I won't submit to any cure—my mind is sound—
since then I'd only be one abject creature more.   7460
CHIRON. Don't miss your chance! Consult this splendid source of help!
Be quick! Dismount! We're here already.
FAUST. What is this place to which, in awesome darkness,
you've carried me through gravel-bottomed streams? Explain!

CHIRON. Between the Peneus, on our right, and on our left,   7465
    Olympus, Rome confronted Greece, whose realm,
    the greater, only stops where desert sands begin;
    the king must flee, the consul is triumphant. –
    Look up! Here is, propitiously at hand
    and bathed in moonlight, the eternal temple.   7470
MANTO (*within the Temple, dreaming*).
        In sacred precincts,
        hark! horse's hoofs are heard
        as demigods approach.
CHIRON. How true!
        Open your eyes and look!   7475
MANTO (*walking*). Welcome! I see I'm not forgotten.
CHIRON. And you're still living in your temple!
MANTO. You haven't tired of your gadding?
CHIRON. You may enjoy your peaceful quiet,
    but I prefer to move about.   7480
MANTO. I let time move while I stay here. –
    And who is this?
CHIRON.   One whom the turbulence
    of this notorious Night has brought our way.
    He is resolved—his wits are crazed—
    to make fair Helen his, although he doesn't have   7485
    the least idea of how and where to start.
    A special case for Aesculapian treatment!
MANTO. I love the man who wants what cannot be.
        (CHIRON *is by now disappearing in the distance.*)
    Enter, bold spirit! Joy shall be yours!
    This tunnel takes us to Persephone,   7490
    who in Olympus' hollow base
    welcomes forbidden pleas in secret audience.
    Here I once smuggled Orpheus in—
    use your chance better! Hurry! Have no fears!   [*Exeunt, descending.*

        SIRENS, *as before on the banks of the Upper Peneus.*
SIRENS. Plunge into Peneus' stream!   7495
        That's the place to float and splash
        while we entertain with song
        these unhappy creatures here. –
        Without water nothing prospers!
        Let us hurry, one and all,   7500

down to the Aegean Sea—
there abundant joys await us.
           (*Violent earthquake-tremors.*)
Seething waves reverse their course,
overflow their river bed—
ground that shakes, obstructed water,   7505
fumes from clefts in graveled shores.
Let us flee! Come, one and all—
this prodigy bodes only ill!
Come as honored merry guests
to a cheerful entertainment   7510
where the gleaming sea swells gently,
where waves softly wash the shore,
and where Luna, twofold shining,
bathes us in her sacred dew!
There, life's uninhibited;   7515
here, you live in fear of tremors;
if you're prudent, quick, away!
All is horror hereabouts.
SEISMOS (*below, making rattling and rumbling noises*).
One more mighty shove is needed,
one good heave of these strong shoulders!   7520
That's the way to reach the surface,
where no one will challenge us.
SPHINXES. What discomfortable tremors!
What a nasty, dreadful rumbling!
How things start to sway and shake,   7525
jolted as they oscillate!
What on earth could be more vexing!
Nonetheless, we will not budge,
even though all hell break loose.
    Now, amazingly, a dome   7530
is emerging from the ground.
This is he who, long-since grizzled,
raised for an expectant mother
from the sea the isle of Delos,
building it amid the waters.   7535
See him strain and push and press,
bend his back and tense his arms
in a stance like that of Atlas,
as he lifts the turf and soil,
ripping from these quiet shores   7540
pebbles, gravel, sand, and clay,
and divides this placid valley
with a gash that mars its mantle.

With sustained, tremendous effort
this colossal caryatid,   7545
buried still up to his chest,
holds aloft a great stone structure.
But there'll be no more disruption:
we've elected to stay here.
SEISMOS. I did all this with no assistance,   7550
    as people will someday acknowledge;
    and if it were not for my shakes and jolts,
    how would this world be such a thing of beauty? –
    How could your mountains stand majestic
    in azure skies' translucent splendor   7555
    had I not shoved them there for you
    to see with picturesque delight?
    When, in the flush of youth, I tried my strength
    under august parental eyes—
    as Night and Chaos watched—   7560
    and, with the Titans as companions,
    played ball with Pelion and Ossa,
    we tired at last of our mad game and set
    both mountains on Parnassus as a two-peaked cap . . .   7565
    Apollo finds it pleasant to stay there
    attended by the godlike Muses.
    For Jove himself, and for his thunderbolts,
    I thus raised high a lofty seat.
    Now, too, with superhuman straining,   7570
    I've pushed up out of my abyss
    and loudly summon to a new existence
    all who would gladly settle here.
SPHINXES. We'd have called this rock primeval
    which here rises like a castle,   7575
    had we not with our own eyes
    seen it struggle from the ground.
    As stones continue pressing into place,
    forest and undergrowth spread up its sides;
    but that is no concern to Sphinxes: 7580
    where we reside is sacrosanct.
GRIFFINS. I see flakes and threads of gold
    glittering in crevices.
    Get to work, you Ants, and mine them,
    lest someone cheat you of this treasure!   7585
GIANT ANTS (in chorus).
        As soon as the Titans
        have finished their mountain,
        scurry on up

as fast as you can!
Then in and out quick! 7590
Every crumb
you can find in these cracks
will have worth.
Hasten along
and don't overlook 7595
the least little bit,
wherever it's hiding.
Be as busy as bees,
keep swarming away;
take only the gold, 7600
leave the rest of the mountain!

GRIFFINS. Bring the gold here! Quick, make a pile,
and we will guard it with our claws;
no better bolts were ever made
for keeping any treasure safe. 7605

PYGMIES. Here we are, installed already,
though we don't know by what logic.
Don't inquire where we've come from,
all that matters is: we're here!
Every country can provide 7610
places where one dwells with pleasure;
if a rock displays a fissure,
dwarfs are certain to be there.
Male and female, eager workers,
model husbands, model wives— 7615
who can say if that's the way
it was once in Paradise?
Here we're perfectly contented
and can thank our lucky star;
Mother Earth is always fruitful 7620
anywhere you choose to go.

DACTYLS. If She could generate
those Pygmies in a single night,
She can produce us mites as well,
who too will form couples. 7625

PYGMY ELDERS. Hurry and settle
where there is space!
Start work at once,
haste is our strength!
While there's still peace, 7630
get your forge built;
furnish our troops
with armor and weapons.

All you Ants busily
running about,   7635
bring us the ore!
As for you Dactyls,
tiny but many,
let your task be
fetching us wood!   7640
Burn it in layers,
carefully covered—
furnish us charcoal!

PYGMY GENERALISSIMO.

Off to war bravely
with bow and arrow!   7645
Shoot me those herons
there by the pond
where in their arrogance
thousands are nesting—
all in one volley,   7650
sparing not one—
so we can wear
helmets with plumes.

ANTS *and* DACTYLS.

Is there no help for us?
We get the iron,   7655
they forge our chains.
It is too soon yet
to make our escape—
meanwhile, comply!

THE CRANES OF IBYCUS.

Murderous shouts and dying moans,   7660
flap of wings that beat in terror!
Even we, high in the sky,
hear the sound of painful groaning.
Now the victims all are dead,
red the waters with their blood.   7665
Avarice in monstrous guise
takes the herons' crowning glory—
see it flutter on the helmets
of the fat-paunched-bow-legged villains!
Allies of our air-borne army   7670
who too cross seas in serried ranks,
join us in a cause of vengeance
that affects near relatives!
Let us make a vital effort!
Swear to hate this scum forever!   7675

Trumpeting, the CRANES *disperse in the air.*

Enter MEPHISTOPHELES *on the plain before Seismos' mountain.*

MEPHISTOPHELES. I had no trouble handling Northern witches,
    but these strange phantoms leave me ill at ease.
    The Brocken's so conveniently laid out,
    and anywhere you are there's company.
    Dame Ilse, on her *Stone,* acts as our lookout,   7680
    and on his *Peak* our *Heinrich* never sleeps.
    Elend may hear the snores of *Schnarcher* now and then,
    but things don't change from one age to the next.
    Here, though, who can be sure of where he is,
    or if the ground won't burst beneath his feet? . . .   7685
    I take a pleasant stroll along a level valley,
    and all at once, behind my back, up pops a mountain—
    the name may be too grandiose, but still
    it's high enough to separate me from
    my Sphinxes—and attracts from up the valley   7690
    flames that dart about to view this novelty. . . .
    My lovely ladies still flit roguishly along,
    luring me toward them, then eluding me.
    Now easy does it! One who has a taste for sweets
    will grab at them in any circumstances.   7695
LAMIAE (*letting* MEPHISTOPHELES *pursue them*).
    Faster and faster,
    no standing still!
    Slow down again
    for a bit of chatter!
    It's quite a lark   7700
    to make this rake
    pay so severely
    for chasing us.
    With such stiff feet
    he only can hobble   7705
    and stumble along;
    we keep escaping
    while he pursues us,
    dragging that leg.
MEPHISTOPHELES (*stopping*).
    Men's lot is cursed! From Adam down   7710
    they've always been led on and gulled!
    We all grow older, but who's any wiser?
    As if I hadn't had enough infatuations! –
    Their tight-laced waists and painted faces tell us
    that these are absolutely worthless creatures.   7715

In what they offer there is nothing healthy;
touch any part of them, it will prove rotten.
We know and see what's all too palpable,
but if the trollops pipe, we dance!

LAMIAE (*stopping*).
Stand still—he's having second thoughts, is pausing, stopping!   7720
To the attack, or he will get away!

MEPHISTOPHELES (*advancing*).
Forward! Don't be a fool and let yourself
be tangled in a web of doubts;
if witches such as these did not exist,
who the devil would want to be a devil!   7725

LAMIAE (*in their most captivating manner*).
Let's parade around this brave Lothario!
Certainly his heart will tell him
which of us inspires his devotion.

MEPHISTOPHELES. I'll concede that by dim light
you apparently are pretty,   7730
so I won't speak ill of you.

EMPUSA (*pushing into the circle of* LAMIAE).
Nor of me, I hope! I'm one of you—
let me join this circle too!

LAMIAE. She's always the unwanted extra
who only spoils the game for us.   7735

EMPUSA (*to* MEPHISTOPHELES).
Your little cousin with an ass's foot,
your dear Empusa, welcomes you;
you merely have a horse's hoof,
but welcome, cousin, just the same!

MEPHISTOPHELES. I thought that here there'd just be strangers,   7740
and find, alas! close relatives;
it's an old, familiar story:
from Harz to Hellas, always cousins!

EMPUSA. My talent is deciding quickly
which of my many shapes to choose;   7745
tonight I thought I'd honor you
by putting on my ass's head.

MEPHISTOPHELES. I note that family feeling means
a great deal to the people here;
regardless of the consequences, though,   7750
I'd like to disavow the ass's head.

LAMIAE. Ignore the nasty thing! She puts to rout
all thoughts of beauty and delight;
and when there's beauty and delight,
if she appears, it's gone at once.   7755

MEPHISTOPHELES. These other cousins, delicate and dainty,
 awaken my suspicions too;
 beneath their rosy cheeks, I fear,
 there may be lurking metamorphoses.
LAMIAE. Find out by trying! There is lots of choice.   7760
 Take your pick! And if you're the lucky kind
 you'll grab the winning ticket.
 Why harp so much upon your eagerness?
 For all your swaggering and boasting
 you are a pitiful gallant. –   7765
 At last he's venturing to join us;
 remove your masks when your turn comes
 and show him what you really are.
MEPHISTOPHELES. I've chosen her who's prettiest . . .
(*Clasping her.*) Alas! A desiccated broomstick!   7770
(*Seizing another.*) And what is this? . . . An awful face!
LAMIAE. Do not pretend you merit something better!
MEPHISTOPHELES. That one's petite—I'd like to make a deal with her . . .
 a lizard's slipping from my hands,
 her slippery braids feel like a snake.   7775
 I'll grab, instead, this tall one then . . .
 and find I hold an ivied thyrsus
 and that her head is its pine cone.
 How will this end? . . . Here's one who's stout—
 perhaps she will afford more solace.   7780
 One last attempt! I'll take the risk!
 She's quite gelatinous, just what
 an Oriental pays high prices for . . .
 but, sad to say, the puffball bursts!
LAMIAE. Now separate and hover in the air!   7785
 At lightning speed, in sable flight
 surround, o bats, on silent wings
 this uninvited witch's son
 with baffling, horrifying circles—
 he'll still be getting off too cheaply!   7790
MEPHISTOPHELES (*shaking himself*).
 I'm not much wiser than before, it seems;
 the world's as crazy here as back up North;
 ghosts in both places are eccentric,
 people and poets equally absurd.
 A masquerade proves here, as everywhere,   7795
 to be but show that entertains the senses.
 I've tried to catch some masks that looked quite charming,
 but what I touched gave me the willies—
 I'd really like to be deluded
 if the illusion only lasted longer.   7800

(*He loses his way in the rubble.*)
Where am I now? Where does this lead?
What was a path is now a wilderness.
I came this way on even roads,
and now am faced by piles of rubble.
This climbing up and down is futile;   7805
where will I find my Sphinxes now?
I never would have thought that things could be so crazy:
a mountain such as this produced in just one night!
Here witches really ride in style,
they bring their own Blocksberg along.   7810
AN OREAD (*from a cliff of pre-seismic rock*).
Come, climb up here! My mountain's old
and still retains its primal shape.
On rugged trail pay Pindus homage,
that has its furthest outcrops here!
As now, I had long stood unshaken   7815
when Pompey fled across this ridge.
The mock-formation over there is an illusion,
and it will disappear at cockcrow.
I often see such fantasies created,
then see them vanish suddenly again.   7820
MEPHISTOPHELES. All honor to a venerable head
whose lofty crown of mighty oaks
does not allow the brightest moonlight
to penetrate the darkness of your leaves. –
But there, beside the underbrush,   7825
an unpretentious light is moving.
How nicely things work out—
it is indeed Homunculus!
Where have you been, my little friend!
HOMUNCULUS. Oh, I keep floating on from place to place   7830
and, eager to destroy this vial,
am hoping to achieve existence properly;
but nothing I have seen as yet
encourages me to become a part of it.
I'll tell you this in confidence, however: 7835
I'm on the trail of two philosophers
who, when I overheard them, were discussing Nature.
I want to stick by them, since they
are bound to know what real existence is,
and in the end I'll surely learn   7840
the wisest course for me to follow.
MEPHISTOPHELES. But make your own decision, inasmuch
as anywhere that spectres have a say
they welcome the philosopher;

to please the public with his skill,   7845
he soon creates a dozen new ones.
You'll never learn unless you make mistakes.
If you want to exist, do so on your own!
HOMUNCULUS. Still, good advice is not to be disdained.
MEPHISTOPHELES Farewell, then! Let us see what happens. [*They separate.*
ANAXAGORAS (*entering, to* THALES).
  Your stubbornness makes no concessions;
  are still more reasons needed to convince you?
THALES. The waves respond to every whim of air,
  but stay away from rugged rocks like this.
ANAXAGORAS. That cliff is here because of fire-vapors.   7855
THALES. All living things evolved in water.
HOMUNCULUS (*hovering between them*).
  Please let me come along beside you—
  I'm eager to evolve myself!
ANAXAGORAS. Did you, o Thales, in a single night
  ever produce from mud a mountain such as this?   7860
THALES. Nature, and Nature's living fluxes,
  have never counted days and nights and hours.
  She fashions forms according to set rules,
  and even when they're huge, there is no violence.
ANAXAGORAS. This time there was! A fierce Plutonic fire,   7865
  tremendous outbursts of Aeolian gas,
  broke through the ancient level crust of earth,
  creating instantly a recent mountain.
THALES. But is this part of any lasting process?
  Your mountain's there, so let it be.   7870
  This controversy is a waste of time,
  and only bores a patient audience.
ANAXAGORAS. The mountain teems with Myrmidons,
  who've promptly occupied its crevices—
  Pygmies and Ants and Dactyls   7875
  and other busy little things.
(*To* HOMUNCULUS.) Your aspirations have been modest,
  you've lived in hermit-like confinement;
  if you believe you'd like authority,
  I'll have you crowned their king.   7880
HOMUNCULUS. What does my Thales say?
THALES.   I would advise against it;
  A little world produces petty deeds,
  great men inspire lesser ones to grandeur.
  But look! See that black cloud of cranes!
  They are a menace to the frightened people,   7885
  a threat to any future king.

With lance-like beaks and taloned claws
they fall upon their tiny victims;
these are the lightning flashes of impending doom!
As they stood peacefully beside the quiet pond   7890
the herons suffered ruthless slaughter;
it is that rain of murderous arrows,
now harvested as cruel and bloody vengeance,
which first incited their close kin
to wrath against the wicked Pygmy race.   7895
What use are helmets, shields, and spears,
how do their heron-feathers help those dwarfs?
While Ant and Dactyl soon find cover,
their army wavers, flees, is crushed.

ANAXAGORAS (*after a pause, solemnly*).
Till now I've praised the subterranean powers,   7900
but what's befallen makes me turn to one above. . . .
O you on high who, never aging,
assume three shapes and bear three names,
I beg relief of the distress my people suffer,
Diana, Luna, Hekate!   7905
You who exalt us with profundity of thought,
who seem so calm, yet have such strength of feeling,
unseal your dread abyss of darkness
and, though you hear no charm, reveal your ancient might! (*Pause.*)
    Have I been rashly heeded?   7910
    Has my appeal
    to higher beings
    caused Nature's laws to be suspended?
Now growing larger every moment,
the disc that is the goddess' throne approaches,   7915
a dread and awesome spectacle
as its flames darken and turn red! . . .
Come, mighty sphere, no closer with your threats,
or you'll destroy the land, the sea, and us!
    Then it is true that women once in Thessaly,   7920
placing their trust in sacrilegious magic,
by incantation drew you from your orbit
and wrested from you direst powers? . . .
Darkness has shrouded the bright disc, which suddenly
explodes and flares and showers sparks!   7925
What din, what sounds of hissing,
of thunder heightened by the roar of wind! –
Humbly I fall before your throne—
forgive me who have caused all this!
            He throws himself prostrate.

THALES. The things this man could hear and see!   7930
　　I'm not quite certain what has happened,
　　yet my perception of it is not his.
　　These hours are mad, on that we can agree,
　　but Luna still is resting cozily
　　in the same spot she was before.   7935
HOMUNCULUS. Look at the place the Pygmies occupied—
　　the peak was rounded, now it's pointed!
　　I felt a terrible collision,
　　the impact of the rock that fell out of the moon
　　and instantly, with no respect of persons,   7940
　　crushed friend and foe to death.
　　I can't, however, deprecate creative forces
　　that in the course of just one night
　　produced from nether and from upper regions
　　the mountain we see here erected.   7945
THALES. Don't get worked up! That was but make-believe!
　　Good riddance to those nasty creatures;
　　it's lucky that you weren't their king!
　　Now to the sea, and to a pleasant celebration
　　that welcomes eagerly strange guests like you!   [*Exeunt.*
MEPHISTOPHELES (*climbing the other side of Seismos' mountain*).
　　Here I am forced to struggle through steep crevices
　　and stubborn roots of ancient oaks!
　　Back in the Harz the resin has a hearty smell,
　　with a *soupçon* of pitch—which, after brimstone,
　　is my favorite scent. – But here, among these Greeks,   7955
　　you hardly get a whiff of it;
　　I wouldn't mind discovering, though,
　　what fuel they use to keep their hell-fires going.
A DRYAD. You may be smart enough at home;
　　abroad, you lack a certain pliability.   7960
　　You ought to take your mind off your own country
　　and pay these sacred oaks the homage owed them here.
MEPHISTOPHELES. You can't forget what you have left behind;
　　what we were used to still is Paradise.
　　But tell me, what's the triple shape which crouches   7965
　　there in that dimly lighted cave?
DRYAD. The Phorcides! Approach them if you dare,
　　address them if you're not dismayed.
MEPHISTOPHELES. Why not? – What I now see astounds me!
　　Although it hurts my pride, I must confess   7970
　　that I have never seen such creatures—
　　they're worse by far than mandrakes.

Can one who sees this monstrous trinity
still find the vilest forms of sin
in any way repulsive?   7975
We wouldn't even let them stand beside the door
of the most dreadful of our hells.
When such things flourish in this Land of Beauty,
they're glorified as Classical. –
Stirring, they seem to sense my presence;   7980
their peeps and squeaks are those of vampire bats.
A PHORKYAD. Sisters, give me our eye, so that it may inquire
who dares to come so close to where our temples are.
MEPHISTOPHELES. Venerable ladies! Allow me to approach
and be thrice blessed by you.   7985
I know I call as one who is as yet a stranger,
but if I'm not mistaken, I'm some kind of cousin.
I've seen the oldest gods that mankind venerates,
have paid obeisance to both Ops and Rhea;
just yesterday—perhaps it is now the day before—I saw   7990
the Fates, who are both your and Chaos' sisters;
but never did I see your peers.
I have no more to say, but my delight is great.
PHORCIDES. This seems to be a spirit with some sense.
MEPHISTOPHELES. Still, I'm surprised no poets sing your praises.   7995
And tell me how it is I've never seen
such worthy subjects treated by an artist?
The chisel ought to strive to do you justice,
not Juno, Pallas, Venus, and their ilk!
PHORCIDES. Engulfed in solitude and silent darkness,   8000
we three have never thought about such things.
MEPHISTOPHELES. In any case, how could you, isolated here
where you see no one and no one sees you?
You'd need to live in some great town
where art and ostentation occupy one throne,   8005
where on the double, every day, a marble block
enters this life in some heroic guise,
where . . .
PHORCIDES.   Hold your peace! Don't make us covet glory!
If we learned more, what good would it do us,
born here in darkness, kin to all that is nocturnal,   8010
known hardly to ourselves, to others not at all?
MEPHISTOPHELES. It wouldn't matter in your case, I see,
if you transferred to others your identities.
A single eye and tooth do for the three of you,
and so, with mythological propriety,   8015

you might combine your triple essence in two persons
briefly, and lend the likeness of the third
to me.
A PHORKYAD. How does this strike you? Would it work?
THE OTHER PHORCIDES.
    Let's test it, but retaining eye and tooth!
MEPHISTOPHELES. You've just subtracted the best items: 8020
    how can there be, without them, authenticity?
A PHORKYAD. You only have to close one eye
    and let but one incisor show;
    in profile then you will at once possess
    a perfect sibling-likeness to us.   8025
MEPHISTOPHELES. I'm flattered! But so be it!
PHORCIDES.   Be it so!
MEPHISTOPHELES (*in profile, as* PHORKYAS).   I stand
    before you now as Chaos' well-loved son!
PHORCIDES. There's no denying we're his daughters.
MEPHISTOPHELES. Then I, o shame! will now be called hermaphroditic.
PHORCIDES. How beautiful is our new trinity: 8030
    we sisters have a second eye and tooth!
MEPHISTOPHELES. Since I must hide from public view,
    I'll go and scare the devils down in hell.   [*Exit.*

ROCKY INLETS OF THE AEGEAN SEA

The moon is at the zenith, where it remains. SIRENS, *couched on rocks about
the stage, are fluting and singing.*
SIRENS.   Even though Thessalian witches
    sometimes have on nights of horror   8035
    drawn you down to serve their crimes,
    look from your nocturnal sky
    tranquilly on waves that ripple
    with the gentlest iridescence;
    shed your light on the commotion   8040
    now arising from these waters!
    We are ever-faithful servants—
    lovely Luna, hear our prayer!
NEREIDS *and* TRITONS (*as sea-monsters*).
    Let your clarion tones be clearer,
    make the whole sea resonate,   8045
    summon all who dwell below!
    Dreadful storm-troughs made us flee

to the depths and utter quiet;
your sweet songs have drawn us back.
　　See how we, to our delight,   8050
deck ourselves in chains of gold,
adding to our crowns and jewels
matching clasp and gem-set buckle,
all of which we owe to you!
Guardian spirits of our bay,   8055
by your singing you have brought us
treasures lost in shipwrecks here.
SIRENS.　We are well aware that fish
like to live in ocean coolness,
gliding carefree back and forth.   8060
Still, tonight, when all of you
are in such a festive spirit,
we would like to have you show us
that you're something more than fishes.
NEREIDS *and* TRITONS.
Prior to our coming here
we'd made up our minds to do so.   8065
Sisters! brothers! let's be off!—
we won't have to travel far
to provide convincing proof
that we're something more than fishes.   [*They withdraw.*
SIRENS.　They're off in a trice   8070
on a straight course for Samothrace;
they disappear, sped by the wind.
What can they be intending to do
there where the great Cabiri rule?
Those deities are most peculiar: 8075
they're constantly self-generating,
but can't discover who they are.
　　Gracious Luna, hear our prayer,
do not move from there on high,
lest the darkness disappear   8080
and the daylight banish us!
　　　Enter THALES, *arriving at the shore with* HOMUNCULUS.
THALES. I'd like to take you to old Nereus,
whose cave, in fact, is close at hand,
but he's a very stubborn person,
peevish and uncooperative;   8085
nothing that mankind ever does
will please this grouchy fellow.
But he can look into the future,
and so enjoys all men's respect,

and honor as a seer and pundit;   8090
  he often has provided helpful counsel, too.
HOMUNCULUS. Let's take a chance! I'll give his door a knock—
  that cannot hurt my vial or flame.
NEREUS. Does sound of human voices reach my ear?
  What sudden fury fills my heart with rage!   8095
  Those creatures—striving to be peers of gods,
  yet doomed never to change one bit!
  When I got old, I'd earned celestial leisure,
  yet I still felt impelled to give the best some help;
  but when I saw what, finally, they did,   8100
  it was as if I'd given no advice at all.
THALES. And yet, Sea-Ancient, you're the one we trust.
  You are the sage, so don't send us away!
  Regard this flame—although it may look human
  it will follow your advice implicitly.   8105
NEREUS. Advice! Have people ever heeded it?
  A stubborn ear is deaf to any wisdom.
  However often acts bring bitter self-reproach,
  mankind remains as self-willed as before.
  Paternal admonition—I gave Paris plenty   8110
  before he got entangled with that foreign hussy!
  He stood undaunted on the coast of Greece,
  and I told him what my mind's eye saw:
  smoke filling air deluged with red,
  slaughter and death beneath the glowing rafters—   8115
  Troy's judgment day, held fast in rhythmic lines,
  known for its horror to all succeeding time!
  The shameless youth laughed at an old man's words,
  heeded his own desires, and Ilium fell—
  a giant corpse, its restless agony now over,   8120
  a welcome feast for Pindus' eagles.
  Ulysses, too! Did I not prophesy to him
  the wiles of Circe, the dreadful Cyclopes,
  his dilatoriness, the rashness of his men,
  and much more too! Did that help him   8125
  before, much buffeted and rather late,
  kind currents brought him to hospitable shores?
THALES. Behavior of that sort may vex the sage,
  but a good man will try once more;
  an ounce of thanks will far outweigh   8130
  tons of ingratitude and make him truly happy.
  The advice we beg is urgent for this boy:
  How can he best achieve a real existence?

NEREUS. Don't ruin what I rarely have, a happy mood!
  Now I'm preoccupied with very different matters.   8135
  I've summoned all my daughters here today,
  the Graces of the sea, whom Doris gave me.
  Neither Olympus nor this earth of yours contains
  beauty that moves with equal ease.
  They leap with utter grace of motion   8140
  from water-dragon onto Neptune's horses,
  united with their element so perfectly
  that by its foam they seem to be raised higher still.
  Borne in the opal glow of Venus' conch,
  now Galatea comes, the fairest of them all—   8145
  she who, since Cypria rejected us,
  even in Paphos is worshipped as divine
  and, as her lovely heiress, long has held
  her templed city and sea-chariot throne.
    Be gone! This hour of paternal bliss forbids   8150
  hate in my heart or anger on my lips.
  Away to Proteus, the man of magic powers—
  ask him how life's achieved, how one can change his form!
              He moves from center stage toward the sea.
THALES. We haven't gained a thing by this maneuver
  since Proteus, when he's found, will promptly melt away;   8155
  and even if he answers, what he says
  only leaves you astonished and perplexed.
  Still, his kind of advice is what you need,
  so let's go on and have a try with him!   *[They withdraw.*
SIRENS (*above, on the rocks*).
  What is it we see gliding   8160
  across far-distant billows?
  They are transfigured sea-nymphs
  who gleam with all the brightness
  of sails whose whiteness flutters
  before the shifting breezes.   8165
  You can now hear their voices,
  so let's descend and greet them.
NEREIDS *and* TRITONS.
  What we now bear in triumph
  should satisfy you fully:
  Chelone's giant buckler,   8170
  austere but glorious figures—
  the latter deities
  whose praises you must sing.
SIRENS.   Gods small in size

but great in power,   8175
anciently worshipped
as saviors of sailors.

NEREIDS *and* TRITONS.
     Cabiri give assurance
     our fête won't be disrupted,
     for in their sacred presence   8180
     Poseidon's never hostile.

SIRENS.   We grant you precedence,
     for when ships are wrecked
     you are omnipotent
     protecting their crews.   8185

NEREIDS *and* TRITONS.
     We've brought along three of them,
     but the fourth wouldn't come;
     he claimed that he was the one
     who did the others' thinking.

SIRENS. A god may ridicule   8190
     another god; you must
     respect all gods, must fear
     the harm that they might do.

NEREIDS *and* TRITONS. There really are seven Cabiri.

SIRENS. And where are the other three?   8195

NEREIDS *and* TRITONS. That's something we don't know;
     ask on Olympus where,
     unknown to anyone,
     an eighth may well be living,
     and where, though stay-at-homes,   8200
     they'd graciously receive us.
       Idiosyncratic gods,
     they aspire ceaselessly,
     burning with nostalgic hunger
     for the Unattainable.   8205

SIRENS.   The prayers we raise
     to sun and moon
     reach all the gods,
     and we are well repaid.

NEREIDS *and* TRITONS.
     How it redounds to our great glory   8210
     that we inaugurate this pageant!

SIRENS.   Antiquity's heroes
     come short of your glory,
     great though theirs be;
     although they won the Golden Fleece,   8215
     you've won the Cabiri.

NEREIDS, TRITONS, *and* SIRENS.
    Although they won the Golden Fleece,
    We've ⎫
         ⎬ won the Cabiri!
    You've ⎭
       The NEREIDS *and* TRITONS *proceed out of view.*
HOMUNCULUS. These ugly figures look to me
    like simple earthen pitchers;   8220
    today savants trip over them
    and break their empty noddles.
THALES. This sort of thing is much sought after;
    the patina enhances the coin's worth.
PROTEUS (*concealed*).
    As fabulist I find all this amusing: 8225
    the odder something is, the sooner it gains credence!
THALES. Where are you, Proteus?
PROTEUS (*ventriloquizing so that his voice first sounds close by, then*
distant).   Here! And here!
THALES. I'll pardon an old joke if you
    will spare a friend this pointless talk.
    I know you're not where your voice is.   8230
PROTEUS (*as if distant*). Farewell!
THALES (*aside to* HOMUNCULUS). He's very near. Quick, flash your lamp!
    He's as inquisitive as any fish,
    and in whatever guise he's lurking
    he'll be attracted by a fire.
HOMUNCULUS. I will release a flood of light at once,   8235
    but not so much that it will crack the glass.
PROTEUS (*in the form of a giant turtle*).
    What's this which shines so prettily?
THALES (*covering* HOMUNCULUS).
    That's better! If you wish, you'll get a closer look;
    don't mind the bit of effort it will cost you—
    you simply must appear on two good human feet.   8240
    Whoever wants to see what we are hiding,
    may do so only if we grant permission.
PROTEUS (*as a stately human figure*).
    You haven't lost your knack for clever tricks.
THALES. And you still like to change your shape.
              THALES *uncovers* HOMUNCULUS.
PROTEUS (*with astonishment*).
    A dwarf emitting light! A novel sight!   8245
THALES. He wants advice on how he should develop.
    He came, as I have heard him tell,
    into this world quite strangely, only half complete.
    He's well supplied with mental faculties,

but sorely lacks substantial attributes.   8250
So far he weighs no more than does his vial,
but hopes that he may soon obtain a body.
PROTEUS. Yours was a true parthenic birth,
  for you exist before you ought to.
THALES (*aside*). Unless I err, there is another problem;   8255
  he seems to be hermaphroditic.
PROTEUS. That only makes success more likely;
  however he ends up, all will go well. –
  There is no need for long deliberations:
  you must begin out in the open sea.   8260
  That's where you start on a small scale,
  glad to ingest the smallest creatures;
  little by little you'll increase in size
  and put yourself in shape for loftier achievements.
HOMUNCULUS. The breezes are so gentle here,   8265
  I like the way the air smells fresh and green!
PROTEUS. I well believe that, darling child!
  Further along it gets to be more pleasant still,
  and on that narrow reach of sand
  the air has qualities which words cannot describe;   8270
  out on its tip we'll have a close-up view
  of the marine procession now approaching.
  Come with me there!
THALES.   I too will come.
HOMUNCULUS. Three spirits keeping step! Extraordinary!
  TELCHINES OF RHODES *appear on sea-horses and sea-dragons; they bear*
                          Neptune's trident.
TELCHINES (*in chorus*). We forged for Poseidon the trident he uses   8275
  whenever he quiets tumultuous seas.
  If thundering Zeus deploys heavy clouds,
  Poseidon then counters their horrible rumbling;
  although jagged lightning may strike from above,
  great volleys of waves will be sprayed from below;   8280
  whatever, between them long hurled back and forth,
  has struggled in terror, the Deep then devours.
  Tonight he's entrusted his scepter to us,
  and so we float past you, carefree and festive.
SIRENS. Hail to you who serve Apollo,   8285
        happy devotees of Light!
        Welcome, as the hour inspires
        adoration of Diana!
TELCHINES. O loveliest goddess of all in the sky,
  who hear with delight any praise of your brother,   8290
  you always have graciously listened to Rhodes,
  which joyously sings endless praises to him.

Beginning day's journey, and ending it too,
he gazes upon us with eyes flashing fire.
Our mountains and cities, our waters and shores,   8295
are lovely and bright, and stand high in his favor.
No fog hovers near us, but if it creeps in,
a sunbeam and breeze make our island's air clear.
In hundreds of forms the god sees himself there,
as colossus august, as ephebus indulgent.   8300
Before us no people had ever depicted
the might of the gods in a pure human form.

PROTEUS. Pay no attention to their boasting!
    In the sun's sacred, living rays
    all lifeless works seem futile jests.   8305
    These creatures sculpt and smelt, by nothing daunted,
    and when their work is cast in bronze
    they think it's something highly special.
    What is the upshot of their pride?
    They raised the lofty statues of their gods;   8310
    one earthquake then destroyed them all,
    and they've long since been melted down.
        Terrestrial life in any form
    is nothing but perpetual grief;
    water is more propitious to existence;   8315
    as dolphin, I will bear you now
    to the eternal sea.

                    (*He turns into a dolphin.*)
                    That change was quick!
    There you can count on meeting no ill-fortune;
    I'll carry you upon my back
    and give you in marriage to the ocean.   8320

THALES. Accede to this commendable request
    and start your life at life's beginning!
    And be prepared for rapid changes,
    for you'll evolve according to eternal norms
    changing your shape uncounted times,   8325
    with lots of time before you must be human.

            HOMUNCULUS *mounts* DOLPHIN-PROTEUS.

PROTEUS. Come, still a spirit, with me to the open waters
    where, as a living being, you'll be free
    to move in all dimensions and directions;
    just don't aspire to the higher classes,   8330
    for once you have become a human being
    you've reached the end of everything.

THALES. That's as may be; it's also good, I think,
    when one's time comes, to be a proper man.

PROTEUS (*to* THALES). You mean one like yourself, no doubt!   8335

Your sort does last a certain length of time—
I have been seeing you for many centuries
in circles rife with pallid spirits.

SIRENS (*on the rocks*).

 See the little clouds now forming
 that great ring around the moon!   8340
 They are doves, by love inspired,
 borne on wings of dazzling whiteness;
 Paphos has dispatched them here,
 all its ardent feathered hosts.
 Now our festival is perfect,   8345
 our delight now unalloyed!

NEREUS (*joining* THALES).

 A nocturnal traveler may
 call that ring mere play of light,
 but we spirits have another,
 and the only proper, theory: 8350
 they are doves, and they escort
 Galatea's sea-borne conch,
 flying in a rare formation
 wondrous taught them long ago.

THALES. I can but approve a theory   8355
 that affords this good man pleasure,
 and sustains a quiet faith
 in the warmth of human hearts.

 PSYLLI *and* MARSI *appear on sea-bulls, sea-heifers, and sea-rams*).

PSYLLI *and* MARSI (*in chorus*).

 In Cyprus' deep and rugged caverns,
 not buried under Neptune's jetsam,   8360
 unshaken by the force of Seismos,
 forever fanned by gentle breezes,
 and still enjoying peace and quiet
 as in the earliest of times:
 we guard the chariot of Venus   8365
 and bring in the murmuring darkness,
 on waves intertwining and graceful,
 unseen by today's generation,
 this fairest of daughters to join you.
 Quietly busy, we have no fear   8370
 of Eagle or of Winged Lion,
 of Cross or of Crescent, and do not care
 who lives and rules above
 with what ado and in which ways,
 or how they're killed or driven out   8375
 with fields destroyed and cities sacked.

We bring to you, as we always shall,
the loveliest mistress ever served.
SIRENS. Light of motion, not too hasty,
  with her conch inside your circles,   8380
  now in intertwining lines,
  now in rows and serpentine,
  agile Nereids, draw near,
  sturdy women, sweet though wild!
  bring, o Doris' tender daughters!   8385
  Galatea, your mother's counterfeit:
  earnest and godlike in mien,
  rightly granted life eternal,
  yet, like lovely mortal women,
  graceful, charming, and alluring.   8390
NEREIDS (*on dolphins, passing* NEREUS; *in chorus*).
  Luna, half-light will suffice us;
  shed on these fine youths your brilliance!
  Hoping for paternal blessing,
  we have brought dear husbands here.
(*To* NEREUS.) These are lads whom we have snatched 8395
  from the breakers' fearful maws;
  in warm beds of sedge and moss
  now restored to life and light,
  they are eager to reward us
  with their grateful, fervent kisses.   8400
  Don't rebuff these sweet young men!
NEREUS. To profit twice from one transaction's splendid:
 you practice charity, and have the joys of love.
NEREIDS. Since you praise what we have done
  and approve our being happy,   8405
  let us hold them fast forever
  on our young, immortal breasts!
NEREUS. Although you may enjoy your pretty catch
 and make good husbands of these youths,
 I cannot grant what Zeus alone   8410
 possesses power to bestow.
 The waves, that rock you in their cradle,
 allow no love to last forever;
 so, when affection's spell has ended,
 tenderly put them back on land.   8415
NEREIDS. Although, dear boys, we're fond of you,
  in sadness we must leave you;
  we wanted an undying love,
  but heaven won't allow it.
THE SAILOR. We worthy lads would not object   8420

to more such kindly treatment;
we've never had so good a life,
and ask for nothing better.

GALATEA *approaches on her conch.*

NEREUS. My dearest, you're here!

GALATEA.   What happiness, father!
Linger, my dolphins—I'm held by his look!   8425

NEREUS. Gone by already, they continue on
in sweeping circles—to them,
what are the stirrings of a heart!
Would that they were taking me along!
Still, a single look is so much pleasure   8430
that it makes up for the whole long year.

THALES. Hail! Hail again!
Beauty and truth fill my being,
make perfect my happiness. . . .
All things have their beginning in water!!   8435
Water sustains all things that exist;
may you, Oceanus, rule us forever!
Unless you sent the clouds
and fed the copious brooks,
directed rivers where to go   8440
and filled them properly,
what would mountain and plain, our earth, be like?
You're the support of all living freshness.

ALL (*echo-chorus of all trionfo groups.*)
You are the source of living freshness.

NEREUS. Off in the distance they waver, turn back,   8445
but not enough for our eyes to meet;
In honor of our celebration
the countless host winds round and round,
making its linking circles broader still.
But now I see—I see it once again—   8450
the conch that is the throne of Galatea,
in the midst of all
it shines like a star.
Love is a beacon no crowd can obscure—
no matter the distance,   8455
it gleams bright and clear,
always seems near, always is true.

HOMUNCULUS. All that my lamp illuminates
amid these fostering waters
has grace and beauty.   8460

PROTEUS.   Amid these living waters
your lamp, now bright at last,
resounds with a glorious tone.

NEREUS. Here in the middle of all this host,
   what new revelation are we to see? 8465
   A flame by the conch, at my daughter's feet,
   now mounts high and strong, now burns sweet and low,
   as though it were stirring with pulsations of love.
THALES. That is Homunculus, whom Proteus has taken. . . .
   Those are the symptoms of passion's imperative— 8470
   I almost can hear the loud groans of its travails.
   He'll shatter his vial on her glittering throne—
   there's the flame, there the flash, and already it empties!
SIRENS. What miraculous fire transfigures our waves,
   that break on each other and shatter and sparkle? 8475
   Lights wave and hover, the brightness comes nearer,
   what moves in the darkness is pure incandescence,
   and all is enveloped in eddies of fire.
   Let Eros now rule, the creator of all!
            Hail to Ocean and the waves 8480
            now embraced by sacred fire!
            Hail to Water! Hail to Fire!
            Hail this strange and rare event!
ALL (*all together*). Hail to Air and its soft breezes!
            Hail to Earth's mysterious depths! 8485
            To you four, o Elements,
            here we offer solemn praise!

ACT III

BEFORE MENELAUS' PALACE AT SPARTA

Enter HELEN *and* CHORUS OF CAPTIVE TROJAN WOMEN, *with its Leader*
PANTHALIS.

HELEN. I, Helen, who am much admired, much berated,
    come from the beach where only now we disembarked,
    still giddy from the lively rocking of the waves   8490
    that on their untamed backs, thanks to Poseidon's grace
    and Euros' force, have borne us from the level plains
    of Phrygia to bays that edge our native shores.
    King Menelaus and his bravest warriors
    are now rejoicing, there below, at their return.   8495
    But here I bid you bid me welcome, lofty house
    erected by Tyndareos upon these slopes
    when he, my father, had come back from Pallas' Hill
    and which, while I as happy sister grew and played   8500
    with Clytemnestra here, with Castor too and Pollux,
    he made the most resplendent house in Sparta.
    I hail and greet you, o great double door of bronze!
    It was through you, who opened wide to welcome him,
    that Menelaus, chosen from so many, once
    appeared to me as radiant bridegroom long ago.   8505
    Spread wide your wings again so that, as loyal wife,
    I may fulfil an urgent order of our king.
    Let me come in, and may I leave behind those storms
    which up to now have raged about me fatally!
    For since I left this threshold in a carefree mood   8510
    for Cytherea's shrine, as sacred duty bade,
    and was abducted by the Phrygian pirate there,
    much has occurred that people dwelling far and wide
    delight to tell, but cannot delight the ear of him
    whose story is expanded to fantastic tale.   8515
CHORUS. Do not, great lady, disdain your glory,
        possession of the highest good!
        Supreme felicity is yours,
        beauty whose fame is all-surpassing.
        His name heralds the hero's coming,   8520
        and so he walks proudly,
        but to all-conquering beauty
        the most obdurate man forthwith submits.
HELEN. Enough! I have come with my husband here by ship,
    am sent ahead into his city now by him;   8525
    what purpose, though, he entertains I cannot guess.

Is it as wife that I come here, is it as queen?
Is it as victim of the prince's bitterness,
atoning for the woes the Greeks so long endured?
I am a prize of war—am I a captive too?   8530
I cannot say! For the immortal gods, uncertain,
allotted me as beauty's dubious attendants
fame and a fateful life, who on this threshold now
beside me stand as gloomy, threatening presences.
While in the hollow ship my husband rarely looked   8535
at me, nor did he speak one reassuring word
but sat, like someone brooding mischief, across from me.
No sooner had, however, the first vessels' beaks
arrived to greet Eurotas' deep-bayed shores
than thus, as if inspired by a god, he spoke: 8540
"My warriors here shall disembark in ordered groups
that, when they're ranged along the beach, I will inspect.
But you shall go ahead and shall continue up
the fertile banks of our Eurotas' holy stream,
driving the steeds across the moist fields' loveliness   8545
until you have attained that beautiful plateau
where amid awesome mountains Lacedaemon once
brought under cultivation broad and fertile fields.
Then, enter the royal house that towers there aloft
and muster in my name the maids I left behind,   8550
including their sagacious ancient stewardess.
Let her produce for you the ample treasure-store,
your father's gifts and all that I in war and peace
myself amassed through never ceasing increments.
You will find everything where it's supposed to be: 8555
on his return a prince has the prerogative
of finding in his house, at their appointed place,
all things kept faithfully as he had left them there.
No servant on his own may alter any detail."
CHORUS. Let this increasing, glorious treasure   8560
        refresh your eye, regale your heart!
        The graceful chain and well-wrought crown
        are lying now arrogant and idle,
        but if you enter and challenge them
        they'll have to combat you.   8565
        Beauty competing with gold, pearls, and jewels
        is a sight I shall watch with utter delight.
HELEN. Our master then gave me a further order still:
        "When you have duly verified that all is well,
        in preparation for a holy ritual   8570
        collect as many tripods as you think required,

all vessels the officiant wants close at hand.
Have caldrons ready, cups, and shallow plates as well;
have filled with purest water from the sacred spring
the great tall jars; moreover, let there be dry wood   8575
available, that rapidly accepts the flame;
then, last, be sure there is a knife, well-sharpened, too.
I shall entrust all else, however, to your care.''
These were the words with which he urged me to depart,
but he who ordered thus named nothing that draws breath   8580
which he will slay to honor the Olympians.
This gives one pause, but I'll not worry more about it;
so let such matters all be left to the high gods,
who then shall bring to pass whatever they intend,
whether this be considered good by human minds,   8585
or bad; as mortals we must bear what they allot.
There have been many times when to the earth-bound neck
of consecrated beast hands raised the heavy axe
and could not consummate the sacrificial rite,
stayed by approaching foe or intervening god.   8590

CHORUS. Thought cannot tell you what yet is to be;
      do not be daunted, o Queen,
      but proceed!
      Good or evil comes
      as a surprise to us mortals;   8595
      even foretold, it is not believed.
      Did not Troy burn, did we not see
      death before us, a death of shame?
      Yet are we not here,
      happy to serve and be with you,   8600
      seeing the dazzling sun in the sky,
      and what is fairest on earth,
      you, whose favor is our happiness?

HELEN. Let come, what may! No matter what impends, I must
ascend without delay into this royal house,   8605
long missed, much yearned for, and nearly lost through folly,
which once again—I know not how—I see before me.
My feet no longer bear me with so light a heart
up these high steps that as a child I skipped across.   [*Exit.*

CHORUS. Sisters so sadly   8610
      mourning captivity,
      cast all your sorrows away!
      Rejoice with our mistress,
      rejoice with Queen Helen,
      now again happily   8615

nearing the hearth of her fathers
with somewhat belated,
but all the more confident, step.
    Praise the benevolent
home-bringing gods,   8620
the holy restorers of order!
Rough though his road be,
the prisoner freed
soars on as if pinioned
while, vainly wasting away,   8625
the captive yearns
with arm outstretched from prison-battlement.
    Far from her home
a mortal god laid hold of her,
and from the ruins of Ilium   8630
he has brought her here,
back to the old, now newly resplendent,
house of her fathers
where restored and refreshed,
after raptures and torments   8635
that no words can describe,
she can think of her childhood.

PANTHALIS. Now leave the joyous path of song and melody,
    and turn your gazes to the portal's open leaves!
    What is it, sisters, that I see? Is not our queen   8640
    returning with marked agitation in her step?
                    (*Enter* HELEN.)
    What can it be, great Queen, that has confronted you,
    not with the welcome of dependents, but with dread,
    there in your house's halls? You do not keep it hidden,
    for I see horror and repugnance on your brow,   8645
    and noble indignation struggling with surprise.

HELEN (*who has left the double door open, agitatedly*).
    Zeus's daughter must be far above all vulgar fear,
    and is not touched by terror's lightly passing hand;
    but horror that emerges from the primal womb
    of ancient Night, that surges up like glowing clouds   8650
    of many shapes arising from some mountainous
    abyss of fire, will even shake a hero's heart.
    The Stygian gods have placed my entering this house
    under so dread a sign today that, like a guest
    dismissed, I would be glad to say farewell and leave   8655
    this threshold I so often crossed, so long desired.
    But no! Although I have retreated to the light,

you shall not force me further, whatever powers you be!
I shall devise a lustral rite; then, purified,
the glowing hearth will welcome mistress and her lord.   8660
PANTHALIS. Disclose, o noble Lady, to the maids who serve
and will support you, what has now occurred.
HELEN. What I have seen, you'll see with your own eyes,
unless primordial Night again at once engulfed
her creature in her magic womb's profundity.   8665
But I'll declare it, so that you shall know, in words:
When I, intent upon my mission, reverently
set foot inside the royal house's somber rooms,
I marveled at the stillness of empty passageways.
No sound of busy people moving met my ear,   8670
no quick and purposeful activity my eye,
and I saw neither maid nor stewardess appear
to greet, as once they did, all strangers graciously.
But when I had drawn near the central hearth,
there by the barely warm remains of a dead fire   8675
I saw a tall, veiled woman seated on the ground,
less like someone asleep than one who meditates.
Imperiously I summon her to be at work,
surmising that perhaps she is the stewardess
appointed by my husband's foresight when he left;   8680
but she, not stirring, sits enfolded in her robes;
at last, responding to my threats, she lifts her arm
as if to order me to leave the hearth and hall.
In wrath I turn away from her and hurry toward
the steps that lead to where the nuptial chamber lies,   8685
richly adorned and with the treasure-room close by;
but now the monster quickly rises to its feet,
barring my way peremptorily, and is revealed
as tall and gaunt, with hollow, blood-discolored eyes,
and as a form whose strangeness bewilders sight and mind.   8690
But I speak to the air, since words can only strive
in vain to build and to endow a shape with life.
Look! There it is! It even dares confront the light,
where we command until the royal master comes!
Yet, either Phoebus, beauty's friend, confines to caves   8695
Night's dread abortions, or they are held in check by him.
PHORKYAS *appears on the threshold and stands between the doorposts.*
CHORUS. I have experienced much, though my hair
lies on my forehead in youthful waves!
Many terrible things have I seen,
warfare's distress, Ilium's night   8700
when it fell.

And I have heard, through the dust-clouded tumult
of hard-pressed combatants, the cries of the gods,
fearful to hear, and Discord's voice
echoing brazen over the field   8705
towards its walls.
    Still they were standing, Ilium's walls,
but, alas! the blaze of the flames
already was moving from neighbor to neighbor,
spread by the wind it created,   8710
from one point and then another,
across the whole night-darkened city.
    Fleeing, I saw amid smoke and fire,
amid the motley tongues of flame,
the dread approach of angry gods,   8715
strange, gigantic figures
striding through thick and somber clouds
lighted on all sides by fire.
    Did I see that, or did my mind,
held in terror's grip, imagine   8720
that confusion? What was fact
I cannot say, but this I know
is certain: here with my own eyes
I see this hideousness,
could even touch it with my hands   8725
if I were not held back by fear
from threatening danger.
    Which of the daughters,
then, are you of Phorkys,
his being the family   8730
to which I'd assign you?
Can it be that here is come
one of the Graiae, gray since birth,
who possess one eye and tooth
alternately shared?   8735
    Hideous creature,
how dare you appear now,
here beside beauty,
for Phoebus to judge you?
You may come still further forward!   8740
What is ugly, he does not see,
even as his hallowed eye
never has glimpsed a shadow.
    But, alas, our mortal eyes
are constrained by a sad mischance   8745
to endure the unspeakable pain

that what is condemned as eternally ugly
must arouse in lovers of beauty.
    You are warned that you'll hear our curse
if you brazenly affront us,   8750
hear invective, imprecations, threats
from the mouths of fortunate beings
who owe their form to supernal gods.

PHORKYAS. The saying's old, but what it says profoundly true,
that Modesty and Beauty never go their way   8755
along the earth's green paths together, hand in hand.
In each there dwells inveterate, deep-rooted hate,
so that if in their travels they may somewhere meet,
each turns her back to her opponent then and there.
Then each, with more impetuous step, will hasten on,   8760
Modesty sad, but Beauty insolent and bold
until, if age has not already made her tame,
she is embraced at last by Orcus' hollow night.
Come from abroad, I see, you inundate us here
with arrogance, even as do the noisy cranes   8765
above our heads, whose raucous flight sends down to earth
from long-extended cloud its strident croaking tones
that tempt the quiet traveler to turn his gaze
into the air; but they continue on their way,
and he on his; so will it be with us as well.   8770
    And who are you, that you, like frenzied maenads, dare
surround with drunken uproar here the king's great house?
Who are you, who assail the palace-stewardess
with howling, like a pack of dogs that bay the moon?
Do you presume I do not know your lineage,   8775
you war-begotten, battle-nurtured, callow things,
man-hungry too, as much seducing as seduced,
who sap the strength of citizen and warrior both!
To see you in such numbers is as if I saw
locust swarms plunge and cover green, fresh-planted fields.   8780
Devourers of the toil of others, who destroy
the buds of the prosperity on which you feed!
Wares gained in war, sold second-hand in market places!

HELEN. Who in her presence dares to scold a woman's maids
encroaches on their mistress' authority,   8785
fcr the prerogative is hers alone, to praise
what merits praise and punish what must be condemned.
I am, besides, well satisfied with how they served
and aided me when Ilium's great power
stood under siege, and when it fell; and no less so   8790
while we endured our voyage's vicissitudes,

when people as a rule think only of themselves.
Here also I expect from them the same light-heartedness;
Masters don't ask what their slaves are, but only how
they serve. Be silent, then, and leer at them no more.   8795
If in its mistress' stead you've taken proper care
of the king's house till now, the merit will be yours;
but now that she herself has come, give way to her,
lest there be punishment instead of generous praise.

PHORKYAS. To chide her household is the great prerogative   8800
which the august consort of one the gods have blessed
well merits for long years of prudent governance.
Since you, whom I now recognize, again as queen
and mistress of this house resume your former place,
hold fast the reins long since grown slack, and govern now,   8805
in charge of the royal treasure and of us as well.
But first of all, protect me, older than the rest,
from these who are, when set beside your beauty's swan,
merely a flock of underfeathered, cackling geese.

PANTHALIS. How ugly seems, set next to beauty, ugliness.   8810

PHORKYAS. How shallow, next to wisdom, foolish ignorance.

Members of the CHORUS *now answer in turn, stepping forth singly.*

FIRST TROJAN WOMAN.
Tell us about your parents, Erebus and Night!

PHORKYAS. Then you tell me about your cousin-german, Scylla!

THE SECOND.. Monsters fill up the branches of your family tree.

PHORKYAS. Be off to Orcus, where you'll find your kith and kin!   8815

THE THIRD. Those who might dwell down there were born long after you.

PHORKYAS. You might try to solicit old Tiresias.

THE FOURTH. Your great-granddaughter's daughter was Orion's nurse.

PHORKYAS. The Harpies, I suspect, gave you their filth as pap.

THE FIFTH. What food explains your special lean-and-hungry look?   8820

PHORKYAS. Not blood, for which you have too great an appetite.

THE SIXTH. And you still more for corpses, loathsome corpse yourself!

PHORKYAS. I see the gleam of vampire-teeth in your bold mouth.

PANTHALIS. I could gag yours by simply saying who you are.

PHORKYAS. If you can name yourself, no riddle will remain.   8825

HELEN. I step between you, not in anger but in grief,
to order that these stormy countercharges cease,
since nothing gives the lord and master greater hurt
than faithful servants' quarrels that fester secretly.
For no concordant echo of his bidding then   8830
comes back to him as swiftly executed deed;
instead, it surges like a wilful, noisy storm
about him as, himself confused, he chides in vain.
Nor is this all. In your unseemly quarreling

you've conjured up the spectres of unhappy shapes   8835
which so crowd in about me that I feel I'm pulled
toward Orcus, although I'm here amid these native fields.
Could those be memories? Was I prey to delusions?
Was I all that? am I that now, to be so evermore,
the nightmare-shape of one who devastates great towns?   8840
My servingwomen shudder; you, the eldest here,
still stand composed—give me some reassuring word!

PHORKYAS. To one who's lived in hopes of fortune many years,
the favor of the gods seems, when it comes, a dream.
But you, augustly favored to the uttermost,   8845
have in life's course seen only men inflamed with love
and eager for all kinds of the most daring deeds.
You were still young when eager Theseus ravished you,
as strong as Heracles, and truly handsome too . . .

HELEN. Took me, a slender doe of ten, to Attica,   8850
where in Aphidnus' castle I was prisoner . . .

PHORKYAS. But then, by Castor and by Pollux soon set free,
were wooed by many heroes, each a splendid man.

HELEN. First in my secret favor, though, Patroclus stood,
Pelides' counterpart, as freely I confess.   8855

PHORKYAS. Your father's will wed you to Menelaus, though,
the bold sea-rover and protector of his home.

HELEN. He gave him both his daughter and his land to rule;
the scion of our wedlock was Hermione.

PHORKYAS. Yet while in distant Crete he boldly gained his rights,   8860
an all too handsome guest appeared to lonely you.

HELEN. Why do you bring to mind that semi-widowhood
and the appalling consequence it had for me?

PHORKYAS. That trip resulted too in my captivity,
and in long slavery for me, free-born in Crete.   8865

HELEN. He promptly sent you here as trusted stewardess
of wealth he'd bravely won, and of his castle too . . .

PHORKYAS. Which you had left to seek the city, tower-girt,
of Ilium, and love's delights that never tire.

HELEN. Do not speak of delights! An all too bitter grief   8870
that never, never ends engulfed my heart and head.

PHORKYAS. And yet they say that you appeared in twofold form,
that in both Ilium and Egypt you were seen.

HELEN. Do not confound the chaos of a mind confused.
I don't know, even now, which of those two I am.   8875

PHORKYAS. They also say, that from the realm of hollow shades
ardent Achilles too came forth to join with you,
he who, in spite of fate's decrees, loved you long since.

HELEN. A shade myself, I was conjoined with him, a shade.
That was a dream, the words themselves make this quite clear.   8880

I now grow faint, become a shade to myself too.
       She sinks into the arms of the SEMICHORUS.
CHORUS. Silence! Be silent,
      you evil-eyed evil tongue!
      From such hideous, single-toothed lips,
      from so frightful a throat's abyss,   8885
      what might not surge forth!
        He who's malicious while posing as kindly,
      wolf-fierce under the sheep's woolly fleece,
      seems far more dreadful to me than the jaws
      of the dog that's three-headed.   8890
      Fearfully we wait to hear
      when, how, where it will emerge,
      malice lurking
      deep below in a monster's guise!
        Here now, instead of offering kindness,   8895
      Lethe-bestowing, consoling words,
      you evoke from all of her past
      less of its good than its evils,
      darkening at the same time
      both the present's radiance   8900
      and the future's
      softly shimmering dawn of hope.
        Silence! Be silent,
      so that the soul of our queen,
      now on the verge of flight,   8905
      may stay and may retain
      this form surpassing any form
      on which the sun has ever shone.
        HELEN, *who has recovered, again stands at center.*
PHORKYAS.
  Come! emerge from those passing clouds, o lofty sun of this our day,
  you who veiled were ravishing, and who now reign in dazzling light; 8910
  you can see the world unfolding here before your gracious gaze.
  Even though they call me ugly, I know well what beauty is.
HELEN.
  Though I come, unsteadily, from the void of dizzying faintness
  and, because my limbs are weary, would be glad to rest again,
  it is proper for a queen, just as it is for all mankind,   8915
  even when surprised by danger, to be calm and stout of heart.
PHORKYAS.
  Now that in heroic beauty you are standing here again,
  in your eye we read some bidding; tell us, what is your command!
HELEN.
  Be prepared to rectify the rude delay your wrangling's caused;
  quick! arrange the ritual that has been ordered by my king.   8920

PHORKYAS.
  All is ready in the palace: bowl and tripod, sharpened axe,
  lustral water, needed incense; say what's to be sacrificed!
HELEN. That he left undesignated.
PHORKYAS.   Left unsaid? O word of woe!
HELEN. Why this woe that so affects you?
PHORKYAS.   You, o Queen, are the one meant!
HELEN.   I?
PHORKYAS.   And these.
CHORUS.   O woe and sorrow!
PHORKYAS.   You shall fall beneath the axe.
HELEN. Heinous! yet not unexpected; poor me!
PHORKYAS.   I see no escape.
CHORUS. Woe! And to us what is to happen?
PHORKYAS.   She will die a noble death;
  like the fowler's row of thrushes, you, inside, shall hang and writhe,
  dangling from the lofty rafter that supports the gabled roof.
  (HELEN and the CHORUS stand amazed and terrified, in a striking, care-
                fully arranged group.)
  All phantoms! — There you stand like lifeless images,   8930
  afraid to quit daylight to which you have no claim.
  But mortals too, who all, like you, are only ghosts,
  do not renounce the sacred sunlight willingly;
  no prayer or effort, though, can save them from their doom;
  all men know this, but very few are pleased by it.   8935
  It is enough that you're undone! So, quick, to work!
(PHORKYAS claps her hands, whereupon there appear in the doorway muffled dwarfish figures which carry out with alacrity the commands given.)
  This way, you somber, spherical monstrosities,
  waddle along—there's pleasant mischief to be done!
  Set down the hand-borne altar with the golden horns,
  and lay across its silver edge the shining axe;   8940
  fill water jars, for you will need to wash away
  the hideous, defiling stains of blackened blood.
  Spread out here on the dust the precious rug, so that
  the victim may kneel down in royal dignity
  and, wrapped in it, although with severed head, receive   8945
  all due respect and yet a prompt interment too.
PANTHALIS. Absorbed in thought, the Queen is standing there, aside,
  her women wilt like meadow-grass beneath the scythe;
  but I, the oldest, as my bounden duty bids,
  will seek a word with you, who are far older still.   8950
  Experienced and wise, you seem to wish us well,
  although these silly girls misjudged and flouted you.
  So speak, and say what you can do to rescue us.

PHORKYAS. That is soon said: to save herself, and you to boot
    as adjuncts, will depend entirely on your queen.   8955
    Resolve is needed, and as soon as possible.
CHORUS.
    You who are the wisest sibyl, are the most revered of Fates,
    keep the golden shears from closing, promise us safe days ahead,
    for already we are feeling how our tender limbs will dangle,
    sway, and swing, not pleasantly, that rather would enjoy some dancing,
    then repose on a lover's breast.
HELEN. Let these be anxious! What I feel is pain, not fear;
    but if you know of an escape, you have our thanks.
    To wisdom's circumspection the impossible
    may truly still prove possible. So tell us, speak!   8965
CHORUS.
    Speak and tell us, tell us quickly, how we can escape the horrid,
    nasty nooses that now threaten, like the meanest kinds of necklace,
    to constrict our throats and breathing. We poor things can feel already
    how we'll die of suffocation if you, Rhea, all gods' mother,
    do not deign to pity us.   8970
PHORKYAS. Have you the patience not to interrupt a speech
    that will be long? All sorts of things need to be told.
CHORUS. Patience enough! While listening we'll be alive.
PHORKYAS. The man who stays at home to guard his precious wealth,
    who takes good care to caulk his house's lofty walls   8975
    and to secure its roof against the rain's assault,
    will know prosperity however long he live;
    but he who lightly steps with hasty foot across
    his threshold's sacred limit, heedless of all law,
    on his return may well still find the same old place,   8980
    but all things altered, even if not all destroyed.
HELEN. What is the relevance of these familiar saws?
    You say you have a tale; avoid what must offend!
PHORKYAS. This is narrated fact, by no means a reproach.
    As corsair, Menelaus steered from bay to bay   8985
    and ravaged all the shores and islands that he touched,
    returning with the spoils which now sit there inside.
    Before the walls of Troy he spent ten tedious years,
    and for the voyage home, how long I do not know.
    But where Tyndareos' house towers grandly here,   8990
    and elsewhere in this kingdom, how do matters stand?
HELEN. Is, then, abuse so totally ingrained in you
    that you can never move your lips except in blame?
PHORKYAS. For many, many years no one had occupied
    the valleyed hills that northwards, back of Sparta, rise   8995
    up to Taygetus; there, still a merry brook,

the Eurotas tumbles down, then broadening its stream
flows past our valley's reeds, gives nurture to your swans.
Back in those mountain valleys, quietly, bold men
have settled, a horde emerging from Cimmerian night,   9000
and raised a towered fortress that no one can scale;
from it they harrass land and people as they please.
HELEN. They could accomplish that? It seems impossible!
PHORKYAS. They had the time—it may be twenty years by now.
HELEN. Is there one chief? Is this a league of robber bands?   9005
PHORKYAS. They are not brigands, but they have a single lord.
    I'll not speak ill of him, although I've felt his might.
    He could have taken everything, yet was content
    with what he called, not tribute, but a few free gifts.
HELEN. How does he look?
PHORKYAS   Not bad! I rather like his looks.   9010
    He's lively, forthright, handsome, and, to a degree
    even in Greece exceptional, intelligent.
    They call this race barbarians, but I would doubt
    that any are more cruel than certain heroes who,
    before Troy's walls, showed cannibal proclivities.   9015
    He is magnanimous, I'd trust myself to him.
    His castle, too, is something you should see yourselves!
    It's very different from the heavy masonry
    erected by your forebears any way at all—
    Cyclopes-like, they heaped rough Cyclopean stones   9020
    one on the other; there, however, everything
    is plumb and level, made with regularity.
    Behold it from without, aspiring heavenward
    firm and tight-jointed and as mirror-smooth as steel!
    To scale such walls—why, thought itself slips off and falls.   9025
    Inside there are great, spacious courtyards, closed about
    with structures of all kinds and purposes.
    There you will see shafts, arches, pillars, large and small;
    platforms and galleries for looking out and in;
    and coats of arms.
CHORUS.   And what are they?
PHORKYAS.   On Ajax's shield,   9030
    there was, as you yourselves have seen, a dragon coiled.
    The Seven at the gates of Thebes had on their shields,
    each one, an image filled with rich significance;
    there in nocturnal skies one saw the moon and stars,
    and goddess, hero, ladder, swords, and torches too,   9035
    and all dire threats that to a noble town bring woe.
    Such images, inherited from their forebears,
    are borne in glowing colors by our hero-band;

you will see eagles, lions, and also claw and beak,
the horns of buffalo, wings, roses, peacock-tails, 9040
and golden, argent, azure, black, and crimson stripes.
They hang these things, row after row, in their great halls,
worlds limitless in their immensity and where
you will have room to dance!
CHORUS.   And men with whom to dance?
PHORKYAS. The best! Plenty of lively lads with golden curls 9045
and youth's ambrosial breath—the scent that Paris had
when he dared come too near our queen.
HELEN.   Do not forget
the role you're playing; finish what you have to say!
PHORKYAS. The final word is yours; but say a clear, firm yes,
and I'll surround you with the fortress here and now. 9050
CHORUS. O speak that one short word, and save yourself and us!
HELEN. Am I to fear, then, that King Menelaus might
commit so cruel a wrong and do me injury?
PHORKYAS. Have you forgotten in what dreadful way he maimed
battle-slain Paris' brother, your Deiphobus, 9055
who claimed and took you, widowed then, with stubborn force
as concubine, successfully? Nose, ears, were cut,
and more was mutilated—an atrocious sight!
HELEN. He did do that to him, did it because of me.
PHORKYAS. Because of him, he will now do the same to you. 9060
Beauty may not be shared; who has possessed it whole,
cursing all half-claims, prefers destroying it.
        (*Trumpets in the distance; the* CHORUS *starts in terror.*)
Even as the trumpet's blare, with rending force, lays hold
of ear and bowels, even so does jealousy
claw at the bosom of the man who can't forget 9065
what once he owned, and now has lost and owns no more.
CHORUS.
Do you not hear trumpets blaring, see the weapons as they flash?
PHORKYAS.
Lord and King, I bid you welcome, glad to answer for my conduct.
CHORUS.
What of us?
PHORKYAS.
            You know the truth, that with your eyes you'll see her death
and, indoors, observe your own; no, there is no help for you. 9070
                    Pause.
HELEN. I have thought out what I may safely venture next.
You are a hostile spirit, as I clearly sense,
and so I fear that you will change what's good to bad.
But first I'll follow to the castle, led by you;

the rest I know alone; and what, deep in her heart,   9075
your queen conceals in secrecy while we do this,
no one shall fathom. Now, old woman, go ahead!
CHORUS. O how glad we are to go there,
       and to hasten our step,
       with death behind us   9080
       and a towering fortress'
       inaccessible walls
       rising before us again.
       May it shield us well,
       like Ilium's citadel,   9085
       which after all only succumbed
       to contemptible guile.
(*Spreading mists obscure the background, then the front of the set, as may*
seem appropriate.)
       But, what is this?
       Sisters, look round you!
       Was it not clear just now?   9090
       Streaks of fog are floating up
       from the Eurotas' sacred stream;
       now its lovely sedge-girt banks
       have already vanished from sight;
       nor, alas, do I still see,   9095
       silently gliding, free and proud,
       the elegant swans whose delight
       is companionable swimming.
         Nevertheless,
       I do hear their cry,   9100
       distant and hoarse, the sound
       which men say presages death.
       Let us hope that after all,
       though salvation has been promised,
       it does not foretell our doom—   9105
       doom to us, who are so swan-like
       with our lovely, long white necks,
       and to our swan-begotten queen.
       Alas! o woe to us, o woe!
         Everything is now concealed   9110
       by the fog that closes in,
       even the sight of each other!
       What can be happening to us?
       Are we marching ahead or, with short steps,
       merely floating along?   9115
       Can you see anything? Is that not Hermes
       who hovers before us, his golden wand gleaming,

who summons, who orders us to return
to dreary, twilight-gray Hades,
which, filled to repletion   9120
with impalpable shapes, is eternally empty?
Suddenly the light grows duller; grayed, the lifting fog lacks luster,
is as brown as weathered stonework. Walls appear and block our vision,
freed again to see their starkness. Can this be a pit? a courtyard?
What is certain is, it's dreadful! Sisters, we alas are captives,   9125
as much captives as before!

INNER COURTYARD OF A CASTLE

The enclosed yard is faced with ornate, fantastic medieval buildings.
PANTHALIS. Hasty and foolish females, truly typical!
Dependent on the moment, sport of every breeze,
of good luck and of bad, but bearing neither one
with equanimity! One sure to contradict   9130
another angrily, then others her in turn!
You wail or laugh together only in joy or pain.
Be silent now, and hear what in her noble mind
our mistress may decide is right for her and us.
HELEN. Whatever your name is, where are you, Pythoness?   9135
Emerge now from this gloomy castle's vaulted halls!
And if you went to tell its wondrous hero-lord
that I am here, so that I may be well received,
accept my thanks, and bring me to his presence now;
I want an end of wandering, want only rest.   9140
PANTHALIS. You look about you everywhere, my Queen, in vain;
that sorry creature's disappeared—perhaps she stayed
there in the bosom of the fog from which, somehow,
we got so quickly here without the need to walk.
Or else, perhaps, confused, she wanders through this maze   9145
of many castles strangely blended into one,
seeking its lord, so that you're greeted regally.
But look! Already, up above, there is a bustle
as multitudes of servants hurry back and forth
by doorway and at windows and on galleries;   9150
a fitting, noble welcome is assured the guest.
CHORUS. How my heart is relieved! Look over there and see
with what dignity, lingering on each step,
toward us there descend, in well-ordered march,
all those lovely young men. How, and at whose command,   9155
can so promptly appear, marshaled in regular ranks,
such a magnificent, boyishly masculine troop?
What should I most admire? Is it the grace of their stride,
or the curls of the hair over their radiant brows,

or perhaps their twinned cheeks, red with the blush of the peach   9160
and having the same soft fleece-like down?
I would like a taste, but am afraid to bite,
since in a similar case—horrid even to say—
a mouth was filled with ashes.
    Now they're advancing,   9165
    these loveliest youths.
    What's that they carry?
    Steps of a throne,
    carpet, a chair,
    curtains, and something   9170
    tent-like, ornate,
    making wreaths of clouds
    which billow above,
    over the head of our queen
    who, as invited,   9175
    now has ascended the sumptuous seat.
    Let us advance
    and, properly grave,
    line up on its steps.
    Let us acclaim, and bless it three times,   9180
    the dignity of this reception!

Everything the CHORUS *has described is enacted in due course. After the*
pages and squires have descended in a long procession, FAUST *appears*
above, at the top of the stairs, in the court dress of a medieval lord, and then
descends slowly and with great dignity.

PANTHALIS (*observing* FAUST *attentively*).
    Unless the gods, as they so often do, have lent
    this man but temporarily his winning presence,
    this outward form that so inspires admiration,
    this stately dignity, he always will succeed   9185
    in what he undertakes—in battles that men fight,
    and minor skirmishes with lovely ladies too.
    He is indeed to be preferred to many a man
    that's held in high esteem whom I have seen myself.
    With slow, grave step, respectfully restrained, I see   9190
    the prince approaching; turn around, o Queen, and look!

FAUST (*advancing, with a* MAN, *fettered, at his side*).
    Instead of fitting ceremonial welcome,
    instead of greeting you with reverence,
    I offer you, fast-bound in chains, this servant
    who, failing in his duty, made me fail in mine.   9195
    Before this noblest lady, on your knees!
    so that you may confess to her your guilt.
    This is the man, great Queen, who was appointed

because of rare acuity of vision
to watch on the high tower and scan   9200
the firmament and earth's expanse to see
whatever may appear in either place,
or move into our valley toward this fortress
from the encircling hills—perhaps great flocks
in waves, perhaps an army; them we protect,   9205
this intercept. Today, what negligence!
You come, but he does not announce your presence;
a most exalted guest is not received
with proper honors. By this crime he's lost
his life, should now be lying in the blood   9210
of death deserved, except that it is yours
alone to punish, as you choose, or pardon.
HELEN. Since you grant me the lofty dignity
   of judge and regent—even if this be,
   as I conjecture, meant but as a test—   9215
   I shall fulfill the law's first duty now,
   grant the accused a hearing. You may speak!
LYNCEUS, THE WATCHMAN.
     Let me kneel and gaze upon her,
     whether I'm to live or die,
     for I am the slave already   9220
     of this Lady sent from heaven.
      Waiting for the dawning glory,
     looking eastward for the sun,
     suddenly I saw it rising
     by some magic in the south.   9225
      Drawn that way, my eyes now sought,
     not the valleys or the hills,
     firmament or earth's expanse,
     but this one and only Sun.
      Though endowed with sharp, clear vision,   9230
     like the lynx on its tall tree,
     now I felt as if I strove
     to escape from dream-like darkness.
      How was I to find my bearings,
     see the barbican, the gate?   9235
     But the swirling mists soon vanish,
     for this goddess now appears!
      Turning eye and heart towards her,
     I imbibed the gentler light;
     beauty of such blinding splendor   9240
     blinded me completely too;
      I forgot my watchman's duties

and the horn I'd sworn to sound.
You may threaten to destroy me;
beauty, though, subdues all anger.   9245
HELEN. It is not fitting that I punish guilt
that I have caused. Alas, what cruel fate
I suffer, everywhere so to confound
the hearts of men that they will neither spare
themselves nor anything we venerate.   9250
Stealing, seducing, fighting, snatching back and forth,
demigods, heroes, gods, dead spirits too,
have led me, much bewildered, to and fro;
my single self wrought great confusion, my double more,
and now a third and fourth add woe to woe.   9255
Dismiss this worthy man, let him be freed;
may no blame smite one whom the gods make mad!   [*Exit* LYNCEUS.
FAUST. I am amazed, o Queen, to see together
both the sure archer and the target struck;
I see the bow that sped the arrow forth,   9260
and him it wounded. Arrow follows arrow,
striking me too. I sense their feathered whir
on every side, in every castle room.
What, now, am I? You suddenly make rebels
of my most trusted vassals, and unsafe   9265
my walls. I therefore fear my troops may soon
obey this conquering-unconquered lady.
What choice have I but to entrust to you
myself and what I foolishly thought mine?
Here at your feet in fealty and homage   9270
let me acknowledge as my Lady you,
whose coming won you state and throne at once.
Enter LYNCEUS *with a casket, followed by men carrying other chests.*
LYNCEUS.You see, o Queen, that I return!—
a rich man comes to beg one look
and, seeing you, at once he feels   9275
both penury and princely wealth.
What was I then, what am I now?
What can one wish to have or do?
A piercing gaze has lost its worth
and ricochets from where you sit.   9280
We made our way here from the East
in hordes so vast that those in front
knew nothing of those coming last,
and soon the West had had its day.
If the first fell, the second stood,   9285
and then a third came with his lance—
a hundred's strength sustained each man,

the thousands slain went unremarked.
    We drove ahead, we surged along,
were masters everywhere in turn,   9290
and where one day I ruled as lord,
another robbed and stole the next.
    We'd take a hurried look around,
then one would seize the prettiest girl,
the next a bull with good, firm legs;   9295
no horse was ever left behind.
    But what I liked was looking for
the rarest items to be found,
and what some other person had   9300
was only withered grass to me.
    I went in search of precious things
and followed where my keen eye led;
I looked in every sack and bag,
no chest held secrets for my eyes.
    And so I soon had piles of gold   9305
and, best of all, of precious stones:
this emerald now alone deserves
to shine resplendent on your heart.
    This oval drop from ocean depths
should float between your ear and lips,   9310
where rubies would be put to flight,
made pallid by your roseate cheek.
    And so I bring before your throne
a treasure without counterpart;
let us now lay here at your feet   9315
the yield of many blood-stained frays.
    Although I bring you many chests,
I have still others, made of iron;
let me become your pursuivant,
and I will fill your treasure vaults.   9320
    No sooner are you on this throne
than mind and wealth and sovereignty
already are your slaves and bow
before your beauty's perfect form.
    What I clung to and claimed as mine   9325
is liberated now, is yours;
I thought it precious, grand and fine,
but now I see it had no worth.
    What I possessed has disappeared,
is grass that withers when cut down.   9330
O let one gladdening look from you
give its full value back to it!
FAUST. Quickly remove these spoils your bravery has gained;

leave unreproved, yet not rewarded either.
For all is hers already that this castle 9335
hides in its depths; to offer her some part
can have no point. Go and arrange our treasures
in ordered piles; display a glorious picture
of splendors yet unseen! Make vaulted ceilings
glitter like fresh-created skies; create 9340
new paradises filled with lifeless life!
Anticipating her each step, unroll
a chain of flowered carpets! Let her step
encounter gentle ground, her eye alight
on splendor that will blind all but the gods. 9345
LYNCEUS. Your command is without force,
    to obey it, almost farce
    since our lives and wealth now are
    subject to her beauty's power.
    The whole army has been tamed, 9350
    swords are blunted, strong arms lamed;
    set beside this glorious form,
    even the sun is dull, lukewarm;
    set against such loveliness,
    all is empty nothingness!   [*Exit.* 9355
HELEN (*to* FAUST).
I wish to speak with you, but you must come
up here, be at my side. The empty seat
summons its owner and ensures me mine.
FAUST. First let me·kneel and by my act of homage,
noble lady, obtain your grace, then kiss 9360
the hand that raises me to sit beside you.
Confirm me as co-regent of your realm
that knows no bounds, and in one person gain
a worshiper, a vassal, a protector!
HELEN. I see and hear so many marvelous things; 9365
I am amazed, would ask you many questions.
Could you explain why that man's way of speaking
sounded so strange to me—strange and yet pleasant?
Sounds seem to be in concord with each other,
and when one word's been welcomed by the ear, 9370
another comes to give it a caress.
FAUST. If you already like the way our peoples speak,
I'm sure their singing will delight you too,
will fully satisfy both ear and mind.
Delay is dangerous—let's practice it at once; 9375
responses are what tempt us to employ it.
HELEN. Then tell me how I too can learn the art.

FAUST. It's simple: let the words well from your heart.
And when your soul is filled with yearning's flame,
you look around and ask
HELEN.   who feels the same.   9380
FAUST. There is no past or future in an hour like this,
the present moment only
HELEN.   is our bliss.
FAUST. It is all things we ever could demand.
What confirmation does it need?
HELEN.   My hand.
CHORUS. Who would dare to blame our princess   9385
        for the friendliness she shows
        toward this castle's lord?
        Let us not forget that all of us
        still are captives—as so often
        since the shameful fall of Troy   9390
        and in the fearsome labyrinth
        of woes through which we've journeyed.
            Women who are used to lovers
        make their choice without delay,
        for they have great expertise.   9395
        To shepherd boys with golden hair,
        or to swarthy fauns perhaps—
        it depends on circumstance—
        they cede impartially all rights
        to their voluptuous limbs.   9400
            She and he are now sitting closer
        and lean against each other;
        shoulder to shoulder, knee next to knee,
        hand in hand, they are lulled
        on their throne's   9405
        deeply cushioned magnificence.
        Majesty can allow itself
        the carefree display
        to the eyes of its people
        of its private affections and joys.   9410
HELEN. I feel so far away and yet so near,
and only want to say: I'm here! I'm here!
FAUST. I tremble, faint of breath, can hardly speak;
all is a dream, and time and space have fled.
HELEN. My life seems past, and yet is somehow new;   9415
I know you not, a stranger, but I live in you.
FAUST. Do not be puzzled by a fate uniquely yours!
Though life be but a moment, our duty is to be.
                Enter PHORKYAS, *precipitously.*

PHORKYAS. Must you study in love's primer,
    ponder what it means to dally,   9420
    idly muse on lovers' pratings,
    even though the time is wrong?
    Don't you feel a coming storm?
    Listen to the trumpet sounding,
    danger is not far away.   9425
    Menelaus with his legions
    is approaching to attack you;
    arm yourselves for bitter fighting!
    Overwhelmed by all these victors,
    mutilated like Deiphobus,   9430
    you will rue your chivalry.
    Once these cheaper goods are dangling
    there will be a fresh-honed axe,
    for your lady, at the altar.
FAUST. Rash interruption, odious intrusion! Even   9435
   when dangers exist I hate foolish impetuousness.
   Bad news makes fairest messengers ill-favored,
   but you, the ugliest, enjoy ill tidings only.
   This time your effort's wasted, though, and so you may
   shatter the air with empty sound. Here is not danger,   9440
   and any danger would be but an empty threat.
(*Signals, explosions from the towers, trumpets and cornets, martial music.*
               A powerful armed force marches past.)
    Now you shall quickly see assembled
    a loyal company of heroes:
    he alone deserves his lady's favor
    who has the strength to give her full protection.   9445
(*To the leaders of the troops, who detach themselves from their columns
                  and come forward.*)
    With your bated, quiet anger
    you surely will gain victory—
    you youthful blossoms from the North,
    you, from the East, the flower of strength.
      Encased in steel, its armor flashing,   9450
    the host that crushed so many states
    appears, and then the earth is shaken;
    they march away, and thunder still is heard.
      We came to Pylos, there we landed;
    old Nestor is alive no longer,   9455
    and soon our unchecked army sunders
    the bonds uniting petty kings. –
      No more delay! Back from these walls
    drive Menelaus to the sea!

There, as was his fatal inclination,   9460
he can rove, waylay, and plunder.
    I am—this Sparta's queen commands—
to hail each one of you as Duke;
lay hills and valleys at her feet,
and what she gains will be your fiefs.   9465
    With walls and ramparts, German Prince,
you must defend the bays of Corinth;
you, Goth, are ordered to attack
Achaia with its hundred passes.
    Our Frankish troops shall move on Elis,   9470
the Saxons are assigned Messene,
and Normans, when they've cleared the sea,
shall bring Argolis glory.
    Then, settled down, you will reserve
the might of arms for foreign foes—   9475
this under Sparta's sovereignty
which is our queen's ancestral home.
    While she sees each of you enjoy
dominions that shall want for nothing,
her throne will guarantee your rights,   9480
assure you of enlightened justice.

FAUST *descends from the throne; the Princes form a circle about him to*
receive special commands and instructions.

CHORUS. He who wants the fairest as his,
    let him above all be able
    and, in his wisdom, attend to his weapons.
    With flattery he may have won   9485
    what he most prizes on earth,
    but it is not easily kept:
    devious flattery can lure her away,
    robbers' daring tear her from him;
    lest this occur, he must have foresight!   9490
      This is why I praise our prince,
    and rate him higher than others:
    so wisely has he chosen brave companions
    that men of strength stand ready
    to obey his every nod.   9495
    What he orders, they loyally do—
    each benefits himself and gains
    liberal thanks from his master—
    thus both vassal and lord gain glory.
      Who, now, can tear her away   9500
    from his power and possession?
    She is his, and he surely deserves her—

doubly, we think, since we share
the protection he gives her: impregnable walls
and, without, an invincible army.   9505
FAUST. Now they have all been splendidly rewarded;
each holds in fief, as generous gift,
some prosperous land. Let them march off!
We, at the center, will stand fast,
and they will eagerly protect   9510
this almost-island in the dancing waves
that by a slender chain of hills
is linked to Europe's outmost mountain spur!
May every nation share the joys
of this, the sunniest land of all,   9515
that now is conquered for my queen,
to whom it lifted once its eyes
when as Eurotas' rushes whispered,
she burst resplendent from the shell
to dazzle her royal mother's eyes   9520
and those of her two brothers also.
This land that looks to none but you,
that offers you its whole abundance—
prefer it, as your native land,
to all the realms that now are yours!   9525
Although its jagged heights and ridges
must be content with cold rays from the sun,
one still can glimpse rocks tinged with green
and goats that forage for their scanty fare.
A spring wells forth, the streams unite and plunge,   9530
and soon ravines and slopes and meadows all are green.
Upon the many hills that dot the plain
you see spread out the moving flocks of sheep.
Cattle, careful not to crowd each other,
come singly to the precipice's edge;   9535
still, there is shelter for them all within
the many caves that arch the walls of rock.
Pan guards them there, while nymphs as living creatures dwell
in the moist freshness of shrub-filled ravines
and, in their urgent search for air and light,   9540
the close-set trees raise high their heavy branches.
Primeval woods! The mighty oak stands motionless
with boughs that branch capriciously;
the generous maple with its sugar-sap
rises uncluttered and bears its weight with ease.   9545
And in the shaded stillness the warm flow
of mother's milk provides for lamb and child;

on nearby plains ripe fruit is found,
and honey trickles from the hollow branch.
 Contentment is a birthright here,   9550
and cheerful cheek and lip express serenity;
all are immortal where they are,
for they are satisfied, are healthy.
 And so, in this untroubled brightness,
each precious child attains maturity.   9555
We see this miracle, and are compelled to ask:
must these be gods, or are they mortal men?
 Among the shepherds here, and in their guise,
Apollo was no fairer than the fairest,
for when the sway of nature is unhindered   9560
all realms of being merge as one.
     (*He seats himself beside* HELEN.)
 Now that we have achieved this oneness,
let what is past, be past forever!
Remember the high god who gave you being,
that only in this primal world do you belong!   9565
 No mighty fortress need confine you!
Arcadia, while near to Sparta,
is a domain of ever-youthful vigor
where we can dwell in perfect bliss.
 When you were lured to flee to this fair soil 9570
fate granted you its greatest favor!
Our thrones shall now become a bower,
our happiness Arcadian and free!

The stage set changes completely. Enclosed arbors rest against a series of
grottos. A

SHADED GROVE

extends to the cliffs that rise on all sides. FAUST *and* HELEN *are not visible.*
About the stage lie members of the CHORUS, *sleeping.*
PHORKYAS. I do not know how long these girls have been asleep,
 or whether in their dreams they can have dreamt the things 9575
 that I have seen so clearly with these very eyes.
 This being so, I'll wake them. They will be amazed,
 and you their bearded elders too, who sit down there
 hoping these marvels may be plausibly explained. –
 Up from your beds! Just hurry, give your curls a toss! 9580
 And clear your eyes of sleep! Stop blinking! Hear me speak!
CHORUS.
 Go ahead and speak! Do tell us all the marvels that have happened!
 What we would most like to hear is something quite incredible,

since we find it very boring to keep looking at these cliffs.

PHORKYAS.

Are you children bored already, though you've scarcely rubbed your

eyes?

Listen, then! Here in these caverns, grottos, bowers, was provided
for our lord and for our lady, just as for idyllic lovers,
shelter and security.

CHORUS.   What, there! Inside?

PHORKYAS.   There, isolated

from the world, they called on me, alone, to serve them privately.
Highly flattered, I stayed near them, but did not abuse their trust;   9590
thus I kept my eyes averted, going off one way or other
to collect roots, barks, and mosses, since I know their special virtues,
and the pair was left alone.

CHORUS.

You make it sound as if inside there one might find entire worlds—
lakes and streams, and woods and meadows. You are quite a story-

teller!

PHORKYAS.

Yes, one might, you innocents; down there are depths no man has fath-

omed!

Musing, I investigated rooms and courtyards never ending.
Suddenly a peal of laughter echoes through the spacious grottos;
lo! a boy is leaping from our lady's lap into her consort's,
then from there back to his mother; I am deafened by alternate   9600
sounds of cooing and caresses, of love's silly, playful banter,
sportive cries, and shouts of joy.

Naked, faunlike but not bestial, a true wingless genius,
he leaps down and hits the ground there, and the solid earth, reacting,
bounces him a long way upwards, and his second or third leap   9605
lets him touch the vaulted roof.

Then his mother cries, much worried: Keep on bouncing all you please,
but be sure you don't try flying; power of flight has been denied you!
And his caring father warns him: Earth possesses the resilience
which propels you ever higher; let your toe but touch the ground,   9610
and at once you will be strengthened like the son of Earth, Antaeus!
Then he leaps atop these massive cliffs and, like a batted ball,
soon is bouncing every which way from one ridge-crest to another.
Suddenly he disappears, gone in the fissure of a gorge,
and it seems that we have lost him. Mother weeps as father comforts;
worrying, I shrug my shoulders. But he reappears, and how!
Are there treasures lying hid there? He has donned, now, flowered

robes,

sumptuous and dignified.

From his arms there dangle tassels, ribbons flow about his breast;

like a miniature Apollo, in his hands the golden lyre,   9620
he steps to the cornice-rim, all self-assurance; we're astounded.
And his parents, captivated, clasp each other, heart to heart.
How his head is bathed in radiance! What the gleam is, is uncertain—
is it goldwork, or the blazing of a never-daunted soul?
Every gesture, every motion, now proclaims him, still a boy,   9625
future master of all beauty, one within whom there shall live
all eternal melody; it is as such that you shall hear,
and as such that you shall see him, to your infinite amazement.
CHORUS. This, then, is your marvel,
      daughter of Crete?   9630
      Can you never have listened
      to what the poets have taught us?
      Have you not heard the rich store
      of Ionia's legends,
      ancient tales of heroes and gods,   9635
      the old fables of Hellas?
        All that happens today,
      whatever it be,
      is but a dreary echo
      of the great days of our forebears;   9640
      the story you tell can't compare
      with what pleasing invention,
      more believable than truth,
      sang of the son of Maia.
        Chattering gossips, his nurses,   9645
      foolishly lacking in foresight,
      wrap the infant just born,
      prettily little but sturdy,
      in purest, downiest diapers,
      in richly embroidered swaddling bands.   9650
      In no time, however, the rascal,
      little but sturdy and cunning,
      is freeing his tender limbs,
      fully supple already,
      and the purple shawl that confined him,   9655
      he leaves in place of himself—
      like a butterfly ready for life
      and unfolding its wings as it agilely
      slips from pupal confinement
      and ventures, wantonly fluttering,   9660
      into the sunlit air's radiance.
        Even so he, agile indeed,
      demonstrates promptly now
      by his skill and adroitness

that as guardian genius he always   9665
    will favor the thief and the rascal,
    and all who are eager for profit.
    Soon from the Lord of the Sea he has stolen
    the trident and, right from its sheath,
    slyly Ares' own sword,   9670
    as well as Phoebus' arrow and bow,
    and the tongs of Hephaestus,
    and would, but for fear of fire,
    take even Zeus' lightning, his father's;
    but he does, by tripping him up,   9675
    vanquish Eros as wrestler
    and steal, while Cypria holds him,
    from off her bosom the girdle.

Pleasing, purely melodic music of stringed instruments is heard from the grotto. All listen attentively, and soon seem deeply affected by it. – From this point to the pause after v. 9938 there is full musical accompaniment.

PHORKYAS. Hear those strains of lovely music,
    liberate yourselves from myth!   9680
    Do not cling to ancient gods—
    a sorry lot that's now passé.
        What you say, no more has meaning;
    we today are more exacting:
    nothing can affect our hearts   9685
    that does not have its source in feeling.
                    PHORKYAS *moves back to the cliffs.*

CHORUS.   Dreaded creature who can like
    these ingratiating sounds,
    we, who've been restored to life,
    know that we are moved to tears.   9690
        Let the sun's light lose its splendor
    now that dawn is bright within us
    and we find within ourselves
    what the world will not provide.

Enter HELEN, FAUST, *and* EUPHORION *in the costume already described.*

EUPHORION. If you hear the songs of children,   9695
    their delight is yours as well;
    when you see me dance to music,
    your parental hearts dance too.

HELEN. Love, to make us humans happy,
    brings a worthy pair together,   9700
    but to make their pleasure perfect
    it creates a precious Three.

FAUST. All our wishes are fulfilled:
    I am yours, and you are mine;

as we now stand here united   9705
   may we be so evermore!
CHORUS. For this couple there are promised
   many years of family happiness
   in the aura of their child.
   It is all profoundly touching!   9710
EUPHORION. Let me try skipping,
        then let me try leaping!
        Now what I want most,
        want most of all,
        is to go high,   9715
        high up in the sky.
FAUST.   Try to be careful,
        don't take any risks!
        We do not want
        our darling to fall   9720
        and to be badly hurt—
        we wouldn't survive that!
EUPHORION. I won't stick around
        on the ground any longer;
        let go of my hands,   9725
        don't touch my hair,
        leave my clothing alone!
        They're mine, are mine!
HELEN.   Stop and remember
        to whom you belong,   9730
        think how you're hurting us,
        how you're destroying
        the wonderful family
        we three established!
CHORUS.   Their oneness, I fear   9735
        won't last much longer!
HELEN AND FAUST.
        Please, for your parents' sake
        try to control
        this violent excitement.   9740
        Have a nice quiet time
        here in the country!
EUPHORION. Simply to please you
        I'm holding back,
    (*He weaves through the* CHORUS, *drawing them into a dance figure.*)
        am quietly dancing   9745
        with these happy girls.
        Is this kind of motion
        and music all right?

HELEN.   Yes, that's what we like;
           show those young beauties   9750
           how one should dance.

FAUST.   I wish this were over!
           All these mad antics
           make me uneasy.

CHORUS (*singing, as it performs intricate figures with* EUPHORION).
           When your arms move   9755
           with such delicate grace
           and you are tossing
           that bright curly hair,
           when your foot lightly
           glides over the ground   9760
           and, linked all together,
           we whirl and we dance –
           then, lovely boy,
           you've accomplished your aim:
           all of our hearts   9765
           are now become yours.
                       Pause.

EUPHORION. You shall be all
           light-footed does—
           hurry, away,
           to start this new game!   9770
           I'll be the hunter,
           you the ones chased.

CHORUS.   In order to catch us
           you won't need to run,
           for all we desire,   9775
           our ultimate hope,
           is to embrace
           so handsome a creature!   [*Exeunt.*

EUPHORION. Off through the grove
           in every direction!   9780
           I can't bear to have
           what's easily gained;
           only what's conquered
           affords true delight.   [*Exit.*

HELEN AND FAUST.What temerity and madness—   9785
           there's no hope of moderation!
           Hear the sound of hunting horns
           echo in the wood and valley—
           what disorder! What an outcry!

CHORUS (*entering singly, in haste*).
           He raced past each one of us;   9790

scorning us derisively,
now he's dragging back with him
the wildest girl there is among us.
            Enter EUPHORION, *carrying a young girl.*
EUPHORION. Here I bring this stalwart girl
            and shall enjoy what I have won;   9795
            for my pleasure and delight
            I embrace her struggling breast,
            kiss the mouth that shrinks from me,
            demonstrate my stronger will.
GIRL. Let me go! I too possess   9800
            strength of mind and force of soul—
            peer of yours, a woman's will
            does not have to be so pliant.
            Do you think that I am helpless?
            Fool, to trust your arm so much!   9805
            Keep your hold as I enjoy
            letting you burn with flames that scorch!
            (*Bursting into flame, she rises out of sight.*)
            Follow me into the air,
            or into the chilly grave,
            if you'd catch the prize you've lost!   9810
EUPHORION (*shaking off the remnants of flame*).
            How can I stay here,
            cramped by these cliffs
            in the midst of a forest—
            youth is still vital!
            There *are* winds that roar   9815
            and billows that thunder.
            I hear them now distantly!
            O, to be near!
            EUPHORION *leaps ever farther up the cliffs.*
HELEN, FAUST, AND CHORUS.
            Must you play the mountain goat!
            Our great fear is that you'll fall.   9820
EUPHORION. Higher still—I must climb higher,
            gain an ever broader view!
            Now I know where I am!
            This is the center   9825
            of Pelops' island,
            kin to both earth and sea.
CHORUS.   Can't you endure
            peaceful mountains and woods?
            Let us now gather
            grapes in the vineyards,   9830

                    grapes on the hillside,
                    figs, and gold apples.
                    Stay and be good
                    in this land that's so good!
EUPHORION. Do you dream that there's peace?   9835
                    Dream on, if you must!
                    War! is the countersign,
                    Win! the echoing shout.
CHORUS.   He who in peace-time
                    wants war again,   9840
                    has bidden farewell
                    to hope and its joys.
EUPHORION. Those this endangered land
                    bore to face danger,
                    free and courageous,   9845
                    not stinting their blood,
                    filled with a holy zeal
                    nothing can quench—
                    may, for these fighters,
                    hope be rewarded!   9850
CHORUS. Look! Look up! How high he's climbed,
              though he does not seem to dwindle:
              a warrior on his way to triumphs,
              wielding steel, in brazen armor.
EUPHORION. Walls and moats do not protect them,   9855
                    everyone is self-reliant—
                    the sure fortress for survival
                    is man's unrelenting will.
                    If you want to live unconquered,
                    off to battle, lightly armed!   9860
                    Let your wives be Amazons,
                    and a hero, every child!
CHORUS. May sacred Poetry
                    always rise heavenward!
                    Shine, fairest star,   9865
                    from the distance forever!
                    Yet we still glimpse the light
                    and still hear the song,
                    have cause to rejoice.
EUPHORION. No, this is not a child you see,   9870
                 I am a young man fully armed;
                 companion of strong, free, bold men,
                 in spirit I have shared their deeds.
                    Away!
                    See there,   9875

the path to glory lies before us!

HELEN *and* FAUST. You're no sooner summoned into life
and enjoy a day's serenity
than you yearn, from dizzying steps,
for a place of hurt and pain. 9880
Don't you care
for us at all?
Is the joy we share a dream?

EUPHORION. Hear that thunder on the sea!
It re-echoes through the valleys; 9885
might meets might, in dust, on water—
troop after troop knows agony.
Now, at last,
men understand:
Death! is an imperative. 9890

HELEN, FAUST, *and* CHORUS.
Dreadful word that makes us shudder!
Do you also need to die?

EUPHORION. Should I watch from far away?
No! Their distress and cares are mine.

HELEN, FAUST *and* CHORUS.
Rash pride and peril 9895
together mean death.

EUPHORION. Not so! Wings spread
to sustain me!
I must get there–
let me have flight! 9900

*He flings himself into the air. For a moment his garments support him and
his head radiates light; a luminous tail follows him.*

CHORUS. Icarus! Icarus!
Grievous event!

A handsome young man falls at the feet of HELEN *and* FAUST; *the body
suggests a well-known figure, but disappears immediately as the aureole
rises skywards like a comet while the garments remain on the stage.*

HELEN *and* FAUST. Brief joy has ended
in merciless pain.

EUPHORION (*from below*). Mother, don't leave me here 9905
down in the darkness, alone!
Pause.

CHORUS (*dirge*).
Not alone, no matter where you are!
for we know who you must be;
you may hasten from this life,
but our hearts are always with you. 9910
It is hard to express sadness

for a fate we praise and envy:
whether day was bright or dreary,
your bold song had lofty beauty.
   Although born for this world's blessings,   9915
endowed with strength and of high lineage,
soon you sacrificed your birthright
and an early blossom died:
eyes that clearly saw the world,
empathy with every feeling,   9920
ardent love for woman's worth,
and a music all your own.
   But your headlong rush enmeshed you
in the snare that saps our will,
and you made yourself the foe   9925
of propriety and law;
yet at last a pure high purpose
filled your soul again with substance;
you had hopes of great achievement—
you were not fated to succeed.   9930
   Who can succeed? Somber question
that, as all mankind lies bleeding,
speechless, on a day of doom,
muffled fate declines to answer. –
Now strike up new songs once more,   9935
be no longer deeply bowed;
earth will engender songs again
as it always has before.

            Complete pause. The music ceases.

HELEN (*to* FAUST).

An ancient saw, alas! holds true for me as well:
beauty and happiness can form no lasting union.   9940
The bond of love, the tie to life, are torn asunder;
I mourn for both and, with a sorrowful farewell,
I fling myself, this one more time, into your arms. –
Persephoneia, now receive this youth and me!

  HELEN *embraces* FAUST *and vanishes, leaving her robes and veil in his*
                                 arms.

PHORKYAS (*to* FAUST).

Hang on to what, after all this, is left you!   9945
That dress—hold on to it! Already daemons
eager to drag it to the underworld,
are snatching at its corners. Hang on tight!
No longer your lost goddess, still it has
celestial attributes. Turn to account   9950
this priceless gift and soar on it aloft!

As long as you endure it will transport you
through the skies, far from the common world.
We'll meet again—far, far away from here.

HELEN'S *garments, dissolving into clouds, envelop* FAUST, *lift him up, and
carry him away.*

PHORKYAS (*picking up* EUPHORION'S *clothes and lyre and advancing to the
proscenium, where he raises them aloft*).

Here is another lucky find! 9955
I'm well aware the flame's gone out,
but doubt the world feels any loss.
Enough is left to get your poets started
and make for bitter competition in their trade;
although I can confer no talents, 9960
at least I have some clothing I can lend them.

PHORKYAS *sits down beside a column of the proscenium.*

PANTHALIS. Come, quickly, girls! No more befuddled by that hag
from ancient Thessaly, we're rid at last of magic spells
and of that roar of jingling, complicated notes
that disconcert the ear and, even more, the mind. 9965
Now down to Hades! where our queen, with measured tread,
has gone so swiftly. Let her faithful servants' feet
follow directly, step by step, the path she trod.
We'll find her at the throne of the Inscrutable.

CHORUS. Queens, as well we know, remain happy everywhere; 9970
even in Hades they outrank all others,
are proud companions of their peers
and intimates of Queen Persephone.
We, however, in the background—
distant fields of asphodel— 9975
placed beside long rows of poplars,
and a mass of barren willows,
what entertainment will we have?
Some bat-like kind of squeaking,
dreary words in ghostly whispers! 9980

PANTHALIS. Those who have earned no fame and lack high purpose
belong to elemental matter—so, begone!
My ardent, loyal desire is to join my queen;
no less than merit, faith preserves identity. [*Exit.*

CHORUS. We have been restored to the day and its light; 9985
that we are persons no longer,
we are well aware—
but to Hades we need never return.
Now, as ever-living Nature
claims us spirits as her own, 9990
we make our valid claims of her.

A PART OF THE CHORUS.

Here amid these myriad branches, softly stirring, gently rustling,
we shall lure with our endearments, from the roots, the springs of life
into each bough and, now with leafage, now with blossoms in

abundance,
ornament the fluttering tresses, freed to prosper in the air.　　　9995
When the fruits drop, there will gather gladdened herds and happy

people,
pressing briskly, coming quickly, eager to collect and taste them;
all will then bend down around us, as if to the primal gods.

A SECOND PART.

We, in gentle undulation, will caress these precipices
clinging to their even surface, now a distant-gleaming mirror;　　　10,000
to all sounds we'll be attentive, to song of birds, to reedy pipings,
prompt to answer all the voices, even Pan's terrific cry;
murmurs we return as murmurs; when it thunders, then our thunder
doubly, triply, tenfold answers with its own augmented roll.

A THIRD PART.

Sisters! We, more fond of motion, will pursue the hurrying streams,
lured to seek those distant ranges with their hills so richly mantled;
going always downwards, lower, with meandering waves we'll water
first the pasture, next the meadows, then the garden by the house
whose existence is denoted by the tips of cypress rising
over landscape, placid water, and the shore along a river.　　　10,010

THE FOURTH PART.

You may go as suits your wishes! Gently sighing, we'll encircle
closely planted slopes and hillsides where the well-staked vine grows
green; there the vintner's constant presence will afford us demonstration
of his loving patient labors and their never sure success.
As he toils with hoe or shovel, while he's hilling, pruning, tying,　　　10,015
all the gods receive his prayers—Phoebus, though, most frequently.
The voluptuary, Bacchus, disregards his faithful servant
and reclines in cave or arbor, prattling with the youngest faun;
all that he has ever needed for his semi-drunken visions
can be seen beside his grottos, in their everlasting coolness　　　10,020
stored for him in wineskins, amphorae, and other vessels.
After all the gods together—Helios the most of all—
have piled high the grapes they fanned and moistened, warmed and heated,
suddenly there's life and motion where the quiet vintner labored,
noise amid the year's new leafage, scurrying from vine to vine.　　　10,025
Baskets creak and buckets rattle, dossers groan on bearers' backs;
all moves toward the giant winevat and the treaders' sturdy dance;
thus, then, is the sacred plenty of the pure-born juicy berry
rudely crushed; to foam and splatter, all becomes an ugly mash.

Now we hear a piercing clangor, brasses clash and gongs are struck:
from the veil of mysteries, lo! Dionysus has emerged;
he appears with his attendants, satyrs whirling satyresses,
and all the while there's the wild braying of Silenus' long-eared beast.
No decorum any longer—it's been crushed by cloven feet!
All the senses whirl, are giddy, every ear is cruelly deafened.   10,035
Drunkards grope for cups and glasses, heads are splitting, paunches bursting;
but if someone urges caution, he but makes their passions wilder:
to provide new wine with storage, last year's wineskins must be emptied!
The curtain falls. PHORKYAS, *in the proscenium, rises to a gigantic height,
then steps down from the cothurni, pushes back mask and veil, and stands
revealed as* MEPHISTOPHELES, *prepared to comment on the play, as much
as may be necessary, in an epilogue.*

Act IV

HIGH MOUNTAINS

Rugged, serrated peaks. A cloud floats in and touches a peak, then settles on
a projecting ledge; it then divides.
FAUST (*stepping forth from the cloud*).

As my eyes see the utter solitude below
I step with care onto the margin of these peaks   10,040
and send away the cloud that during sunlit days
softly transported me across the land and sea.
It slowly separates from me without dispersing.
The greater part, a massive sphere, is pressing eastward,
followed by my admiring and astonished gaze: 10,045
although its changing billows, as they move, divide,
it seems to shape a figure. – Yes, my eyes are right! –
I see, stretched out in sun-gilt splendor on a couch,
a gigantic, yet still godlike, woman's form.
In its majestic loveliness it hovers there   10,050
within my sight, resembling Juno, Leda, Helen!
Already it moves on! Like distant icy masses
piled high upon each other, there in the east it stays,
a dazzling symbol of these fleeting days' vast import.
    Yet one bright tenuous streak of mist still hovers near   10,055
and cheers me with its cool caress on heart and brow.
Lightly it rises, hesitates, goes higher still,
and draws together, – Am I entranced by a mirage
of what, when young, I valued most, but lost long since?
Deep in my heart youth's first rich springs well up; I see   10,060
the image of love's dawn, its carefree happiness—
that swiftly felt, first, scarcely comprehended vision
which, had it lasted, would surpass all other treasures.
Like inward beauty of the soul the lovely form
grows clearer, rises, not dissolving, to the ether,   10,065
and draws away with it my best and inmost self.
A seven-league boot plumps itself down, immediately followed by another;
after MEPHISTOPHELES *has stepped down from them, they stride quickly*
away.
MEPHISTOPHELES. I'd call that making proper progress! –
But tell me now, what's gotten into you
and made you land amid the horror
of these hideous maws of rock?   10,070
I know them well, though not in this location,
since they once paved the floor of hell.
FAUST. You're never at a loss for silly legends,
and now, I see, you're going to offer me another.

MEPHISTOPHELES (*with gravity*).

When God, our lord—for reasons I well understand—   10,075
banished us from the skies down to those lowest depths
where all about a glowing core
eternal fire feeds on its own flames,
we found ourselves, despite—too much—good light,
in very cramped, uncomfortable quarters.   10,080
We devils all began to cough,
emitting puffs from top and bottom;
sulphuric fumes inflated hell
with such a vast amount of reeking gas
that very soon the earth's flat crust,   10,085
thick though it was, could only crack and burst.
What we see now is upside down,
the bottom's now become the top—
this is the basis of those glorious doctrines
that turn all values topsy-turvy.   10,090
And so we fled our over-heated dungeon
and gained new, greater freedom as princes of the air.
I have disclosed a mystery, one long concealed
and only recently revealed to all the world. (Eph. 6, 12.)

FAUST. I—I'll always see in mountains silent grandeur   10,095
and do not ask about their whence or why.
When Nature, from herself, created nature,
she made this globe complete and perfect;
pleased with its peaks and its abysses,
she set the mountains and the rocks in line,   10,100
then formed the easier slopes below
and drew them gently outward to form valleys.
There all is verdant growth, and for her happiness
chaotic madness is redundant.

MEPHISTOPHELES. How you talk! You think that's all as clear as day, 10,105
but one who saw it all knows better.
I was down there when the abyss was seething
and welled up raising floods of flame,
when Moloch's hammer, welding rock to rock,
cast bits of shattered mountains far and wide.   10,110
The heavy chunks lie where they don't belong,
and what ballistic force can be the explanation?
Philosophers and scientists are at a loss:
there is the rock, they say, you'll have to let it lie,
since we are hopelessly confounded by it.   10,115
Only the honest common people know the truth
and, in their ancient wisdom,
are not to be dissuaded from it:

the rock's a miracle, and credit's due to Satan.
My travelers, with the crutch of their credulity,   10,120
hobble along to Devil's Rocks and Bridges.

FAUST. It's interesting to see, I must admit,
the view that devils have of nature.

MEPHISTOPHELES. A fig for yours! Be nature as it may,
I'll stake my life on this: the devil was on hand!   10,125
Our kind are specialists in what's colossal,
upheaval, chaos, violence—you see their signs about you. –
But let me now return to clear and simple language.
Back here upon our earth, has nothing pleased you?
You've now surveyed, in measureless expanses,   10,130
the kingdoms of the world and all their glory. (Matt. 4.)
Yet I suppose, since nothing ever suits you,
that you saw nothing you desired.

FAUST. You're wrong! Something important aroused my interest.
Try guessing!

MEPHISTOPHELES. That won't take too long.   10,135
I'd pick some capital whose center
sustains itself by dreary trade,
with crooked narrow streets and gabled peaks,
a crowded market filled with onions, cabbage, beets,
and meat stalls where flies hang about   10,140
to feast upon the greasy joints;
there you are sure, at any time,
to find activity and noisesome odors;
next, broad streets and spacious squares
pretending to gentility;   10,145
and finally, outside the city gates,
suburbs stretching on for ever.
To top all that, I'd love to watch
the carriages, the noisy traffic,
the teeming ant-like colonies   10,150
that never cease their to and fro.
And if I drove or if I rode,
I'd always be the cynosure
of people by the hundred thousands.

FAUST. That could not ever satisfy me!   10,155
It's nice to see the population grow,
the people make a fairly decent living,
and get some culture and more education—
but you are only training rebels.

MEPHISTOPHELES. And then, aware of my importance,   10,160
I'd build a chateau in some pleasant spot,
converting wood and hill, champaign and farmland,

into a park of great magnificence
with velvet lawns before its walls of verdure,
straight paths, correctly managed shadows,   10,165
cascades that plunge in pairs down rocks,
and jets from every kind of fountain
that rise imposingly while at their sides
a thousand piddling sprays are hissing.
I'd also have less formal residences   10,170
for rendezvous with lovely ladies
and in them spend time without end
in pleasantly gregarious solitude—
I speak of *ladies* for a simple reason:
I always think of beauties in the plural.   10,175
FAUST. Sardanapalus—tawdry, but still quite in fashion!
MEPHISTOPHELES. Perhaps I'll guess what's fired your ambition—
something sublime and daring, I am sure!
Did you, while floating near the moon, not have
the lunatic desire for a lunar voyage?   10,180
FAUST. No, not at all! Here in this world
there still is room enough for deeds of greatness.
Astounding things shall be achieved—I feel
in me the strength that will sustain bold efforts.
MEPHISTOPHELES. So what you want is to win glory?   10,185
It's obvious that you have been with heroines.
FAUST. I wish to rule and have possessions!
Acts alone count—glory is nothing.
MEPHISTOPHELES. Nevertheless, there will be poets glad to tell
posterity what splendid things you did   10,190
and with their folly kindle other folly.
FAUST. What you call folly is no threat to you.
What do you know of human aspirations?
How can your bitter, sharp, and hostile temperament
know what it is that mankind needs?   10,195
MEPHISTOPHELES. Have it your way! What you want will be done;
make me the confidant of all your various whims.
FAUST. The ocean far below attracted my attention;
it surged and rose to towering heights,
then it abated, scattering its waves,   10,200
that hastened to assault the low, broad shore.
And I was vexed—for arrogance,
unbridled blood, will always cause
uneasy feelings in a spirit
that, though free, respects all laws and rights.   10,205
I thought it chance, but looking close I saw
the surge desist, and then roll back and leave

the goal it had so proudly reached;
at certain times what happens is repeated.
MEPHISTOPHELES (*ad spectatores*).
    There's nothing new in this for me to learn;   10,210
    I've known that for a hundred thousand years.
FAUST (*continuing, with passion*).
    The surging sea creeps into every corner,
    barren itself and spreading barrenness,
    expands and grows and rolls, and covers
    a long expanse of ugly desolation.   10,215
    Imbued with strength, wave after wave holds power
    but then withdraws, and nothing's been accomplished—
    a sight to drive me to despair,
    this aimless strength of elemental forces!
    This has inspired me to venture to new heights,   10,220
    to wage war here against these forces and subdue them.
       It can be done! – Although the tides may flood,
    when there's a hill they gently press beyond it;
    however arrogant their motions,
    the slightest mound confronts them proudly,   10,225
    the slightest depth attracts them to itself.
    And so I quickly worked out plans,
    resolving to obtain a precious satisfaction:
    to bar the shore to the imperious sea,
    narrow the limits of the ocean's great expanse,   10,230
    and force the waters back into themselves.
    I've worked out every step within my mind;
    this is what I want, what you must help me do!
A distant sound of drums and martial music is heard from the right-rear of
the audience.
MEPHISTOPHELES. That should be easy! Do you hear distant drums?
FAUST. War once again! Bad news for all who're sensible!   10,235
MEPHISTOPHELES. With war or peace, what's sensible
    is to derive advantage from it.
    You wait and watch for the right moments.
    This is your opportunity. Now, Faustus, seize it!
FAUST. Spare me your enigmatic nonsense!   10,240
    Get to the point, explain what you're proposing!
MEPHISTOPHELES. On my way here it came to my attention
    that the kind Emperor is having problems.
    You know what he is like. When we provided him
    with entertainment and false riches,   10,245
    he thought the whole world could be had for money.
    He was still young when he came to the throne,

and so he drew the false conclusion
that it was proper and commendable
to practice two activities at once—   10,250
to govern, and to lead a life of pleasure.
FAUST. A grave mistake! A ruler's happiness
    must be derived from how he rules;
    he must have lofty strength of purpose,
    but none must know his purposes;   10,255
    his whisper in a faithful ear
    becomes some deed at which mankind will marvel;
    thus he may hold supremacy
    and merit it. – The cult of pleasure is degrading.
MEPHISTOPHELES. That's not our man. He cultivated pleasure!   10,260
    Meanwhile, the empire fell apart in anarchy
    as great and small all feuded with each other,
    as brother banished or slew brother,
    and castle fought with castle, town with town,
    the guilds with the patriciate,   10,265
    and bishops with their chapter and their parish;
    all men were enemies at sight.
    In church they murdered and assassinated;
    outside the towns, no merchant traveled safe.
    Audacity became a common trait—   10,270
    to live was self-defense. – Thus things went on.
FAUST. You mean they staggered, fell, got up again,
    then went head over heels, collapsing in a heap.
MEPHISTOPHELES. And no one dared deplore the situation,
    for all now had the will and right to be important.   10,275
    The paltriest were anybody's equals
    until, at last, the best got tired of the madness.
    Men of ability rebelled, and said:
    Let him be ruler who'll establish order;
    the Emperor can't and won't, so let's hold an election   10,280
    and have a new one give our land new life
    and guarantee each subject's safety;
    thus, in a world that starts afresh,
    we shall let righteousness and peace be wed.
FAUST. That sounds quite clerical.
MEPHISTOPHELES.   Well, there were clerics   10,285
    who, to protect their well-fed paunches,
    played a more active part than did the others.
    Turmoil increased, then it was sanctified,
    and so the Emperor, whose heart we'd lightened,
    marches this way, perhaps to his last battle.   10,290

FAUST. I feel for his distress; he was so kind and easy.

MEPH. Let's see how things are going—while there's life, there's hope!
We'll get him out of this confining valley;
once he is safe, he'll have a thousand chances more,
and who knows how the dice will fall next time?   10,295
If he should win, he'll win his vassals back.

They cross the next lower range of mountains and view the disposition of the army in the valley below, from which the sound of drums and military music arises.

MEPHISTOPHELES. I see they've occupied a good position;
with us beside them, victory is certain.

FAUST. But what can we provide? Illusions,
the empty make-believe of magic!   10,300

MEPHISTOPHELES. The stratagems that win all battles!
Do not relapse into faint-heartedness,
remember what great plans you have:
if we preserve his throne and lands for him,
you'll kneel before the Emperor and get   10,305
the boundless shore you seek as fief.

FAUST. You have performed a lot of feats so far,
so go ahead and win a battle too!

MEPHISTOPHELES. No, you will win it; you shall be
the general in charge today.   10,310

FAUST. It is absurd to put me in command
of matters I don't understand at all.

MEPHISTOPHELES. Leave such things to your General Staff;
you, as field marshal, won't have any worries.
I long since saw war's horrors coming   10,315
and, to help out, created a war-council
of primal mountains' primal-human forces;
he's lucky, who has gathered them together.

FAUST. What's that I see there, bearing arms?
Have you involved the mountaineers?   10,320

MEPHISTOPHELES. No! But I do, like Peter Quince,
provide the quintessence of all of them.

            Enter the THREE MIGHTY MEN. (2 Sam. 23, 8.)

MEPHISTOPHELES. Here come my fellows now! As you can see,
each is a different age and has
a different kind of clothes and armor;   10,325
you'll find that they are worth their salt.

(*Ad spectatores.*) Today you cannot find a child who doesn't dote
on suits of armor or a uniform,
and since they're allegories too,
these wretches will but please the better.   10,330

BULLY (*young, wearing light armor and dressed in motley*).
Whoever tries to stare me down

will feel my fist where he had teeth,
and if he tries to run away,
I'll grab the coward by his hair!
GET-QUICK (*mature, well armed and richly dressed*).
   It's folly to seek pointless brawls—   10,335
   they're nothing but a waste of time.
   Never forget to grab the booty,
   and settle other matters later!
HOLD-ON (*well on in years, heavily armed and unostentatiously dressed*).
   That, too, won't get you very far—
   in the torrential stream of life   10,340
   great wealth is quickly dissipated.
   It's well and good to take, but better still to keep;
   let this old fellow manage things,
   and your reserves will never be depleted.
                  (*All descend to a lower level.*

ON A FOOTHILL

Drums and martial music from below; the imperial tent is being pitched. –
Enter the EMPEROR, *the* GRAND-MASTER, *as* COMMANDING GENERAL, *and*
                     BODYGUARDS.

GENERAL. I still believe it was a prudent plan   10,345
   to have withdrawn and concentrated all our forces
   in this well-situated valley;
   I have high hopes that this will prove the proper choice.
EMPEROR. We'll have to wait and see what happens;
   this half-retreat chagrins me nonetheless.   10,350
GENERAL. Observe, my liege, where our right flank is placed.
   Terrains like this are the tactician's dream:
   the hills, not steep, yet not too easy either,
   will help our troops and cause the enemy trouble;
   we're half concealed here on this rolling land;   10,355
   their cavalry will never dare approach us.
EMPEROR. I can't withhold approval any longer;
   stout arms and hearts now have a chance to test their strength.
GENERAL. Here, at our center, where the fields are flat,
   you see our phalanx, ready to attack;   10,360
   high in the air their pikes reflect the sunlight
   and glitter through the morning haze.
   Thousands of men aflame with love of glory
   there form a great, dark, heaving square!
   This tells us how tremendous are our numbers;   10,365
   I have no doubt they'll split the enemy's forces.
EMPEROR. This is the first time that I've seen them all so well;

an army such as this is worth one twice its size.

GENERAL. About our left flank nothing need be said;
    our bravest men are holding that steep cliff,   10,370
    upon whose rocks you see the flash of weapons,
    and which protects this valley's vital pass.
    It's there that I expect the enemy
    will suffer bloody, unforeseen disaster.

EMPEROR. There they advance, those lying kinsmen   10,375
    who called me Uncle, Cousin, Brother
    as they kept taking ever greater liberties
    and robbed my throne of honor, my scepter of its power,
    who next laid waste our lands with feuds,
    and who have now all joined against me in rebellion.   10,380
    Many have not made up their wavering minds,
    but they will rush along in any torrent's wake.

GENERAL. A trusted man, sent out to reconnoiter,
    is hurrying downhill; let's hope his news is good!

A SCOUT. Thanks to boldness and to cunning   10,385
        we've succeeded in our mission,
        gotten through the lines and back;
        but our news is not too good.
        Many subjects swear they're loyal,
        many troops vow their allegiance;   10,390
        foreign and domestic dangers are
        the excuse for their inaction.

EMPEROR. What egoism teaches is self-preservation,
    not gratitude, affection, duty, honor.
    Do you forget that, when accounts are settled,   10,395
    your neighbor's burning house may burn you out as well?

GENERAL. Here comes a second scout, but his descent is slow,
    his limbs are trembling with fatigue.

SECOND SCOUT. For a while we watched, well pleased,
        riot marching in confusion;   10,400
        suddenly, to our surprise,
        a new emperor appeared,
        and in order multitudes
        now are marching through the field.
        Sheep-like, all are following   10,405
        the false flags that were unfurled!

EMPEROR. An anti-emperor's a benefit to me;
    at last I really feel I'm Emperor.
    I donned this armor simply as a soldier,
    but now I wear it with a nobler purpose.   10,410
    Although at your most splendid tournaments
    all was provided, what I missed was danger;

you only recommended tilting at the rings
while I, with eager heart, desired jousting;
and had you not dissuaded me from waging wars,   10,415
my brilliant exploits would long since have won me glory.
I felt my self-reliance was confirmed
when I beheld myself inside that sphere of flame;
the fearful element pressed in about me,
illusion only, but one truly grand.   10,420
I've had confusing dreams of victory and fame;
I'll now make up what I have wantonly neglected.

HERALDS *are dispatched to challenge the Anti-emperor to single combat. –*
Enter FAUST, *in armor, with half-closed visor, and the* THREE MIGHTY
MEN, *armed and attired as already described.*

FAUST. We hope you won't object to our appearing;
prevision's useful even in untroubled times.
You know that mountain people are deep thinkers,   10,425
can read what nature's written in the rocks.
Spirits, who left the lowland long ago,
are fonder now of mountain rocks than ever;
through labyrinthine crevices they toil
in vapors laden with the gas of precious metals;   10,430
they analyze, they test, they synthesize,
obsessed with making substances unknown before.
With deftness only spirits can possess
they fashion clear transparent forms;
then, in the crystal's everlasting silence,   10,435
they see what happens in the world above.

EMPEROR. I've heard and credit what you say;
but tell me, my good man, how it applies to us.

FAUST. At Norcia lives a Sabine necromancer
who is your loyal, faithful servant.   10,440
How fearful was the fate that menaced him!
The faggots crackled, tongues of fire had appeared;
surrounded by dry piles of interlocking boards,
to which they'd added pitch and sulphur-matches,
he was beyond the help of man, or God, or devil;   10,445
but you released him, Sire, from fiery bondage.
That was in Rome. As your eternal debtor,
he follows your career with deep solicitude.
Ever since then unmindful of himself, he now
consults the stars and underworld for you alone.   10,450
He charged us urgently to hasten to your aid.
Great forces are at work there in the mountains,
where nature is omnipotent and free;
dull-witted priests denounce such things as magic.

EMPEROR. When we salute, on festive days,   10,455
    the cheerful guests who come to share good cheer,
    we watch with pleasure as they push and crowd
    and make our halls seem insufficient.
    But no one is more welcome than the worthy man
    who offers us his help and strength   10,460
    at this precarious morning hour
    controlled by fate's uncertain scales.
    However, at this solemn juncture,
    lift from your ready sword that valiant hand
    and so pay tribute to a moment when, by thousands,   10,465
    men march to fight against or for me.
    A man does things himself! And he who wants a crown and throne,
    must demonstrate that he is worthy of them.
    So let this ghost that's risen up against us,
    that dubs itself the Emperor and claims our lands,   10,470
    that calls itself the army's duke, our princes' liege,
    be thrust by my own hand into the underworld!
FAUST. However that may be, you would be ill-advised
    to risk your person in this noble enterprise.
    Your helmet, with its crest and plume,   10,475
    protects the head that gives our hearts their strength.
    Without a head, what use are limbs?
    If it is sleepy, they all droop;
    if it is hurt, they all share in the wound,
    but are restored as soon as it recovers.   10,480
    The arm is prompt to use its innate strength
    and raise the buckler, lest the head be harmed;
    the sword assumes responsibility at once,
    parries with vigor and returns the blow;
    and then the foot shares aptly in their triumph—   10,485
    it's planted quickly on the slain foe's neck.
EMPEROR. That is my wrath exactly; that's how I'd like to treat him,
    and make his insolent head my footstool.
THE HERALDS (*returning*).
      We enjoyed but scant respect
      and acceptance over there;   10,490
      for our brave and noble challenge
      they had scorn and ridicule:
      "Emperor! He's now forgotten—
      you've an echo in your valley;
      'Once upon a time,' we say,   10,495
      if we think or talk of him."
FAUST. This has turned out as they desired
    who are your best, most loyal supporters. –

The enemy approach, we're eager to see action;
bid us attack, the moment is propitious.   10,500
EMPEROR. At this point I relinquish my command.
(*To the* GENERAL.) Your duties, Prince, are yours again.
GENERAL. Have our right wing advance!
    Before they reach the top, the enemy's left,
    now climbing up this hill,   10,505
    shall flee our tried and true young troops.
FAUST. Permit this lively and courageous youth
    to join these ranks of yours at once;
    assimilated to them, he'll display
    his sterling strength and character.   10,510
            FAUST *points to a figure at his right.*
BULLY (*stepping forward*).
    The man who lets me see his face won't turn away
    with jaw and cheekbones still intact;
    and if he turns his back, his head and hair
    will soon be flopping from a hideous neck.
    And if, while I rampage, your men   10,515
    rain blows with sword and mace,
    the enemy will drop in quick succession
    and drown in their own blood.   [*Exit.*
GENERAL. Let them be followed by the center, slow and prudent;
    our phalanx's total strength will thus engage the foe—   10,520
    our furious forces there, a little to the right,
    have already dealt their battle-plan a blow.
FAUST (*pointing to the second* MIGHTY MAN).
    Let this man too be covered by your order!
    With his élan, he'll give the rest an impetus.
GET-QUICK. The heroism of our Emperor's troops   10,525
    shall have a partner, thirst for plunder;
    and so let's make our common goal
    the Anti-Emperor's sumptuous tent!
    He will not boast a throne much longer,
    with me now at the forefront of this phalanx.   10,530
QUICKLOOT (*camp-follower, clinging to his side*).
    Although I have no marriage lines,
    this is the man whom I love best.
    What a rich harvest now awaits us!
    A woman's never gentle if she's grabbing,
    and if she is a thief, she's merciless—   10,535
    forward to victory, and no holds barred!   [*Exeunt both.*
GENERAL. As was to be expected, their right flank
    attacks our left full-force. To the last man
    our troops are to resist this furious attempt

to take the pass's narrowest stretch.   10,540
FAUST (*beckoning to the left*).
 My lord, pray do not overlook this man;
 it will not hurt to add more strength to strength.
HOLD-ON (*stepping forward*).
 Don't give your left wing further thought!
 Nothing that's held is lost when I am with it;
 though old, I can be trusted as custodian,   10,545
 and even lightning will not break my hold.   [*Exit*
MEPHISTOPHELES (*descending from above*).
 See in the background there of jagged rock
 how now from every gorge armed men
 are issuing in throngs that crowd
 the narrow pathways even more;   10,550
 with helmet, armor, sword, and shield
 they form a rampart at our rear
 that's ready to attack on signal.
(*Aside, for those in the know.*).
 You're not to ask where *they* come from. –
 The fact is, I have not been idle;   10,555
 I've emptied every arms-collection hereabout;
 these suits of armor stood or sat astride
 as if they still controlled this world;
 once knights and kings and emperors,
 they're only empty snail's shells now;   10,560
 ghosts often have used them as finery
 and helped revive some medieval fashions.
 Regardless of what devil's in them,
 today they're sure to be effective.
(*Aloud.*). Hear how they're working up a rage   10,565
 and clank when shoving one another!
 Beside our standards, tattered flags now wave
 that long have waited for some breezes.
 Remember that these are old stock,
 who gladly get involved in modern broils.   10,570
*A tremendous peal of trumpets is heard from above; the enemy forces are
seen to waver.*
FAUST. Darkness has covered the horizon,
 and only here and there are to be seen
 ominous flashes of glowing red;
 weapons already gleam with blood;
 the rocks, the woods, the air, and the whole sky   10,575
 turn crimson too.
MEPHISTOPHELES. Our sturdy right flank holds its own;
 I even see, surpassing all in height,

that nimble giant, Jack the Bully,
plying his trade with customary vigor.   10,580
EMPEROR. Where I saw only one arm raised
  I now can see a dozen flailing;
  what's happening defies the laws of nature.
FAUST. Haven't you heard of those streaks of fog
  that drift along the coasts of Sicily?   10,585
  There, in broad daylight, halfway up the sky,
  mirrored with shimmering clarity
  in exhalations of a special kind,
  one sees a strange mirage:
  cities are swaying to and fro,   10,590
  and gardens floating up and down,
  as image after image cleaves the aether.
EMPEROR. I find it nonetheless disquieting to see
  the tips of all the spears emitting sparks,
  and nimble little flames   10,595
  dancing along our phalanx's glittering lances.
  This is too spectral for my taste.
FAUST. Forgive me, Sire, but those are after-traces
  of long-since vanished spirit beings—
  a light the Dioscuri cast,   10,600
  by whom all sailors used to swear;
  for us they're making one great final effort.
EMPEROR. But tell me whom we owe it to,
  that in our interest Nature has assembled
  her greatest prodigies in this one place.   10,605
MEPHISTOPHELES. To whom but to that noble seer
  whose heart is mindful only of your welfare!
  The violence your enemies have threatened
  caused him the most profound distress.
  His gratitude insists that you be rescued,   10,610
  though this might mean his own destruction.
EMPEROR. To celebrate, the Romans took me everywhere in triumph;
  at last I was important, and I wished to prove it;
  and so, not really thinking, I saw fit
  to give his white beard somewhat cooler air.   10,615
  Because I spoiled their entertainment,
  the clergy ceased to be my strong supporters.
  Now, after all these years, am I to see
  the consequences of a carefree deed?
FAUST. Instinctive kindness is a good investment: 10,620
  look there, up in the sky; unless I err,
  your friend's about to send a portent!
  Now watch; its meaning will be soon made clear.

EMPEROR. An eagle's soaring high above us,
    pursued and threatened by an angry griffin.   10,625
FAUST. Keep watching! To my mind, this augurs well:
    a griffin's but a beast of fable—
    how can it so forget its limitations
    that it dares challenge a real eagle?
EMPEROR. Now they are wheeling in great circles   10,630
    about each other; now each rushes
    at the same instant at the other,
    eager to claw the other's breast and throat.
FAUST. See how the hateful griffin, torn and mauled,
    has suffered all the hurt; see how,   10,635
    with drooping lion's tail, it plunges
    into the trees atop that hill and disappears.
EMPEROR. May the event confirm the omen,
    which I accept amazedly.
MEPHISTOPHELES (*looking toward the right*).
    Pressure from sustained assaults   10,640
    forces them to yield the field,
    and in aimless skirmishes
    they are pushing toward their right;
    this disrupts the battle-order
    of their main contingent's left.   10,645
    Our unwavering phalanx's spearhead,
    moving right, with lightning speed
    dashes toward that weak position.
    Now, like splashing storm-tossed waves,
    equal forces in their furious rage   10,650
    meet together in this duel;
    this surpasses all our hopes,
    we've already won the battle!
EMPEROR (*on the left, to* FAUST).
    Look! I think there's something wrong;
    on the left our outpost's threatened.   10,655
    I don't see them hurling stones;
    lower ledges have been scaled,
    higher ones have been abandoned.
    See! – Concerted masses of the foe,
    pressing ever nearer now,   10,660
    may have seized the pass already—
    end result of godless efforts!
    In vain are all your stratagems.
                              Pause.
MEPHISTOPHELES. There is my pair of ravens coming—
    I wonder what their message is?   10,665

It's possible that something's wrong.

EMPEROR. What do these dismal birds portend?
　　The way their sable sails are set,
　　they've come from that fierce mountain-fray.

MEPHISTOPHELES (*to the ravens*).
　　Perch here, close to my ears.　　　　　　　　　　　　　　10,670
　　No one is lost who has your patronage;
　　advice you give is good to follow.

FAUST (*to the* EMPEROR).
　　You've surely heard how homing pigeons
　　return from the most distant lands
　　to where they nest and feed their young.　　　　　　　　10,675
　　Here it's the same, with an important difference:
　　a dove may carry peace-time mail,
　　but war requires somber messengers.

MEPHISTOPHELES. The news they bring is dire:
　　see how, up on those heights of rock,　　　　　　　　　10,680
　　our soldier-heroes stand endangered!
　　The near-by heights already have been scaled,
　　and should the pass itself be taken,
　　our own position will be critical.

EMPEROR. Then I am now betrayed completely!　　　　　　10,685
　　The net into which you have drawn me
　　gave me the horrors from the very start.

MEPHISTOPHELES. Do not despair! All is not lost.
　　Patience and cunning will resolve the plot—
　　things often look their worst, close to the end.　　　　　10,690
　　I've messengers on whom I can rely;
　　command that I be given the command!

GENERAL (*who has moved to the* EMPEROR'S *side*).
　　That you allied yourself with these two men
　　has bothered me right from the start;
　　no lasting good can come from magic.　　　　　　　　　10,695
　　I can't control the course of battle;
　　since they began it, let them end it;
　　I'm giving back the marshal's baton.

EMPEROR. Keep it until some better time
　　that fortune may bestow on us.　　　　　　　　　　　　10,700
　　This villain and his raven-friends
　　fill me with horror and disgust.

(*To* MEPHISTOPHELES.)
　　I can't entrust this staff to you,
　　who do not seem the proper man;
　　but take command, avert defeat,　　　　　　　　　　　10,705
　　and let what can be done, be done!

The EMPEROR, *with the* GRAND-MASTER, *withdraws into his tent.*

MEPHISTOPHELES. I hope his baton will protect him;
    it wouldn't be much use to us—
    it had some cross or other on it.

FAUST. What must we do?

MEPHISTOPHELES.   All has been done! –   10,710
    Now, my black cousins who're such eager servants,
    be off to the great mountain-lake, and ask—
    politely—the undines to lend us a mock-flood.
    They know the trick, that is a woman's secret,
    of separating semblance from reality,   10,715
    so all will swear that what they see is real.
                            Pause.

FAUST. It's clear our ravens' flattery
    has stirred your water sprites profoundly;
    I see a trickle there already.
    Freshets are gushing forth in various places   10,720
    where only bare, dry rock was seen;
    their victory is now defeat.

MEPHISTOPHELES. They are amazed by this strange welcome,
    their boldest climbers are dumbfounded.

FAUST. Now one great rushing stream turns into many brooks,   10,725
    that soon reissue doubled from their gorges
    and form a mighty waterfall;
    this torrent comes to rest upon a bed of rock
    and fills its broad expanse with raging foam,
    then plunges tier by tier into the valley.   10,730
    What good is gallant, hero-like resistance
    when this vast flood will sweep them all away?
    I am myself appalled by its fierce surging.

MEPHISTOPHELES. I see no part of these aquatic lies—
    the human eye alone can be deceived—   10,735
    but am amused by what is happening.
    Whole mobs are now in headlong flight;
    the fools believe that they are drowning,
    and though they stand and breathe on solid ground,
    run ludicrously about with swimming motions.   10,740
    There's now confusion everywhere.
               (To the ravens, who have returned.)
    I shall commend you to our Lord and Master;
    but if you'd like to show that you yourselves are masters,
    speed to the glowing forge at which,
    with endless energy, the dwarfs   10,745
    strike sparks from ores and metals.
    Persuade them, with a long oration,

to lend you fire, of the kind our Master likes,
that glows, and sparkles, and explodes.
There's nothing special when, on summer nights,   10,750
you see heat lightning in the distance
and falling stars shoot flashing from the zenith,
but summer lightning in a maze of bushes
and stars that hiss along wet ground
are not an every-day occurrence.   10,755
But don't make an inordinate effort—
start with entreaties, then give orders.

The ravens leave, and what is described by MEPHISTOPHELES *is seen occurring.*

MEPHISTOPHELES. Now let dense blackness shroud the foe,
their every step be an uncertain groping
as sparks flit waywardly about them   10,760
and sudden lightnings daze their vision!
That hardly could have been improved on;
but horrid noises are required too.

FAUST. The empty armor from funereal halls
regains its vigor here in the fresh air;   10,765
that continuous clank and rattle up above
provides a strange, discordant note.

MEPHISTOPHELES. The fact is that they can no longer be restrained;
you hear the sound of knightly cudgels
just as one did back in the good old days.   10,770
Arm-guards and leg-pieces have once more become
the Guelfs and Ghibellines, and hasten
to start their endless feud again.
Inheriting their fixed opinions,
they are immune to reconciliation;   10,775
you now can hear their bluster everywhere.
When all is said and done, at diabolic revels
it's party hatred that is most effective
and is their culminating horror.
Let its abhorrent, frightening voice,   10,780
at times so shrill and stridently satanic,
spread panic throughout all the valley.

Warlike tumult in the orchestra, finally changing into lively military tunes.

THE ANTI-EMPEROR'S TENT

A throne and lavish trappings. Enter GET-QUICK *and* QUICKLOOT.

QUICKLOOT. We are here first, then, after all!

GET-QUICK. No raven's flight can match our speed.

QUICKLOOT. There is so much wealth piled up here!   10,785
  Where should I start? Where can I stop?

GET-QUICK. The place is crammed so full with stuff,
  I don't know what to reach for first!

QUICKLOOT. That tapestry's just what I need—
  my bed is often much too hard.   10,790

GET-QUICK. Here's a steel mace with lots of spikes,
  exactly what I've long wished for.

QUICKLOOT. This scarlet cloak with a gold hem
  is like what I've been dreaming of.

GET-QUICK (*taking the mace*).
  With this you don't waste any time,   10,795
  you knock them dead and keep right on. –
  Your sack's already filled enough,
  but what you've grabbed is not worth much.
  Leave all that rubbish where it is,
  and take one of these little chests;   10,800
  they hold the pay that's due the troops,
  each one of them's chock-full of gold.

QUICKLOOT. This is a fiendishly great weight!
  I cannot lift or carry it.

GET-QUICK. Hurry, crouch down! Bend over more—   10,805
  your back is strong, I'll put it there!

QUICKLOOT. That hurts! I'm truly done for now—
  the load is going to break my back!
                    The coffer falls and bursts open.

GET-QUICK. Your gold's now piled there on the ground;
  get to work quick and snatch it up!   10,810

QUICKLOOT (*crouching down*).
  Quick, sweep it here into my lap!
  There'll still be plenty of it for us.

GET-QUICK. That is enough! Now hurry up!
                    (QUICKLOOT *rises.*)
  This is too much! Your apron leaks;
  no matter where you stand or walk,   10,815
  you'll scatter money like a spendthrift.
                Enter BODYGUARDS *of the rightful emperor.*

GUARDS. What are you up to in this sanctum,
  ransacking the imperial treasure?

GET-QUICK. We've risked our lives and limbs for you,
  and take as pay our share of loot.   10,820

That is what's done in enemy tents,
and we are in the military.
GUARDS. That's not what's done when we're around—
being soldiers and dirty thieves.
To serve our emperor, a soldier man   10,825
must also be an honest soldier.
GET-QUICK. We know your kind of honesty,
you call it requisitioning!
We're all on the same footing here;
the password of our trade is: give!   10,830
(*To* QUICKLOOT.) Clear out, and take what you have got;
we are not welcome here as guests.   [*Exeunt.*
A GUARD. Why didn't you, right then and there,
slap that smart aleck in the face?
SECOND GUARD. It's hard to say; I lacked all strength,   10,835
and they were somehow ghost-like, too.
THIRD GUARD. Something was bothering my eyes;
my head was swimming, things were blurred.
FOURTH GUARD. I can't exactly tell you either:
It's been so sultry all day long,   10,840
oppressive, hot, uncomfortable;
as one man stood, his neighbor fell;
just groping, you would strike a blow,
and with each blow some foe was felled;
gauze seemed to hang before our eyes,   10,845
our ears heard buzzing, hisses, roars;
that never stopped, and now we're here
with no idea how it was done.
The EMPEROR *enters with* FOUR PRINCES; *the* BODYGUARDS *retire to the*
background.
EMPEROR. It does not matter how! What counts is that we've won
and that the scattered foe is fled across the plain.   10,850
Here is the empty throne, and crowding in about us
is treason's treasury, wrapped up in tapestries.
We, with the full protection of our honor guard,
await as Emperor the envoys of all nations;
from all directions come reports to make us joyous,   10,855
our realms are pacified, all gladly swear allegiance.
Although our battle did involve some use of tricks,
the fact remains that we were those who did the fighting.
Sometimes coincidence, we know, will help combatants:
a stone falls from the sky, blood rains upon the foe,   10,860
and rocky caves emit mysterious, loud noises
that make the enemy less, and us much more, courageous.
The vanquished are the butt of never-ending taunts;

the victor, in his triumph, lauds Him who favored him,
and of their own free will all voices join with his   10,865
as countless throats intone "We praise Thee now, our God."
I turn my pious eyes in highest praise however—
a thing I've rarely done—to where my own heart lies.
In youth a carefree prince may give his days to pleasure,
but with advancing years he learns the moment's worth.   10,870
To make secure forthwith my line, this court, our realm,
I join my lot with that of you four worthy men.
(*To the* FIRST PRINCE.)
     We owe to you, o Prince, the army's wise deployment
and, at the crucial point, its bold, heroic guidance;
perform the tasks of peace the times will now require;   10,875
I here give you this sword and dub you Lord Arch-Marshal.
ARCH-MARSHAL.
     When once your loyal troops, now civil war is over,
have made our borders strong, made safe your throne and person,
grant us the privilege of serving you at table
as celebrating guests crowd through ancestral halls.   10,880
Before you I will bear, beside you hold this sword,
attendant at all times upon Your Majesty.
EMPEROR (*to the* SECOND PRINCE).
     You, sir, who are both brave and sweetly courteous
shall be Arch-Chamberlain. This is no easy office,
for you will be the head of our domestic staff,   10,885
that fails to serve me well when servants quarrel and bicker;
henceforth may they have you as their respected model
of how to please one's liege, one's court, and all one's fellows.
ARCH-CHAMBERLAIN.
     To do what you enjoin will make all nobly eager
to lend good men support and treat the less good kindly,   10,890
and be undevious, reserved without deceit.
My true reward, o Sire, is how you've read my heart.
May I imagine, too, your coming celebration?
When you prepare to feast, I'll fetch the golden basin
and hold your rings for you so that on that great day,   10,895
your hands may be refreshed as I am by your gaze.
EMPEROR. My mood is still too grave for thoughts of celebration,
yet be it so! Joy, too, may serve a proper need.
(*To the* THIRD PRINCE.)
     I've chosen you Arch-Steward, who henceforth shall be
in charge of hunting grounds, of barnyard and of manor.   10,900
Have carefully prepared, according to the season,
whatever then is best to make my favorite dishes.
ARCH-STEWARD.
     No duty shall more please me than keeping a strict fast

until you can be served a dish that suits your taste.
The kitchen staff and I shall make it our joint effort   10,905
to get exotic fare and expedite the seasons—
although such luxuries do not mean much to you,
whose preferences are what's nourishing and simple.
EMPEROR (*to the* FOURTH PRINCE).
　Since banquets seem the theme that none of you avoid,
　you, my young hero, shall be changed to a cup-bearer.   10,910
　As Arch-Cupbearer now, make sure that in our cellars
　the best of wines are kept in plentiful supply.
　Be temperate yourself, and when there's merriment
　do not be led astray because occasion's offered!
ARCH-CUPBEARER.
　My Lord, young people will, if only they are trusted,   10,915
　achieve maturity before you notice it.
　I too can see myself at your great celebration,
　when I will lavishly adorn the royal buffet
　with ceremonial plate, of gold and silver only,
　but for your use will save the loveliest cup of all,   10,920
　of clear Venetian glass, in which delight awaits you;
　it adds to the wine's taste, prevents intoxication.
　Some might rely, besides, upon its precious magic,
　but your sobriety protects you, Sire, still better.
EMPEROR. What I've conferred on you here in this solemn moment,   10,925
　you've heard with confidence from lips that you can trust.
　The Emperor's word alone enforces these donations,
　but to attest the fact a formal deed's required
　that bears his signature. To phrase it properly,
　here comes the proper man exactly when he's needed.   10,930
　　　　　Enter the CHANCELLOR-ARCHBISHOP.
EMPEROR. As soon as a great vault's entrusted to its keystone,
　it is securely built for all time still to come.
　You see four princes here. We've been discussing how
　our house and court may have a surer permanence.
　For matters that concern the empire as a whole   10,935
　you five together shall have full authority.
　In lands you hold you must surpass all other men,
　and so I here extend your borders to include
　the legacies of all who were unfaithful to us.
　Thus, loyal friends, I grant you many fine estates,   10,940
　together with the right, when chance permits, to add
　by purchase or exchange, or by succession, to them;
　it further is decreed that you may exercise
　without impediment all territorial rights.
　The verdicts that you give as judges will be final,   10,945
　and no man shall appeal to any higher court.

All taxes, tributes, rents, safe-conducts, tolls, and fiefs,
the royalties of mines, salt-works, and mints, are yours.
To demonstrate to all my gratitude's extent,
I've raised you to a rank next only to my own.   10,950
ARCHBISHOP. Let me in all our names express our heartfelt thanks!
You make us powerful, and strengthen your own power.
EMPEROR. I wish to grant you five an even higher honor.
I still live for my state, still have a zest for life,
but my great forebears' seal now turns my prudent gaze   10,955
from eager aspirations to that which looms ahead.
When, in my turn, I bid the ones I love farewell,
your duty let it be to say who's my successor.
Raise him, when he is crowned, aloft the holy altar,
and so shall end in peace what was so stormy here.   10,960
ARCHBISHOP.
With pride deep in their hearts, but humble in their bearing,
there bow before you here the first of this earth's princes.
As long as loyal blood still courses through our veins,
we'll be the body which obeys your slightest wish.
EMPEROR. And so now, to conclude, let all I've here enacted   10,965
for every age to come be ratified in writing.
You have full sovereignty in each of your estates,
with the condition, though, that none may be divided.
However you increase what you've received from us,
it shall descend upon your eldest sons entire.   10,970
ARCHBISHOP. To parchment I'll at once commit this statute which,
both for the Empire's weal and ours, is so important;
fair copy, seals, can be prepared in chancery;
your signature will then attest its sanctity.
EMPEROR. I now shall let you leave, so that you may, each one,   10,975
with tranquil mind reflect upon this glorious day.

            [*Exeunt the* FOUR SECULAR PRINCES.

ARCHBISHOP (*remaining, and speaking with pathos*).
The Chancellor withdrew. The Bishop still remains,
impelled by grave concern to seek your ear and warn it;
paternal feelings fill his heart with fears for you!
EMPEROR. What can, in this glad hour, cause you to feel alarm?   10,980
ARCHBISHOP. It grieves me bitterly to see your hallowed head
at such a time as this in covenant with Satan.
Although you seem, indeed, secure upon your throne,
you flout, alas! the Lord and flout our Holy Father.
The Pope, once he's informed, will pass a penal judgment   10,985
that shall with sacred bolts destroy your sinful realm.
He still remembers how, when you were celebrating
your coronation day, you set that sorcerer free.
To Christendom's great hurt, it was your diadem

that first shed mercy's rays upon that evil head. 10,990
But beat your breast and give, from your ill-gotten fortune,
to things of holiness a modest mite again;
confirmed in piety, donate to holy efforts
that broad expanse of hills where your pavilion stood,
where evil spirits formed a league for your protection, 10,995
and to the Prince of Lies you lent a willing ear;
include the whole extent of mountain and thick forest,
its slopes of alpine green that offer fattening pasture,
its limpid lakes of fish, and all the brooks that plunge
with swift meanderings into the vales below; 11,000
to this add the broad valley's meadows, flats, and bottoms—
contrition, so expressed, will gain you absolution.
EMPEROR. My grievous fault fills me with terror so profound
that any boundaries shall be what you decide.
ARCHBISHOP. But, first, the place that sin has so defiled must be 11,005
proclaimed at once as sacred to God's service.
The mind already sees great walls that quickly rise,
the shafts of morning sun that flood the choir with light,
the edifice that grows and widens to a cross,
the soaring, lengthening nave, a joy to all the faithful 11,010
who in their fervor now pour through the solemn doors—
from lofty towers that aspire heavenwards
the bells' first summons has sung out through hill and valley,
and penitents approach to start their lives anew.
At this great consecration—may its day be soon!— 11,015
your presence, Sire, will be the chief and crowning glory.
EMPEROR. Let this work's magnitude proclaim a piety
that praises God our Lord and frees me of transgression.
Enough! I can feel now my sense of exaltation.
ARCHBISHOP. As Chancellor I shall soon settle all details. 11,020
EMPEROR. Bring me a formal deed of transfer to the Church,
and I'll be overjoyed to sign my name to it.
ARCHBISHOP (*taking his leave, but then turning back at the entrance to the
tent*). You will, besides, devote to the work's furtherance,
in perpetuity, all local revenues:
tithes, tribute, rents. The costs of proper maintenance 11,025
are great, and so are those of careful management.
To speed construction in so desolate a place
you'll give us from your loot some of the gold you won.
Moreover, we shall need—a fact I won't gloss over—
wood from a long way off, and lime and slate and such like; 11,030
the people shall haul these, instructed from the pulpit;
the Church will bless the man whose team toils in her service. [*Exit.*
EMPEROR. The burden of my sin is large and hard to bear;
those scoundrel sorcerers are doing me great harm.

ARCHBISHOP (*returning again, with as low a bow as is possible*).
   Your pardon, Sire! That man of dubious character   11,035
   received in fief our coasts; on them the ban will fall
   unless, in penitence, to our consistory
   there too you cede the tithes, the rents, the dues, the taxes.
EMPEROR (*with annoyance*).
   That land does not exist, it's only high sea still.
ARCHBISHOP.
   The right time always comes for patient and just causes.   11,040
   For our part, we expect your promise to be valid.   [*Exit.*
EMPEROR (*solus*).
   At this rate I'll have soon signed all my realm away.

ACT V

A BROAD LANDSCAPE

Enter a TRAVELER

TRAVELER. Yes, they're there, the same dark lindens
   now grown old, but sturdy still. –
   After all these years of travel,   11,045
   I shall see my friends again!
   It's the old familiar place—
   in that cottage I found shelter
   when the storm and wave had cast me
   on the sand-dunes over there.   11,050
   I should like to greet the couple
   who were very helpful then,
   but already rather old
   to be still my hosts today.
   They were worthy, pious people!   11,055
   Shall I knock or shall I shout?
   Greetings if, as kind as ever,
   doing good still gives you pleasure!
              Enter BAUCIS, *a little woman, very old.*
BAUCIS. Softly, softly, welcome stranger!
   Quiet! let my husband rest!   11,060
   Long naps give the old the power
   to be active when awake.
TRAVELER. Are you, mother, then still here
   to receive my thanks again
   for the way you and your husband   11,065
   saved my life when I was young?
   Are you Baucis, who so promptly
   offered half-dead lips new life,
              (*Enter her husband,* PHILEMON.)
   you Philemon, who so bravely
   rescued from the sea my goods?   11,070
   That my dire adventure ended
   happily, I owe alone
   to your quickly kindled beacon
   and your bell's clear silver sound.
      Now let me walk into the open   11,075
   and survey the boundless sea,
   there to kneel and say a prayer—
   for my heart is much oppressed.
              He strides forward on the dune.
PHILEMON (*to* BAUCIS).
   Quick! and lay the table for us

where it's pretty in the garden.   11,080
Let him hurry and be startled—
he will not believe his eyes.

                    He joins the TRAVELER.

PHILEMON. See! the place where angry waves
    mistreated you so cruelly
    has been laid out as a park,   11,085
    is a counterfeit of Eden.
    Age prevented me from helping,
    as I would have done before;
    even as my strength kept failing,
    so the waters too withdrew.   11,090
    Under cautious masters, workmen
    daringly built dams and channels,
    limited the ocean's rights
    to obtain them for themselves.
    See how meadows, fields, and gardens,   11,095
    woods and villages all flourish. –
    But now come and have your meal,
    for the sun will soon be gone. –
    Far away I see sails seeking
    a safe harbor for the night!   11,100
    Birds know how to find their nests—
    there is where the port now is.
    That is why the sea's blue edge
    only shows there in the distance,
    and left and right you see extending   11,105
    densely populated land.

        The three seat themselves at a table in the small garden.

BAUCIS. Silent still? And you take nothing
    to relieve your thirst?
PHILEMON.   Our friend
    is curious about this marvel;
    since you like to talk, you tell him.   11,110
BAUCIS. *Marvel* is the word to use!
    Even now I'm still uneasy;
    I'm convinced that the whole business
    was not done with proper means.
PHILEMON. Can the Emperor have sinned   11,115
    who gave him these shores as fiefdom?
    Did a herald with a trumpet
    not proclaim it everywhere? –
    The first foothold was established
    not far distant from our dunes—   11,120
    tents and huts! – But soon a palace

rises, there amid the green.
BAUCIS. In the daytime noisy workmen
    hacked and shoveled, all in vain;
    where, at night, small fires flickered,   11,125
    there was a dam the following day.
    Human lives were sacrificed,
    groans of torment filled the darkness;
    fires flowed down to the sea—
    there, at dawn, was a canal.   11,130
    He's a godless man who covets
    both our cottage and our grove;
    boasting that he is our neighbor,
    he would have us be his serfs.
PHILEMON. But in exchange he's offered us   11,135
    an estate in the new land.
BAUCIS. Do not trust land in a marsh,
    stick to where the ground is high!
PHILEMON. Let's go over to the chapel—
    there we'll see the sun's last light—   11,140
    toll the bell, then kneel and pray,
    trusting in our fathers' God!

PALACE

Before the Palace is a spacious formal park with a great rectilinear canal.
    FAUST, *now an extremely old man, walks back and forth, meditating.*
LYNCEUS (*as* WATCHMAN, *through a speaking-trumpet*).
    The sun is setting; some last sails
    are making briskly for the harbor.
    A good-sized boat in the canal   11,145
    will reach this quay at any moment. –
    Your colored pennants flutter gaily,
    your masts and rigging show no damage—
    the grateful sailor gives you thanks,
    and fortune welcomes your well-timed return.   11,150
             The little chapel-bell tolls on the dune.
FAUST (*starting*).
    Confound that bell's atrocious sound,
    as painful as an unexpected shot!
    Ostensibly my realm is boundless,
    but at my back vexation, taunting,
    reminds me with these irritating noises   11,155
    that my great holdings have a blemish:

that linden grove, its old brown cottage,
and the dilapidated chapel are not mine.
Although I would enjoy its restful quiet,
I cannot bear the thought of shade that's not my own,   11,160
that pricks the eye and stabs the flesh like thorns—
oh, would that I were far from here!
Lynceus (*as above*).
See how the painted ship approaches gaily
as evening breezes swell its sails!
How agilely that moving tower bears   11,165
chests, crates,and bales along its course!
There appears a splendid vessel, richly laden with colorful exotic wares;
on it are Mephistopheles *and the* Three Mighty Men.
Mephistopheles *and the* Mighty Men (*in chorus*).
Here we will land—
have landed already.
We greet our master,
hail our patron!   11,170
They disembark, and the cargo is unloaded.
Mephistopheles. As can be seen, we've proved our worth,
and praise from you would give us pleasure.
We started out with two ships only,
but now we're back in port with twenty.
Our cargo clearly demonstrates   11,175
what great success we have achieved.
On the open sea your mind is open,
and no one gives a fig for prudence;
you have to grab things in a hurry:
you catch a fish or catch a ship,   11,180
and once you've three in your possession,
you soon have caught a fourth as well;
the fifth then hasn't got a chance,
since it's a fact that might is right—
not *how* but *what* will be the only question asked.   11,185
Unless I'm all at sea about maritime matters,
war, trade, and piracy together are
a trinity not to be severed.
The Mighty Men. No thanks or welcome!
No welcome or thanks—   11,190
as if we brought
our master trash!
He looks askance
and finds repugnant
these treasures   11,195
worthy of a king.

MEPHISTOPHELES. Do not expect
    still more rewards—
    you know you took
    your share already!   11,200
THE MIGHTY MEN. That does not count
    in any way;
    we all demand
    our equal shares.
MEPHISTOPHELES. Put all our treasures   11,205
    on display
    in the great rooms
    of the main floor!
    When he goes up
    and sees this wealth,   11,210
    sees more exactly
    what it's worth,
    I'm sure he won't
    be stingy then,
    will give our squadron   11,215
    many a feast. –
Our merry company will all be here tomorrow,
and I'll take proper care of them.
                      (*The cargo is removed.*)
(*To* FAUST.) Your brow is grave, your look is somber,
    despite this news of great success.   11,220
    August sagacity has won its crown of triumph:
    the ocean and your shore are now at peace,
    and from this strand the willing sea
    allows your ships a speedy journey—
    admit that here, here from this palace,   12,225
    you have the whole world in your reach.
    This is the spot where all began,
    here stood your first rude wooden shack;
    a little ditch was dug where now
    is seen the splash of busy oars.   11,230
    Your courage, and your workmen's zeal,
    make you victorious on sea and land.
    And right from here . . .
FAUST.   Confound your *here* —
    that's what's so terribly oppressive!
    I have to tell you, you who know so much;   11,235
    it causes me such endless heartache,
    it's something I can bear no longer!
    And yet, I feel ashamed to say it.
    Those old folk there ought to give in;

I want those lindens part of my estate;   11,240
the few trees spoil, because I do not own them,
everything that I possess on earth.
Among their branches I would like to build
a platform with a panoramic vista
and so obtain an unobstructed view   11,245
of all that I have now accomplished—
survey with one inclusive look
this masterpiece the human spirit has wrought
to augment, by intelligent planning,
the space its peoples have for living.   11,250
    The worst of torments we can suffer
is to feel want when we are rich.
The tinkling bell, the lindens' scent,
make me feel buried in a crypt.
The freedom of an invincible will   11,255
is blunted by this pile of sand.
How rid myself of this obsession—
the bell will ring, and I'll be frantic!

MEPHISTOPHELES. It's only natural that something so annoying
    should sour life for you. The fact is not   11,260
    to be disputed: any cultivated ear
    must find such clinking noisome.
    And yet that damned ding-dong-ding-dong,
    casting its damp pall on serenest evening skies,
    intrudes itself upon whatever happens   11,265
    from first immersion to interment,
    as if, between that ding and dong,
    life were a dream to be forgotten.

FAUST. Such wilful, obstinate resistance
    so blights the acme of success   11,270
    that, with intense regret and pain,
    one has to tire of being just.

MEPHISTOPHELES. Why let yourself be bothered so by this?
    You surely know, by now, how best to colonize.

FAUST. So be it! Go and rid me of their presence—   11,275
    you know the pretty piece of property
    that I have designated for their use.

MEPHISTOPHELES. We'll carry them off, then set them down;
    there! you see them settled once again;
    a nice new place will reconcile them   11,280
    to any violence they suffer.

        He whistles shrilly; the MIGHTY MEN *enter.*

MEPHISTOPHELES. Come! There is an order from our master.
    The party for the fleet will be tomorrow.

THE THREE. The old man's welcome wasn't generous—
  a lively party's our just due.   11,285
MEPHISTOPHELES (*ad spectatores*).
  Here's an old story, ever the same—
  Naboth's vineyard once again. [1 Kings 21.]

The Darkness becomes complete.

LYNCEUS (*the keeper on the palace watchtower, singing*).
  Sight is my birthright;
  assigned to this tower
  to watch is my task,   11,290
  and the world is my joy.
  I gaze into the distance
  or look at what's near—
  the moon and the stars,
  the forest with deer.   11,295
  In what I behold
  there always is beauty;
  content with it all,
  I'm content with myself.
  Oh fortunate eyes!   11,300
  whatever you've seen,
  whatever the outcome,
  you have known beauty!
                      (*Pause.*)
I have not been stationed here
simply for my private pleasure—   11,305
what's this threat of monstrous horror
from the dark world down below!
Through the lindens' twofold night
I see flashing sparks explode;
incandescence, fanned by breezes,   11,310
swirls in ever greater rage.
Woe! the fire's in the cottage
that so long was damp with moss;
quick assistance is what's needed,
but no rescuers are near.   11,315
Will that dear, that kind old couple,
once so careful with their fires,
be the victims of that smoke!
What a terrible disaster!
Blazing flames—and glowing red   11,320
the moss-covered timberwork—

let us hope that those good people
have escaped from the inferno!
Tongues of flashing light are climbing
through the leaves and up the branches;   11,325
withered boughs that burn and flicker
soon are blazing, then cave in.
Is this what my eyes should see!
Why must I be so far-sighted?
Now the chapel too collapses,   11,330
burdened down by falling branches.
Coiling flames with serpent tongues
have the treetops in their grasp.
To their roots the hollow trunks
blaze scarlet in the glow they cast. –   11,335
(Long pause. Song.)
What was once a joy to see
now belongs to ages past.
FAUST appears on the balcony, looking toward the dunes.
FAUST. What is that dolorous song up there?
The message has arrived too late.
My watchman grieves; my inmost being   11,340
is offended by this impatient action. –
Although the stand of lindens may now be
reduced to ugly half-charred trunks,
a lookout soon can be erected
that will grant me a boundless view.   11,345
From it I'll also see the home
that gives new shelter to those two old people
who, grateful for my generous indulgence,
will spend their final days in happiness.
MEPHISTOPHELES and the MIGHTY MEN (appearing below).
As fast as possible, we have returned;   11,350
excuse us if there was a bit of trouble.
We knocked, then beat upon the door,
but still no one would open it;
we kept on rattling and pounding,
then the rotted door fell down;   11,355
we shouted and made angry threats,
but still we met with no response.
And as so often in such cases,
they did not hear, they would not listen;
but we refused to brook delay,   11,360
and, as you wished, soon cleared them out.
The couple didn't suffer much,

they simply dropped down dead with fright.
A stranger who was hiding there
put up a fight—we knocked him flat.   11,365
During this short but savage struggle,
with embers scattered all about
some straw ignited. Now it's blazing,
the pyre on which all three must die.
FAUST. Were your ears deaf to what I said?   11,370
I wanted an exchange, not theft.
My curse upon your senseless savagery—
may each of you bear his part of it!
MEPHISTOPHELES *and the* MIGHTY MEN (*in chorus*).
The ancient truth is loud and clear:
Obey with grace when Force commands!   11,375
But if you're bold and must resist,
then risk your house and home and—life.   [*Exeunt.*
FAUST (*on the balcony*).
The stars conceal their glittering light;
the fire dies down to a faint glow,
then a damp breeze rekindles it   11,380
and brings to me the smoke and vapor.
An order quickly given, too quickly executed! –
What are these shadows drifting toward me?

At the last stroke of midnight, FOUR GRAY WOMEN *appear in the courtyard.*

THE FIRST. My name is Want.
THE SECOND.   And mine is Debt.
THE THIRD. My name is Care.
THE FOURTH.   And mine, Distress.   11,385
THREE (*together*). The portal is locked, we cannot get in;
    the owner is wealthy, it's no place for us.
WANT. I'd be but a shadow.
DEBT.   And I would be canceled.
DISTRESS. Those whom life pampers have no eyes for me.
CARE. You, sisters, are helpless, have no right to enter.   11,390
    But Care, through the keyhole, will slip quickly in.   [*Disappears.*
WANT. Away, then, gray sisters, away now from here!
DEBT. As close as I can I'll stick to your side.
DISTRESS. And to your heels as close as she can, Distress.
THE THREE. See the clouds gather, the stars disappear!   11,395
    Look there, look off there! Far away in the distance
    our brother is coming – it's he, it is – – – Death.   [*Exeunt.*

FAUST (*within the palace*).

I saw four come, but only three depart;
I could not catch the sense of what they said.
I heard one word that sounded like *distress,*   11,400
the somber rhyme that followed it was – *death.*
It had a hollow, muted, spectral sound.
I have not fought my way to freedom yet!
If I could rid my path of magic,
could totally unlearn its incantations,   11,405
confront you, Nature, simply as a man,
to be a human being would then be worth the effort.
    That's what I was before I probed obscurities,
blasphemed and cursed my world and self.
Now the air holds so many spectral shapes   11,410
that there's no knowing how to shun them.
Though reason grant us happy, lucid days,
the nights entangle us in webs of dream;
as, gladdened, we return from springtime fields,
some bird will croak—an omen of ill-fortune!   11,415
Enmeshed in superstition all our lives,
when something happens it's a sign or warning.
And so we stand alone and frightened. –
There the door creaks, and yet no one appears.
(*Shaken.*) Is someone here?

CARE.   The question asks for *Yes.*   11,420

FAUST. And who are you?

CARE.   I'm here—that's all that matters.

FAUST. Begone!

CARE.   This is my proper place.

FAUST (*at first angry, then addressing himself in a moderated tone*).

Take heed to use no incantation!

CARE. Even though no ear may hear me,
    in your heart my voice is loud;   11,425
    I appear in many masks,
    and I wield a vengeful power:
    the companion-cause of fear
    whether you're on land or sea;
    always met with, never sought,   11,430
    always cursed, but never banished.
Have you not ever, then, known Care?

FAUST. I've never tarried anywhere;
I snatched from fortune what I wanted,
what did not please me I let go,   11,435
and disregarded what eluded me.
I've only had desires to fulfill them,

then wished anew, and so I've stormed amain
my way through life; once grand and vigorous,
my days are spent with prudent caution.   11,440
I know this mortal sphere sufficiently,
and there's no seeing into the Beyond;
he is a fool who casts a sheep's eye at it,
invents himself some peers above the clouds—
let him stand firm and look at what's around him: 11,445
no good and able man finds this world mute!
What need has he to float into eternity—
the things he knows are tangible!
Let his path be this earth while he exists;
if spirits haunt him, let him not break stride   11,450
but, keeping on, find all life's pains and joys,
always, in every moment, never satisfied!
CARE. Once I make a man my own,
    nothing in this world can help him;
    everlasting darkness falls,   11,455
    suns no longer rise or set—
    though no outward sense has failed,
    all is darkness in his heart,
    and however great his treasures,
    there's no joy in their possession.   11,460
    Good and bad luck both depress him,
    he is starving though there's plenty;
    source of joy or spot of trouble,
    it's postponed until the morrow—
    caring only for the future,   11,465
    he gets nothing done at all.
FAUST. Stop! In this way you won't get at me!
    I will not listen to this madness.
    Begone! Your wretched litany
    might well seduce a man of wisdom.   11,470
CARE. Whether he should go or come
    is something he cannot decide;
    in the middle of a street
    his stride will break, he'll grope his way;
    more and more he is bogged down,   11,475
    everything seems more distorted;
    to himself, to all, a burden,
    when he breathes he feels he's choking,
    neither stifled nor yet living,
    torn between despair and hoping.   11,480
    All is one unceasing round
    of things not done, of odious duties,

of sense of freedom, then depression;
broken, unrefreshing sleep
leaves him without will to move   11,485
and prepares him for damnation.
FAUST. Ill-omened spectres! Time and time again
this is the way you work on human kind,
transforming even days that are indifferent
into an ugly tangle of enmeshing torments.   11,490
We can't, I know, be rid of daemons easily—
their ties upon us never can be severed—
but I shall not acknowledge, Care, not ever,
your vast, insidious power.
CARE. Then feel it now, and hear the curse   11,495
with which I turn away from you:
throughout its whole existence your human race is blind—
now, Faustus, it's your turn at last.
            She breathes upon him and vanishes.
FAUST (*blinded*).
The darkness seems to press about me more and more,
but in my inner being there is radiant light;   11,500
I'll hasten the fulfillment of my plans—
only the master's order carries weight. –
Workmen, up from your beds! Up, every man,
and make my bold design reality!
Take up your tools! To work with spade and shovel—   11,505
what's been marked off must be completed now!
Prompt effort and strict discipline
will guarantee superb rewards:
to complete a task that's so tremendous,
working as one is worth a thousand hands.   11,510

———————

The large outer courtyard of the palace is now lit by torches. – Enter
        MEPHISTOPHELES, *leading a group of* LEMURES.
MEPHISTOPHELES. Come, hurry here! Come in! Come in,
        you tottery Lemures,
        you patched-together, half-live creatures
        of sinew, ligament and bone.
LEMURES (*chorus*).
        Here we come, and promptly too,   11,515
        half under the impression
        that this concerns a lot of land
        of which we'll take possession.
            We see the poles and pointed stakes,

the chain to measure sections,   11,520
    but why we have been summoned here
    is something we've forgotten.
MEPHISTOPHELES. No fine surveying's needed here;
    just use the standard of your bodies:
    he who is tallest must lie down full length,   11,525
    you others make a ridge of turf around him;
    then, as they did for our forefathers,
    dig a long four-sided hole!
    From palace into these cramped quarters—
    that's the inane conclusion of all this.   11,530
LEMURES (*digging, with derisive gestures*).
    In youth when I did live and love,
    I thought that all was pleasant;
    when there was song and merriment,
    my feet would take to dancing.
       But then malicious Age appeared   11,535
    and smote me with his crutch;
    I tripped beside an open door—
    why must be graves left open!
FAUST *emerges from the palace, groping his way past the door posts.*
FAUST. How good to hear the sound of shovels!
    The mass of workers serve my pleasure,   11,540
    uniting land again with land,
    imposing borders on the ocean,
    confining it in rigid bonds.
MEPHISTOPHELES (*aside*).
    And yet with all your dams and levees
    your striving serves no one but us;   11,545
    in fact, you're now preparing a grand feast
    for the water-daemon, Neptune.
    All of your kind are doomed already; –
    the elements have sworn to help us;
    the end will be annihilation.   11,550
FAUST. Overseer!
MEPHISTOPHELES. Here!
FAUST.   Use every means you can
    and get a plentiful supply of laborers;
    use benefits and discipline to spur them on,
    make payments, offer bonuses, conscript them!
    And day by day I want to be informed   11,555
    how the canal I've started is advancing.
MEPHISTOPHELES (*sotto voce*).
    The word I heard was more banal:
    they mentioned graves, not some canal.

FAUST. A marsh stretching along those mountains
    contaminates what's been reclaimed so far;   11,560
    to drain that stagnant pool as well
    would be a crowning last achievement.
    If I can furnish space for many millions
    to live—not safe, I know, but free to work
    in green and fertile fields, with man and beast   11,565
    soon happy on the new-made soil
    and settled in beside the mighty hill
    a dauntless people's effort has erected,
    creating here inside a land of Eden—
    then there, without, the tide may bluster to its brim,   11,570
    but where it gnaws, attempting to rush in by force,
    communal effort will be quick to close the breach.
    To this idea I am committed wholly,
    it is the final wisdom we can reach:
    he, only, merits freedom and existence   11,575
    who wins them every day anew.
    And so, beset by danger, here childhood's years,
    maturity, and age will all be vigorous.
    If only I might see that people's teeming life,
    share their autonomy on unencumbered soil;   11,580
    then, to the moment, I could say:
    tarry a while, you are so fair—
    the traces of my days on earth
    will survive into eternity! –
    Envisioning those heights of happiness,   11,585
    I now enjoy my highest moment.
FAUST *falls backward and is caught by the* LEMURES, *who lay him on the*
ground.
MEPHISTOPHELES. No pleasure sates him, no success suffices,
    and so he still keeps chasing shapes that always change;
    this final, mediocre, empty moment—
    the poor wretch wants to cling to it.   11,590
    He who resisted me with such great vigor
    —time triumphs—lies here on the sand an old, old man.
    The clock stands still –
LEMURES.   Stands still? As deathly still as midnight!
    Now its hand falls.
MEPHISTOPHELES.   It falls, and all is finished.
LEMURES. So all is over.
MEPHISTOPHELES.   *Over*—a stupid word!   11,595
    Why over?
    What's over, and mere nothing, are the same.
    So what's the point of making all our effort

to snatch what has been made into our nothingness!
"All's over!"—what's the inference from that?   11,600
That things might just as well have never been,
but chase around in circles as if they did exist.
I'd much prefer Eternal Emptiness instead.

INTERMENT

ONE OF THE LEMURES (*solo*).
　　Who built me such a wretched house
　　with shovel and with spade?   11.605
LEMURES (*chorus*).
　　For an insentient guest in burlap
　　it's far too nicely made.
ONE OF THE LEMURES (*solo*).
　　Why is the room so badly furnished?
　　Where are the chairs, the table?
LEMURES (*chorus*).
　　All items were on short-term loan,   11,610
　　and creditors are many.
MEPHISTOPHELES. The body's here, and if its spirit tries escaping
　　I'll promptly show my blood-signed title to it—
　　although, alas! today they have so many ways
　　to cheat the devil of his souls.   11,615
　　Our good old-fashioned methods give offense,
　　and modern ways won't help us much;
　　once I'd have acted on my own,
　　but now I'll need to call upon assistants.
　　　Things have come to a pretty pass!   11,620
　　Established usages and ancient rights—
　　there's nothing we can count on any more!
　　The soul used to emerge when someone breathed his last;
　　I'd lie in wait and, like the nimblest mouse,
　　snap! it was clenched within my claws.   11,625
　　But now it hesitates to leave that dreary place,
　　its noisome home inside a worthless corpse.
　　But in the end the feuding elements
　　will ignominiously evict it.
　　And though I fret for days on end, the questions   11,630
　　when, how, and *where* continually plague me;
　　old Death has lost his former mettle,
　　so even *whether* has been long in doubt.
　　I've often coveted some limbs in *rigor mortis*—
　　illusion only! They stirred and began to move again.   11,635
　　　　(*He makes fantastic gestures of conjuration, in the manner of a
　　　　　　　　　　squad-leader.*)

Here, quickly! On the double! When you come,
you fellows with straight horns, and you with crooked ones,
you sterling coins from our infernal mint,
bring the hell-mouth along as well.
Hell, to be sure, devours with many different jaws,   11,640
according to one's rank and status—
though in the future, even for this final fanfare,
people will bother less about the niceties.
    (*The hideous hell-mouth, placed stage-left, opens its jaws.*)
Past gaping tusks the fiery torrent
pours raging from the dome of the abyss,   11,645
and in the background, amid seething vapors,
I see the Flaming City glow eternally.
The red surf surges forward to the teeth,
bearing damned souls that seek salvation;
crushed in the hyena's colossal jaws,   11,650
they must retrace the fearful path of fire.
In the corners, much more could be discovered—
the maximum of horror in a minimum of space!
Try as you will to terrify the sinful,
they think these things are only lies and figments.   11,655
    (*To the* FAT DEVILS, *who have short, straight horns.*)
You there, pot-bellied rascals with the fiery cheeks,
fattened on brimstone, your faces fairly shining!
You bullnecked scoundrels with unturning heads!
watch out below for any phosphorescent glow:
that will be Psyche with her wings—his petty soul—   11,660
but if you pluck them off, she is a loathsome worm.
The moment I have set my mark upon her,
away with her in flaming cyclone!
   It is your duty, fat-paunched rogues,
to pay attention to the lower regions,   11,665
although it is somewhat uncertain
if that is where she would prefer to dwell.
The navel is one place she likes to stay,
so be on guard, or she may slip out there.
    (*To the* THIN DEVILS, *who have long, twisting horns.*)
You giant clowns, file-leaders everyone,   11,670
keep sawing the air—no letting up!—
with arms full length and sharp claws out
to grab the fluttering fugitive.
Her spirit's surely wretched in her present house,
will want to move up right away to something better.   11,675
    A Glory is lowered from above-right.

HEAVENLY HOST. Heavenly messengers,
                  kin to the blest above,
                  come, flying calmly,
                  to bring sinners forgiveness
                  and new life to dust;   11,680
                  provide, as you soar
                  in leisurely flight,
                  all living creatures
                  with tokens of love!

MEPHISTOPHELES. I hear discordant, nasty tinklings—   11,685
  they come from that disturbing light up there;
  such juvenile-androgynous bumbling
  is what the sanctimonious enjoy.
  You will remember how, in our most heinous hours,
  we plotted the destruction of mankind: 11,690
  the vilest method we invented
  exactly suits the needs of their devotions.
    The canting puppies, here they come!
  Those mincing ways have cost us many a soul,
  snatched from us as they wage their war with our own weapons— 11,695
  they're devils, too, but in disguise.
  To be defeated there would be your lasting shame—
  on to the grave, and take your stand beside it!

ANGELS (*in chorus, strewing roses*).
                  Roses so brilliant
                  and aromatic,   11,700
                  fluttering, floating,
                  secretly quickening—
                  on leaf-wings to hold you,
                  with blossoms unfolding,
                  hasten to bloom!   11,705
                    Springtime and crimson
                  and purple, appear!
                  Bring paradise down
                  to him who rests here!

MEPHISTOPHELES (*to the* DEVILS).
  Why do you flinch? Is that good devilish behavior?   11,710
  Stand fast, and let them strew away!
  Back to your posts, you beardless boys!
  No doubt they think that with this snow of tiny flowers
  they'll cool your diabolic ardor,
  but it will melt away before your breath.   11,715
  Now blow, you bellows-devils! – That's enough!
  your breathing makes the whole flock blench. –

Take it easy! Now shut your mouths and noses!
I see that you've been blowing much too hard.
Why can't you ever learn to practice moderation!   11,720
The stuff not only shrivels, it scorches, withers—burns!
Now the bright mass of poisoned flame drifts toward us,
Brace yourselves, close ranks, and stop it! –
The devils' strength gives out! All valor's gone!
They've caught an unfamiliar scent of wheedling warmth!   11,725

THE ANGELS.   These blossoms of happiness,
                 these flames filled with gladness,
                 disseminate love
                 and prepare for the bliss
                 all hearts desire.   11,730
                 In radiant skies
                 what's said will be truth,
                 and heavenly hosts
                 will always know light.

MEPHISTOPHELES. A curse upon these scurvy dolts!   11,735
    My fiends are standing on their heads—
    the fat ones turning cartwheel after cartwheel,
    before they plunge breech-first down into hell. –
    I hope your bath will be as hot as you deserve!
    But as for me, I won't desert my post.   11,740
              (*Fighting off the roses that drift about him.*)
    Will-o'-the-wisps, begone! You, there! You may shine bright
    but, once you're caught, you are a nasty whitish slime.
    Why are you fluttering still? Be on your way! –
    I feel the pinch of pitch and brimstone on my neck.

THE ANGELS.   What you find alien,   11,745
                 be sure to avoid it;
                 what hurts your inward self,
                 you must reject it.
                 But if still it intrudes,
                 we must confront it.   11,750
                 Love only succors
                 those who can love.

MEPHISTOPHELES. My head's on fire, and I've heart-and-liver burn;
    that superdiabolic element
    is far more poignant than the flames of hell.   11,755
    I see why you unhappy lovers moan so overmuch—
    you who, although you're spurned, still twist
    your necks to catch a glimpse of her you love.
        My plight too! What's pulling my head in that direction,
    when that's the side of my sworn foes—   11,760
    I used to find them an offensive sight!

Has some strange thing infected me?
I love to look at them, these loveliest of youths;
what makes me hesitate to curse them?
And if I let myself become infatuated, 11,765
who will be henceforth called a fatuous fool!
Confounded rascals—though I hate them,
I find them only too attractive! –
   You lovely children, may I ask
if you're descendants too of Lucifer? 11,770
You are, I swear, so pretty that I'd like to kiss you;
I have a feeling you would suit me nicely.
I am as much at ease and natural
as if we'd met a thousand times already,
and am as eager as a stalking kitten, 11,775
while you grow lovelier each time I look.
Please don't hang back—look at me at least once!
THE ANGELS. Now that we are advancing, why do you withdraw?
   We're coming closer, and if you can, remain!
      The ANGELS *proceed to occupy the whole stage.*
MEPHISTOPHELES (*forced into the proscenium*).
You call us spirits damned but prove to be 11,780
the actual sorcerers yourselves,
for you seduce both men and women. –
Oh, what a damnable affair!
Is this the stuff that love is made of?
My body is on fire everywhere— 11,785
I hardly feel those burns upon my neck. –
You're hovering without direction—come down here
and use your limbs in ways a bit more worldly;
your grave looks suit you very nicely, I admit,
but just for once I'd like to see your smile— 11,790
that would afford me everlasting ecstasy!
I have in mind the way that lovers look:
it only takes a little movement of the mouth.
You, there, the lad that's tall, I like you best;
that sanctimonious air is not becoming to you, 11,795
so please give me a slightly wanton look!
Another thing! Without offending decency
you could wear less; long pleated robes are prudish –
They're turning – see them from the rear! –
the rascals really whet my appetite! 11,800
THE ANGELS.   Turn into clarity,
      you fires of passion!
      May truth cure all
      who seek self-damnation,

　　　　so that from evil　　　　　　　　　　　　　　11,805
　　　　they win joyous redemption
　　　　and, one with the All,
　　　　are evermore blessed!

MEPHISTOPHELES (*regaining composure*).
　　What's happening to me? – Like Job a mass of boils
　　from head to toe, a horror to myself,　　　　　　11,810
　　and yet triumphant after self-inspection,
　　still confident in both my tribe and self!
　　The parts essential to a devil all are rescued,
　　the love-illusion has become a healing rash;
　　all those atrocious flames have now stopped burning—　11,815
　　and, as is only proper, I curse you one and all!

THE ANGELS.　　　Fires of holiness!
　　　　　　　　　Whom they encompass,
　　　　　　　　　will live in blessed oneness
　　　　　　　　　with all who are good.　　　　　11,820
　　　　　　　　　Let us, together,
　　　　　　　　　ascend and give praise!
　　　　　　　　　The air is now purified,
　　　　　　　　　his spirit may breathe!

　　　The ANGELS *rise, bearing away the immortal part of* FAUST.

MEPHISTOPHELES (*looking about*).
　　But what has happened, where can they have gone? –　11,825
　　You stole a march on me, you puppies! –
　　They're flying off toward heaven with my prey—
　　so that is why they dallied at the graveside!
　　They've robbed me of a great, unequaled treasure;
　　the noble soul that pledged itself to me—　　　　11,830
　　they've tricked me out of it and smuggled it away.
　　　From whom can I now seek redress?
　　Who will procure me what I've duly earned?
　　You've been deceived—and late in life, besides—
　　it serves you right, this is your worst of times.　　11,835
　　I bungled everything disgracefully,
　　and so, o shame! a great investment's wasted—
　　a seasoned devil overcome
　　by vulgar lust, erotic silliness!
　　If one possessing wisdom and experience　　　　　11,840
　　could get involved in childish madness,
　　it is indeed the very height of folly
　　that in the end defeated him.

———————

MOUNTAIN GORGES

Forest, rocks. A solitude with HOLY ANCHORETS *in crevices of the mountain-side.*

CHORUS *and* ECHO. Woods seek to come near
               as rocks press them down,   11,845
               roots try to take hold
               as trees crowd together,
               wave splashes on wave
               as caves give us shelter;
               lions roaming about,   11,850
               silent and friendly,
               respect this asylum,
               love's sanctuary.

PATER ECSTATICUS (*hovering at various levels*).
               Searing eternal bliss,
               love's bond of fire,   11,855
               heart's seething anguish,
               divine surges of rapture—
               arrows, transpierce me,
               lances, subdue me,
               batter me, cudgels,   11,860
               lightning, crash through me,
               so that what's trivial
               may evanesce
               and love's lasting core
               shine as a constant star!   11,865

PATER PROFUNDUS (*in a lower region*).
When the abyss of rock below
weighs down abysses deeper still,
when jetting streams in thousands plunge
into the seething cataract,
when with its strong innate compulsion   11,870
a tree will rise straight to the sky,
it is all-potent Love that gives
all things their form, sustains all things.
    When all about me there is tumult—
woods and ravines a surging sea—   11,875
the roar is pleasant as the streams,
bringing water to a valley,
gush and plunge into the gorge;
the thunderbolts that crashed in flame
to purify the atmosphere   11,880
of poisonous vapors it had nursed—
    these messengers of love proclaim
creative force encompassing us always.

May it enkindle, too, my inner being
where, confused and chill, my spirit   11,885
is consumed, racked by their fetters,
in the tormenting bondage of my blunted senses.
Quiet, o God, my troubled thoughts,
and grant my needy heart Your light!

PATER SERAPHICUS (*at median elevation*).
Lo! a morning-wisp of cloud is floating   11,890
through the spruces' waving hair;
I divine what lives within it—
it's a group of newborn spirits.

BLESSED BOYS (*in chorus*).
Tell us, Father, where we're going,
kindly tell us who we are! –   11,895
We are happy, for existence
seems so easy to us all.

PATER SERAPHICUS.
You are boys!—were born at midnight,
half-endowed with mind and senses—
right away lost to your parents,   11,900
for us angels, source of gain.
Since you feel someone is present
who can love you, come to me;
you are fortunate that on you
earth's harsh paths have left no mark.   11,905
Come down here into my eyes,
organs made to see this world;
you may use them as your own—
gaze upon the landscape here!
                    (*He takes the* BOYS *into himself.*)
Those are trees, and those are rocks,   11,910
that's a stream—its falling waters
tumble down in giant loops
to make short the steep descent.

BLESSED BOYS (*heard as if speaking from within* PATER SERAPHICUS).
That is a tremendous sight,
but this place, it is too gloomy,   11,915
makes us quake with fear and dread.
Kindly let us leave, good sir!

PATER SERAPHICUS. Rise to higher spheres above,
growing imperceptibly
as God's pure sustaining presence   11,920
always works to make you stronger.
Absolute where skies are boundless,
it is this which feeds all spirits:

eternal love's epiphany
that flowers as beatitude.   11,925
BLESSED BOYS (*circling the highest summits*).
          Let us join hands
          to begin a gay round;
          let's dance and let's sing
          and feel pious besides!
          With such godly instruction   11,930
          there's no need to be hesitant,
          and soon we'll behold
          Him we revere.
ANGELS (*hovering in the upper sky with the immortal part of* FAUST).
This worthy member of the spirit world
is rescued from the devil: 11,935
for him whose striving never ceases
we can provide redemption;
and if a higher love as well
has shown an interest in him,
the hosts of heaven come   11,940
and greet him with a cordial welcome.
YOUNGER ANGELS. All those roses, given us
by penitents whose love is saintly,
helped us win our victory
and fulfill our lofty mission,   11,945
helped us seize this priceless soul.
When they fell, the wicked faltered,
when they hit, the devils fled.
Spirits used to hellish torment
felt the pangs of love instead;   11,950
even the old Master-Devil
suffered agony all over.
Hallelujah! We have won!
MORE-PERFECT ANGELS.
          This remainder of earth,
          it's distasteful to bear it;   11,955
          even cremated,
          it would still be impure.
          When a strong spirit
          has taken the elements
          and made them its own,   11,960
          angels can't separate
          two natures conjoined
          in one single entity—
          only Eternal Love
          can disunite them.   11,965

YOUNGER ANGELS. Close to us here,
  I suddenly sense
  spirit-life stirring
  as mists near the mountain-top.
  The clouds, now transparent,   11,970
  reveal Blessed Boys,
  all lively and active;
  free of earth's pressures
  they've formed a circle
  and now are enjoying   11.975
  the upper world's beauty,
  the freshness of spring. –
  As his start toward perfection
  let him who has come
  be their companion!   11,980
BLESSED BOYS. We're glad to receive
  this chrysalid entity,
  since it's you angels
  who give us the surety.
  Let's pull off the floss   11,985
  still clinging to him!
  Filled with life's sacredness
  he's handsome and tall.
DOCTOR MARIANUS (*in the highest and neatest cell*).
    The view here is vast,
    the spirit exalted.   11,990
    There I see women
    floating past upwards—
    I can tell by the glory
    that she at the center
    of their wreath of stars   11,995
    is heaven's High Queen.
(*In ecstasy.*) Sovereign mistress of the world,
  let me, in the azure
  of the heaven's canopy,
  contemplate your secrets!   12,000
  Sanction that which stirs man's heart
  to earnest tenderness
  and bears it aloft to you
  in love's sacred rapture.
   When you give august commands, 12,005
  nothing daunts our courage;
  when we know the peace you give,
  passion soon is quiet—
  Virgin, pure in the best sense;

venerated Mother;   12,010
one coequal of the gods;
Queen we have elected!
   Nebulous cloudlets
   dancing around her
   are penitent women—   12,015
   delicate creatures,
   down at her knees
   breathing the pureness,
   anxious for mercy.
You whom none may ever touch   12,020
always gladly suffer
those who're easily seduced
to confide in you.
 Hard indeed it is to save
those swept away by weakness—   12,025
how can they, desire's slaves,
burst their bonds unaided?
All too quickly feet give way
on a slippery slope!
Who resists a welcoming look,   12,030
is deaf to words that flatter?
   The MATER GLORIOSA *now floats past.*
PENITENT WOMEN (*in chorus*).
   You who soar upward
   to eternity's kingdoms,
   o peerless Being,
   fountain of mercy,   12,035
   give ear to our prayers.
MAGNA PECCATRIX [Luke, 7, 36].
 By the love that shed the tears—
which the Pharisee despised—
to be ointment for the feet
of your son, whom God transfigured;   12,040
by that box of alabaster
with its overflowing fragrance
and the hair that wiped and dried
the sacred limbs so tenderly –
MULIER SAMARITANA [John 4].
 By the well to which of old   12,045
the flocks of Abraham were driven
and the waterpot allowed
to refresh our Savior's lips;
by the pure, abundant waters
that since then spring up from it   12,050

and in everlasting brightness
overflow and flood the universe –
MARIA AEGYPTICA [*Acta Sanctorum*].
    By that holiest of places,
    where our Lord has been entombed,
    and the arm that from its door   12,055
    thrust me back with silent warning;
    by the forty years that I devoted
    to true penance in the desert
    and the peaceful farewell message
    that I wrote down in the sand –   12,060
THE THREE PENITENTS (*together*).
    You who let come near to you
    women who have greatly sinned,
    and augment the gains of penance
    in eternity forever,
    grant unto this good soul also—   12,065
    one who lost her head but once,
    unaware that she did wrong—
    as is fitting, your forgiveness!
A PENITENT *alias* GRETCHEN (*clinging to the* MATER GLORIOSA).
    Deign, o deign,
    you who are peerless,   12,070
    you who are radiant,
    to look down on my joy—
    the love of my youth,
    no longer unhappy,
    has now returned!   12,075
BLESSED BOYS (*circling closer*).
    Already he has grown
    bigger than we,
    and will reward our loving care
    with love still greater:
    as children we were separated   12,080
    from all of life's spheres;
    but this man has gained learning,
    he'll be our teacher.
THE PENITENT (GRETCHEN).
  Amid this host of lofty spirits
  our novice is uncertain he exists,   12,085
  but when he senses there is new life here,
  he soon will be the peer of any angel.
  See him work loose from all the bonds
  that once enveloped him on earth!
  See how his early, youthful vigor   12,090

shows to advantage in ethereal raiment!
Grant me permission to instruct him—
he still is dazzled by the strange new light.
MATER GLORIOSA. Come, rise to higher spheres—
Sensing your presence, he will follow!   12,095
DOCTOR MARIANUS (*prostrate, in adoration*).
                Look up to salvation's eyes,
                tender penitents,
                so that you may gratefully
                be reborn for heaven! –
                May all nobler spirits be   12,100
                eager for thy service;
                Virgin, Mother, Queen, and Goddess,
                keep us in your grace!
CHORUS MYSTICUS. All that is transitory
                is only a symbol;   12,105
                what seems unachievable
                here is seen done;
                what's indescribable
                here becomes fact;
                Woman, eternally,   12,110
                shows us the way.

[Finis.]

NOTES

CHRONOLOGY OF THE COMPOSITION OF *FAUST*

[Dates in square brackets are those of publication.]

1771–1772   Simultaneous interest in Götz von Berlichingen and in the puppet-play hero (cf. *Dichtung und Wahrheit*, Book X [1812] and Book XII [1814]).

1773–1775   "Urfaust." ['The King in Thule,' 1782; *Faust. A Fragment*, 1790 (about 1600 verses correspond to "Urfaust" passages); the subsequently discarded scene 'A Highway," 1794; *Goethe's Faust in ursprünglicher Gestalt*, 1887.]
       Cf. *Faust*, v. 354–605; 1868–2050; 2073–2336—here followed by 'A Highway' (4 verses); 2608–3216; 3374–3619; 3776–3834; 3620–59; 3342–69; 'An Expanse of Open Country'; 4399–4612.

1787–1790   *Faust. A Fragment* [1790].
       Cf. *Faust*, v. 354–605; *1770–1867;* * 1868–2050 (*1882–95, 1904–10, 1964–2000*); *2051–72;* 2073–2336 (*2095ff., 2015–8, 2120–3, 2161–78, 2181–8, 2270–3, 2284–9, 2313–5, 2324f., 2331, 2336*); 2337–2604; 2605–3261; 3374–3586; *3217–3341, 3370–73;* 3587–3619; 3776–3834.

1797–1801   *Faust I* [1808]. (New are *v. 1–353; 598–601, 606–1769; 2366–77; 3290–3; 3835–4334; 4343–98;* some *50* verses in the scene 'Prison'—4405–4612—without equivalents in the prose of "Urfaust."

1800–1801   *Faust II* begun.
       'Helen in the Middle Ages' [1888].—Cf. *Faust*, v. 8489–8802.
       Act I, first two scenes (v. 4613–c.5064).
       Act V, Faust's death (v. 11,151–c.11,603, *passim*).

1816   Résumé of Acts I, III, and IV, originally meant for inclusion in *Dichtung und Wahrheit* [1888].

1825f.   *Helen. Classico-Romantic Phantasmagoria. A* Faust *Intermezzo* [1827].

1827f.   Act IV begun (v. 10,039–66), and Act I continued (text of v. 4613–6036 in definitive form).

---

*Newly written or extensively revised passages in Faust. A Fragment and Faust I are indicated by italic verse-numbers.

1828	Opening scenes of Act II (v. 6566–7004).—*Faust II*, v. 4613–6036, published as a continuation of *Faust I* (to which v. *4335–42* are added).
1829f.	Act I completed (*i.e.*, final revision of v. 6037–6565).
1830	'Classical Walpurgisnight' (v. 7005–8487).
1830f.	Act V completed (v. 11,043–142; c.11,604–12,111).
1831	Act IV completed (v. 10,067–11,042) and, after final revision, the manuscript of *Faust II* sealed for posthumous publication.
1832	*Faust II* [1833] posthumously printed.

GOETHE'S *FAUST* AND THE PRESENT TRANSLATION

Faust is often thought of as the figure who embodies most completely—in proportions determined by the temper of the times—what are considered the best or the worst features of the German national character. He is also universally acknowledged to be the prototypical representative, for better or worse, of all post-medieval civilizations. Both these somewhat contradictory but not mutually exclusive conceptions of what Faust symbolizes ultimately derive from the fact that he is the protagonist of a tragedy which Goethe began in the early 1770's, when he and other young writers were urgently concerned with creating what they hoped would be a literature with distinctively German themes and qualities, but which he subsequently transmuted into a drama expressing humanistic and cosmopolitan values that transcend all nationalisms. Into the tragedy he re-conceived and began to execute in 1788, toward the end of his first sojourn in Italy, Goethe fitted almost all of what he had originally written for his *Faust*. He was guided by the ideal of a new classicism that would reconcile permanently his aesthetic and scientific modes of thought and would reflect the influence, until the completion of the drama in 1831, of what he had come to regard—primarily because of their high artistic achievements—as the exemplary greatness of Greco-Roman antiquity and the Renaissance.

Faust is thus a mosaic, often in one and the same scene, of elements written decades apart—for details the reader is referred to the tabular summary "Chronology of the Composition of *Faust*" (p. 306 f.). Only what Goethe completed, at Schiller's urging and with Schiller's encouragement, as Part One contains passages that grant an occasional glimpse of his original, relatively naive, dramatic conception; although they hardly constitute a tenth of the total text of *Faust,* they are often emotionally powerful or trenchantly witty and give Part One a greater range of tonal intensity than Part Two, which otherwise is distinguished by even more variety of tone and style. Begun in 1800, when Part One was still unfinished, Part Two—nearly twice its length—took Goethe almost exactly the same number of years to complete as had Part One. Although, between 1801 and 1825, he is not known to have written any passage of *Faust,* Goethe continued to make revisions of his plans for it and of the motifs to be used. Thus, in 1816, still uncertain whether he would ever be able to complete the drama, he prepared for inclusion in *Dichtung und Wahrheit* a detailed summary of the action of Part Two as he then conceived it. It was while revising this summary for publication that he was persuaded in early 1825 by Eckermann and others to withhold it, and to undertake instead the completion of Part Two, which is therefore comprised primarily of material actually written in Goethe's last years.

Composed over so many decades, often at moments of immediate response to new ideas and experiences, *Faust* mirrors in varying degrees of intensity the ever-widening interests and concerns of Goethe's long and rich life which are thematically integral to it. Accordingly, despite the unified conception under-lying its dramatic action, themes and motifs are sometimes developed so fully, with such great abruptness, or in such a variety of styles that (to be sure, more for the reader than the theater-goer) their functions become evident only when an earlier context is remembered or a subsequent one illuminates them. Mo-tival repetition and thematic counterpoint are thus often more important, especially in Part Two, than immediate transparency of plot or character development; they offset structural ellipses, integrate what would otherwise be disparate textual elements, and, as a consequence, establish the intercon-nectedness of the several real worlds and their imaginary extensions in which the action of *Faust* takes place. Regardless of any disadvantages attendant upon it, the quasi-organic complexity consequent to Goethe's mode of com-position keeps *Faust* free of the monotonous homogeneity or artificial hetero-geneity that flaws otherwise comparable dramas of epic scope by authors who emulated Goethe's technique of varying dramatic styles and prosodic forms. (Examples would be contemporaries like Tieck, Brentano, Atterbom, and Oehlenschläger, and such later writers as Mickiewicz, Ibsen, Hardy, and Werfel.)

That in *Faust* the primary function of formal variety is to be thematic rather than ornamental best explains why Goethe prefaced his tragedy with three prologues—Dedication, Prelude on the Stage, Prologue in Heaven—which would otherwise be superfluous. Neither the dedication nor the stage-prelude makes any specific reference to Faust or to the plot of *Faust,* and although the heaven-scene announces an untraditional use of the Faust legend—the trag-edy's hero is to prove to be "a good man"—it too says nothing about the action of the play, while all it has to say about Faust will be stated dramatically in either Part One or Part Two of the tragedy proper. The three prologues do serve, however, to establish the thematic and tonal range that is to be a salient feature of *Faust.* The subdued, almost private, elegiac lyricism of Dedication is immediately followed by the realism of the farce-like scene in which the voices of cynical materialism and conciliatory practicality quickly silence the voice of conventionally rhetorical pathos. And after this typically eighteenth-century pseudo-improvisation there comes the timeless symbolism of a miracle-play heaven in which the rapid alternation of hymnlike sublimity, satiric diatribe, and gentle irony demonstrates that intense lyricism can coexist as it were simultaneously with bathos and ridicule.

The great tonal range displayed in these prologues is not without antecedents in dramatic literature—Shakespeare and Calderón, both of whom Goethe much admired, are major earlier masters of it—but it is not to be found in the introductory scenes of what was to be a serious play (and had perhaps never been used with such virtuoso concentration as in Goethe's Prologue in Heaven). By insistently indicating that *Faust* represents a radical break with—or at least radical modification and extension of the functions of—traditional poetic and dramaturgical elements, it underscores the fact that Goethe's drama will deviate radically from tradition in its conception of Faust's character and its use of motifs from an already well-established Faust-legend.

The only writer before Goethe to anticipate the motif of Faust's salvation was Lessing, but although an earnest concern for truth was to save his primarily intellectual hero from the paths of wickedness, traditional motifs were to constitute the main action of his never completed play, which is only a dream that Faust would awaken from as a better and wiser man. With the exception of Paul Valéry, most later writers—e.g. Heine, Gounod's librettists Barbier and Carré, Thomas Mann, Dorothy Sayers, John Hersey—have been more conservative and conventional than Goethe; despite their often generous use of motifs, like the Gretchen action, which are Goethe's sole invention, they have preferred to follow earlier tradition and let Faust sell his soul to the devil and, after twenty-four years of wish-fulfillment, die either literally or figuratively damned. Even Arrigo Boito's *Faust*-opera, by virtue of its title *Mefistofele,* pays homage to that tradition, and although its Faust is "saved," by giving the miracle-play motif of Prologue in Heaven a dramatic function not attached to it in Goethe's tragedy, his work represents a return to the tradition established by Marlowe's morality play of treating the *Faust* theme allegorically.

By virtue of its extremes of tone and style—motivally embodied in Prologue in Heaven as the polarity of light (Divine Reason) and darkness (human and Mephistophelean finitude)—Goethe's tri-partite introduction establishes thematic variation and contrastive parallel as basic structuring principles of the tragedy that follows. The flexible application of these principles not only makes congruous the coexistence of present and past, of reality and dream, of temporality and timelessness, of life and art, of actuality and vision; through small and large parallelisms it also keeps certain longer scenes and several loosely connected scene-sequences from being a mere congeries of discrete elements and, most importantly, integrates with Part One of *Faust* a Part Two not radically different in dramatic and other techniques, but very unlike it in the proportions in which these are used. Thus the brief dream-play that in Part One concludes Faust's Walpurgis Night visions adds little to them and means nothing to him, while that, well over ten times its length, which follows the visions of his "classical" Walpurgisnight significantly extends the symbolic exteriorization of his growing ability to be objective, especially about himself. Analogously, Part Two has many more, and many much longer, passages of strictly regular verse than does Part One, most immediately noticeable being those from which rhyme is absent; whereas in Part One only one of its three unrhymed passages (23 verses in iambic pentameter) is metrically regular, in Part Two there are five scenes with longer passages in variously regular unrhymed meters (in all nearly 1100 verses, including 101 iambic pentameters).

A motival technique much more important in Part Two than in Part One is the use of iconic and pictorial elements. Although Goethe occasionally employs this technique in Part One, chiefly in passages composed after his espousal of conscious classicism, and then chiefly as an ornamental surrogate for or supplement to detailed stage directions, in Part Two he uses it not only more extensively and more insistently, but also to all intents and purposes exclusively as a sign indicating that what is described—usually a motif from classical or Renaissance art—is to be displayed or imagined as Faust envisions it. This obviously holds true for the iconic elements of the long masque he stages for the Emperor, but elsewhere in the drama—whether or not Faust is an active participant or even present—its importance is far greater, since it establishes that what is happening must be looked at from Faust's point of view and in terms of how it mirrors a given stage of his development as a dramatic character. Insofar as they are chiefly "classical," the iconic motifs in *Faust* often reflect Goethe's personal artistic preferences, but if they have an extra-dramatic function, it is not to document his aesthetic judgments or his knowledge of art history, but to underscore the secular-humanistic and humane-liberal values he lets Faust share with himself—values which, as he wrote Part Two of his tragedy, seemed threatened by a romantic cult of the irrational and by the forces of political, social, and religious reaction too often supported in the post-Napoleonic decades by consciously conservative exponents of romanticism. However ornamentally used, the iconic motifs of *Faust* are thus never merely incidental; like its motifs from myth and history, music and literature, philosophy and science, they represent elements that, by being archetypally significant, illuminate and bring into focus the themes and values given symbolic substance in Goethe's uniquely universal drama.

Even the most scrupulous translation, whether prose or verse, will fail to convey some distinctive feature of an original text—a shade of meaning, a degree of emphasis, a sound effect, a level of tone, etc. A translator may be aware of all such textual features, but since no two languages are sufficiently alike to permit the simultaneous transfer of more than some of them from one language to another, the translator of a particular text has to decide which of its features it is most important to retain in translation. Translating, unless merely piecemeal hackwork, is thus a hermeneutic process, and a translation represents the results not only of textual analysis and linguistic (chiefly historico-lexicographical) interpretation, but also, and far more significantly, since this will determine what the translator retains in translation, of critical evaluation.

Faust as translated here will, I hope, give the English reader fully adequate equivalents of those features of the text which I have already indicated I regard as most important. Its language is present-day English, not so much because there was in Goethe's day no contemporary literary equivalent of Goethe's German that could be recreated, but because only modern English permits the reading or reciting of the text at a tempo approximating that possible with the German original. Accordingly, I have consciously introduced slightly old-fashioned words or turns of phrase only when it seemed appropriate to provide the counterpart of a German archaism, have eliminated *thee* and *thou* except when God is addressed (even though this has occasionally meant the addition of words to clarify whether a *you* is singular or plural), and have reproduced inversions only when they are thought-structuring rather than German-grammatical. And although I always sought the closest possible English approximations of the rhythms of Goethe's text, I have not hesitated to sacrifice metrical regularity to idiomatic clarity.

Most translators of *Faust* into English (some ninety of the hundred, including myself on two earlier occasions, who have heretofore translated either the entire text or generous portions of it) seem to have subscribed to the view that the distinguishing feature of poetry is rhyme. Although they sometimes have demonstrated a keen ear for Goethe's rhythms or substituted for them effective rhythmic patterns of their own, simply by employing rhyme—either rhyme schemes modeled upon those of the German text or, occasionally, ones of their own choosing—they have made it a far more conspicuous prosodic element in their translations than it is in the original German. In *Faust,* as in most of Goethe's verse, rhyme is minimally obtrusive, since it ordinarily functions only to mark line-closure, i.e., to indicate the length of rhythmic units. To write doggerel, convoluted English, or non-English ("translatese") for the sake of having rhyme gives as false an impression of how and what Goethe wrote as does mistranslation of lexical and syntactic elements. Aware of this, a handful of translators chose to disregard Goethe's use of verse and were content to reproduce the tonal range of *Faust* only to the extent that it can be conveyed through prose. A few others tried using blank verse as the sole equivalent of what in *Faust* is great metrical variety. In each case, but especially in the second, the result has been a rhythmic homogenization that is not only minimally functional but, sooner or later, monotonous as well.

To avoid the pitfalls of rhyme, the limitations of prose, and the losses attendant upon metrical transposition or homogenization, in this translation I have made extensive use of what Randall Jarrell called "metered verse" (and used for his translation of Part One of *Faust*). By dispensing with rhyme it almost always permits the translator to reproduce the rhythms and to convey adequately the prosodic variety of Goethe's German without recourse to inappropriate inversions or distortions of meaning. It not only allows inconspicuous transition to rhyme when rhyme—usually because it is mentioned—is demanded by the text of *Faust;* it is also so distinctively flexible that, when metrical regularity must contrast functionally with it, this regularity is immediately recognizable. I have therefore made it a basic principle to introduce no "undemanded" rhyme into my translation. To do so in order to imitate a rhymed couplet marking a scene-closure would be to attach a greater degree of importance to it than it has in an already rhymed context. To do so when rhyme is simply a signifier of lyric intensity, as in Gretchen's monologue at her spinning-wheel, would be to intrude into the text a dramatically incongruous *Singspiel* or opera-like element as well as to diminish the functional effectiveness of other metrically regular passages meant—and marked—for singing. And to do so with these metrically regular passages would, in a now normally unrhymed context, make them unwarrantedly more conspicuous than are their German equivalents. (That, whatever its functional importance, rhyme is inconspicuous in *Faust* can most easily be confirmed by consulting the German counterpart of Bartlett's *Familiar Quotations,* Büchmann's *Geflügelte Worte;* of the 50 *Faust* passages cited in my edition of it, only 15 are two lines or more in length, and only two of these 15 constitute rhymed couplets.)

In the present translation metered verse usually corresponds to what in the original are either octosyllabic couplets or irregularly rhymed passages of lines with as few as one and as many as six stresses. Stanzaic verses are normally, and *terza rima* and non-discontinuous alexandrine couplets are always, reproduced (without rhyme) in more or less exact equivalents of the original meters; as in the German text of Goethe, indentation makes stanzaic verse immediately identifiable. The few irregularly rhythmical unrhymed verses of the German text—they occur only in Part One—have been assimilated to metered verse. Blank verse, and the lines in rhymeless "classical" meters of Part Two, are differentiated from metered verse by their sustained metrical regularity. Goethe's "classical" strophes, which appear only in Act III of Part Two, strictly imitate Greek models and, when there is an antistrophe, repeat its meters. I have not—as, at the expense of clarity of expression, I did in earlier translations—reproduced their metrical patterns exactly, but offer only rhythmic approximations of them; their irregular rhythms distinguish them from stanzaic verses that, even though also rhymeless, are metrically far more regular. Naturalness of idiom has, I believe, never been sacrificed in order to establish stanzaic or metrical regularity, and it is the explanation of why—as is sometimes the case, though less often, in Goethe's German—classical verses are here occasionally hypermetric or have, like some alexandrines, an improperly placed caesura. (Identification of verse forms and their German equivalents is provided, *passim,* in the Explanatory Notes to the text of this edition.)

Although, Goethe says in *Dichtung und Wahrheit* with reference to prose translations of Shakespeare, rhythm and rhyme make poetic works Poetry, "what actually produces a profound and fundamental effect . . . is what remains of a poet when he is translated into prose. It leaves us with the essential substance, which a dazzling exterior . . . may have concealed." How best to be faithful to the substance—the meaning—of *Faust* and convey in English its poetic essence is the fundamental decision that its translator must make. All other decisions are ones that arise in connection with any translation and are, in the case of *Faust,* chiefly syntactic and lexicographical. If the translator is not trapped by "false friends"—does not mistake some lexical or grammatical element for another that resembles it, does not fail to recognize that the semantic value of a word may no longer be what it was in Goethe's day, and does not fall into the trap of using an English word that, although it strongly resembles a German one in the text, has very different connotations—the result can be a reasonably close English counterpart of what *Faust* says and means. The only trap a scrupulous translator may fail to avoid is translating too carefully and too much. As Lessing noted:

> Over-exactness makes any translation stiff; what is natural in one language cannot always be so in another. And when verses are translated (even) a prose translation becomes dilute and skewed. For where is there a successful versifier whom meter or rhyme . . . has not caused to say something otherwise than he would have without their constraints? If the translator cannot discern when this has occurred and lacks the judgment and courage to omit incidentals, to replace a metaphor by its referent, to supplement an ellipsis or introduce one, he will transmit to us all the flaws of a text without the symmetry and euphony that made venial their presence in its original language.

In making my translation of *Faust* I have frequently followed Lessing's implicit advice; the one important exception is that I have kept textual elements apparently incidental to rhyme closure—i.e., that seem only to prepare for or to complete a rhyme—when a context of flexible line-lengths permitted their unobtrusive retention.

The distinctive features of the original text that have been preserved in this translation will, I believe, permit English readers to understand why *Faust* has long been everywhere recognized as one of the world's "Great Books," and why Goethe has earned an acknowledged place beside Homer, Dante, and Shakespeare in the pantheon of Western literature. In a world of time and history, *Faust* is Goethe's timeless vision of what it is to be human. It is the expression of a spirit that transcends any national character, and I hope that my translation into today's English lets this spirit be fully conveyed.

BIBLIOGRAPHICAL NOTE

The translation of Part One, and of Part Two v. 4613–6036 and v. 8488–10,038, is based on the last editions published under Goethe's personal supervision (1827 f.); for the sections of Part Two published posthumously, I have normally followed the first edition (1832), which, despite minor deviations from Goethe's manuscript text, best reproduces his often helpfully idiosyncratic punctuation. Line numbering, as in all modern German editions of *Faust,* is that of Goethe, *Werke,* 1. Abt., XIV–XV (Weimar, 1884 f.): a few discrepancies occur when idiomatic English did not permit line-for-line equivalents of the German text.

As of 1981, 12 English translations of *Faust* were in print.

There are two prose translations of both Parts, one by B. Q. Morgan, and the other by Barker Fairley; the latter, somewhat free and often deliberately elliptical, occasionally omits—it may be presumed, inadvertently—short sections of the text.

The verse translations of both Parts that offer more or less close approximations of the original meters and rhyme schemes are those by Bayard Taylor, Philip Wayne, Charles Passage, and Walter Arndt; a revision of Taylor's translation by Stuart Atkins; and the W. H. Bruford revision of the translation of Theodore Martin. With these may be included the abridged version of Louis MacNeice, a translation of about two-thirds of the text; its most notable omissions are *Dedication, Prelude on the Stage,* Mephistopheles' interview with the Student, *Auerbach's Wine-Cellar, Walpurgis Night's Dream, A Great Hall* (the Court Masquerade), the scene between Mephistopheles and the Baccalaureate, slightly more than half of "Classical Walpurgisnight," the entire first section of Act III, and about one-third of Act IV.

There are also in print two translations of Part One almost entirely in "metered verse," by Carlyle F. MacIntyre and by Randall Jarrell (with v. 3374–3413 by Robert Lowell), and a rhyming translation of it by John Prudhoe.

Information in English about Faust, and commentaries on and interpretations of *Faust,* can be found under the entries "Goethe" and "Faust" in any library catalogue or general encyclopedia, and in many editions of *Faust* (including the translations of Arndt and Taylor-Atkins). The selective bibliography in Vol. III of Goethe, *Werke,* "Hamburger Ausgabe," ed. Erich Trunz (München: C. H. Beck), which is updated every two or three years, is international in its coverage and, in addition, lists all comprehensive Faust-bibliographies to date.

Illustrations of many of the works of art alluded to in *Faust* are reproduced in the Passage translation and in the German editions with commentary by Georg Witkowski.

EXPLANATORY NOTES

All references are to line numbers (in *italics*) — When not reproduced in the translation, distinctive verse forms are identified. If not identified in the notes, and not printed as stanzas, unrhymed iambic verse represents iambic lines (usually with four to six stresses) variously rhymed—e.g., *aa, abab, abba,* etc.

1–32 (and *59–74*) ottava rima (iambic pentameter, rhymed *ababab cc*).

2 young 25 years earlier (1772, since these lines were written when Goethe undertook, in 1797, to complete *Part I*).

17 songs (Germ. *Gesänge*—also: the books of an epic poem).

21 tragic song in texts printed in Goethe's lifetime: *Leid* (sorrow); in some modern editions: *Lied* (song), a manuscript reading.

26 spirit realm realm of the spirit (of dream, imagination, and poetry—*not:* of spirit creatures).

27 aeolian harp traditionally: the lyre of the heart, of uncontrollable feeling.

33–242 Director: financial principal of an acting troupe. *Poet-Playwright* (Germ. *Theaterdichter*): primarily an adapter of others' works to the troupe's resources. *Player of Comic Roles* (Germ. *Lustige Person*): actor-clown, a figure that largely disappeared from the German stage in the course of the 18th century. Time: first two-thirds of that century (*53:* late afternoon performances had long ceased to be customary when Goethe began completing Part I).

156 f. variation of the Renaissance commonplace that the gods are the invention or creation of poets.

243–353 parallels to Job 1 f.

243–70 hymn stanzas (rhymed *abab*).

285 f. Renaissance commonplace (e.g., Macchiavelli); cf. the Earl of Rochester: "Reason, an *ignis fatuus* of the mind, / Which leaves the life of nature's sense behind."

312 What'll you bet? Equivalent of the formulaic phrase of challenge introduced by Luther in translating Job 1, 11; it replaces "and" in the English version of "and he will curse thee to thy face."

354–807 Time: primarily 16th century (especially *354–85*), with some 18th-century elements (feeling for landscape; Storm-and-Stress satire in Wagner episode). Pictorial models: Thomas Wyck, *Alchemist's Laboratory*; Rembrandt, *The Astrologer* (an adaptation of the latter was used as frontispiece to *Faust: Ein Fragment,* 1790).

360 Doctor university professor (with privileges of the nobility).

420 Nostradamus a French astrologer-prophet and younger contemporary of the historical Faust (here as an alchemist-mystic).

434 signs symbols of planets and elements.

442 sage a mystic or mystagogue.

446 roseate dawn here figurative: a moment favorable for mystic insights.

449 forces stars, angels.

460–513 Earth Spirit (Germ. *Erdgeist*) not the alchemical-mystic *anima terrae,* but a symbol of the divine-creative spirit as this manifests itself in terrestrial activity.

469–74 unrhymed verse.

482 fearful overwhelmingly large (in a stage design sketched by Goethe: a colossal Olympian head).

737–41, 449–61, 785–807 rhymed chorale (hymn).

749–61, 785–96 Pictorial model: Raphael, *The Transfiguration.*

808–1177 Time: 16th century (*998* plague of 1525), with 18th-century elements in the first folk scene *808–902* (e.g., *862* refers to Russo-Turkish Wars, 1768–74 and 1787–92—in the 16th century the Turkish threat was not so remote). First use in the text of a stage set representing several different places simultaneously.

878 Saint Andrew's night Nov. 29 (patron saint of the unmarried).

1043 Lily an acid.

1046 Young Queen the sublimate produced (the elixir or panacea, the Philosopher's Stone).

1178–1529 Time: 16th century (*1220 ff.* recall Luther's translation of the New Testament, printed 1522).

1255 fire-red eyes fiery eyes are a striking feature of the dog in the elder Matthäus Merian's *The Devil Appears as a Dog to Cardinal Crescentius* (engraving).

1258 Solomon's Key collection of spells, incantations, etc.

1272 Spell of the Four i.e., the four elements Fire, Water, Air, and Earth, here identified with nature spirits.

1273 Salamander not the mythically incombustible animal, but—in Paracelsus' writings—a being that inhabits fire.

1333 Lord of Flies (Hebr. *Beelzebub*), *Destroyer (Satan), Liar* (Gr. *diábolos,* slanderer).

1366 the indestructibility of matter became an accepted principle in the later 18th century (and was scientifically demonstrated, c. 1780, by Lavoisier).

1447–1505 rhymed (except for two verses).

1507 sleep hypnotic sleep (as of Miranda in *The Tempest,* I, ii, 185–304).

1530–2072 Time: 16th century (with later elements: 17th-century wigs, *1807;* mid-18th century student scene, *1868–2050;* ascent in 1783 of the hot-air balloon of the brothers Montgolfier, *2069 f.*).

1607–26 verses of one to four stresses (all but three lines rhymed).

1705 its hand may fall the clock's mechanism—or the clock itself—be broken.

1712 doctoral banquet Goethe at one time planned to write a scene with a comic disputation (traditional at academic celebrations), but the reference now serves only to underscore the fact that the long Easter recess is over— that considerable time has elapsed since the first scene with Mephistopheles.

1808 shoes such patten-like shoes (Ital. *zoccoli*) were fashionable in 16th-century Venice.

1911 Collegium Logicum required introductory lecture course on logic.

1941 encheiresis naturae (18th century GK.-Lat. scientific jargon; the form in the text is accusative) Nature's knack of combining substances so that they are endowed with life (as opposed to products of distillation, crystallization, etc.).

2000 jot or tittle (Germ. *Jota,* the Greek letter *iota*); an allusion to the bitter conflict between Homoiousians and Homoousians (Eccl. Hist.).

2048 "Ye shall be as God, knowing good and evil"—Gen. 3, 5 (Vulgate, with *Deus* substituted for the plural *dii,* gods).

2073–2336 Time: 18th century (the German Holy Roman Empire no longer significant, *2090 ff.*; political absolutism questioned, *2211 ff.*; effect of electric shock on nervous system—Galvani, 1789—*2324* and *2331*).

2113 witches' sabbath (Germ. *Blocksberg* = the Brocken, in the Harz Mountains, where the witches' sabbath is held on Walpurgis Night).

2189 Rippach town in which Master Jackass (Germ. *Hans* [sc. *Arsch* or *Dumm*]) was said to live.

2337–2604 Pictorial models: illustrations in books on witchcraft; David Teniers, the younger, *Witch's Kitchen with Young Apes Playing with a Ball;* H. B., *Witch's Kitchen with Apes* (Dresden Gallery—formerly attrib. to Adriaen Brouwer).

2369 (cf. *10,121*) allusion to rock-formations called Devil's Bridges.

2429 ff. Faust presumably sees a nude in the style of Titian, Giorgione, or Paris Bordone.

2530 ff. The Witch's preparations are traditional, but the ringing of glasses is a feature of later, 18th-century spiritualist séances (e.g., Cagliostro).

2759–82 ballad-like quatrains (rhymed *abab*).

3037 Sancta simplicitas saintlike naivety.

3217–50 blank verse.

3318 her song an actual folksong ("Were I a little bird, I'd fly to thee").

3337 lilies (Germ. *Rosen*—Luther's translation of Song. Sol. 4, 5, has "roses").

3374–3413 lyric monologue (except for four lines, rhymed *xaxa, xbxb,* etc.).

3537 interest in physiognomy (and phrenology—Gall) developed in the second half of the 18th century (cf. n. to *4323*).

3540 radical (Germ. *Genie*) writer of the German Storm-and-Stress period (mid-1770's).

3587–3169 verses of one to four stresses (all but two lines rhymed), with many echoes of the Stabat Mater (particularly popular in the 18th century in the setting for two voices by Pergolesi).

3673 pearls omens of tears and misfortune.

3682–97 folksong motif (cf. Ophelia's "Tomorrow is Saint Valentine's day," *Hamlet*, IV, v, 49–56).

3776–3834 The German text is unrhymed (verses of one to six stresses).

3788 agonies of purgatory (having died, unshriven, in her sleep).

3798f., 3813ff., 3825ff. (from the Latin hymn, *Dies Irae,* sung in requiem masses) "The day of wrath shall dissolve this world into ashes. / When therefore the Judge shall take His seat, whatever is hidden shall appear, nothing shall remain unpunished. / What shall I, wretched man, then say? what protector supplicate? when scarcely the just may be secure!"

3835–4398 Time: dream-present, with steadily increasing number of allusions to persons and events of the late 18th century. – *Schierke* and *Elend* are towns at the base of the Brocken. – Pictorial models: illustrations in books and broadsides on witchcraft. – Stage set: several different places.

3855 will-o'-the-wisp ignis fatuus (cf. n. to *285f.*).

3962 Baubo a lewdly amusing nurse in the Greek mysteries of Demeter.

3996–4007 the voice of a recidivist (in the Enlightenment the Renaissance and Reformation were regarded as the beginning of modern rationalism).

4072–91 untraditional figures (persons disadvantaged by the political and intellectual changes of the late 18th century).

4096 Huckstress-Witch A huckstress is a figure in Renaissance Italian carnival processions.

4144–75 (and *4267–70, 4319–22*) Friedrich Nicolai, a life-long exponent of rationalism and prolific author of semi-autobiographical travel books, in 1799 reported his (earlier) cure of hallucinations by use of the treatment described by Mephistopheles.

4211 Prater a park in Vienna that became a popular fairground in the later 18th century.

4223–4398 quatrains (rhymed *abab* except for two that are rhymed *xaxa*). – *Intermezzo* an interlude—comic or satiric—given between the acts of an *opera seria;* here a satiric masque (masquerade). From *Midsummer-Night's Dream* the figures Oberon, Titania, Puck; from *The Tempest,* Ariel.

4224 Mieding court cabinet-maker who served as stage manager of the Weimar theater until his death in 1782.

4227 Herald the announcer—and often describer—of figures in a masque or pageant.

4259 Materializing Spirit grotesque (and "unorganic") poetry.

4271 Orthodox an orthodox Christian like Count F. L. von Stolberg, who condemned Schiller for glorifying "The Gods of Greece" in a poem so titled.

4275 Artist Goethe, who planned a third trip to Italy in 1797; military-political developments, however, made it impractical.

4279 Purist language-purist, and prude.

4295 Weathervane backbiting opportunist.

4303 Satiric Verses (Germ. *Xenien:* title of satiric distichs by Goethe and Schiller published in 1796; they aroused much anger among the butts of the satire—e.g., Hennings, *4307–18*).

4307 Hennings (cf. n. to *4303*).

4311 Would-Be Apollo (Germ. *Musaget,* Gr. *mousagétes,* Apollo as leader of the Muses—the title of a collection of Hennings' poems).

4315 Spirit of the Age (Germ. *Genius der Zeit*) title of a journal edited by Hennings that was changed in 1801 to *Genius des 19. Jahrhunderts* (Spirit of the Nineteenth Century).

4323 Crane J. C. Lavater, Swiss Protestant pastor and leading 18th-century physiognomist (cf. *3537*), friend of Goethe in the 1770's and early 1780's whom Goethe later came to distrust.

4327 Worldling (Germ. *Weltkind*) Goethe's name for himself as a secularist.

4331 group representatives of various systems or types of philosophy *(4343–62)*.

4347 Idealist J. G. Fichte or a Fichtean (cf. n. to *6736*).

4367 Adroit those who survive social and political change (beginning with the French Revolution) successfully.

4371 Awkward maladroit French emigrés.

4375 Will-o'-the-Wisps those who have risen socially as a result of political change.

4379 Shooting Star a political idealist disillusioned by the actualities of revolution.

4383 Massive the masses who have not fully adjusted to their new importance.

4394 Hill of Roses site of the castle of Oberon in C. M. Wieland's verse romance *Oberon* (1780).

p. 113 avenger of blood executioner (cf. Deut. 19, 12). That devils cannot release prisoners magically is traditional folklore.

4399–4404 unrhymed.

4405–4612 rhymed (except for 18 random verses).

4412–20 the song (by Goethe) with its Atreus-like motif is based on a German folktale.

4590 the white rod a wand broken after the decree of execution has been publicly read.

4613–78 rhymed (4613–20, 4634–65 *abab*). *Ariel* (cf. n. to *4223 ff.*) and the *Spirits* personify the curative powers of nature and time.

4666 Horae goddesses of (the orderly passage of) the seasons. Pictorial model: Guido Reni, *Aurora*.

4679–727 In terza rima (i.e., pentameters rhymed *aba bcb* etc.)—a verse form used in Italian for epic (e.g., Dante, *Divine Comedy*) and lyric poetry, and in Spanish drama of the Golden Age for lyric monologues (e.g., Calderón, Cervantes).

4728–6565 rhymed (when quatrains: *abab* or, occasionally, *abba*). Time: early 16th century (eve of the Reformation).

4743–50 Perhaps Mephistopheles' self-introduction (fool as privileged critic), perhaps preliminary allusion to Faust as potential savior of the Emperor (cf. *4895 f.*).

4938 subsoil earth below the level reached by a plow (Roman law).

4979 f. The shriek of the mandrake root when pulled from the ground was said to be fatal unless the agent used was a black dog.

5065–5986 The *Masquerade* is a mixture of carnival masquerade, pageant, and allegorical masques (cf. n. to *4223–4398*) staged by Faust, the last of which—the triumph of the Emperor as Pan—ends in a mock-tragic conflagration modeled after a historical incident in the life of Charles VI of France. Almost all the figures who appear are standard types in Italian (Renaissance) carnival processions. For the role of the *Herald,* cf. n. to *4227*.

5136 Theophrastus Greek botanist (pupil of Aristotle).

5299 The Graces Pictorial model: Andrea Boscoli (drawing).

5305 Pictorial model: Primaticcio, *The Three Fates as Youthful Nudes* (a motif occurring without nude figures, e.g., in *The Fates* by Heinrich Meyer, painter-collaborator of Goethe).

5357 Alecto identified, as traditionally since the Renaissance, with Calumny.

5378 Asmodeus In Tobit 3, 8 (Apocrypha) the demon who kills the husbands of Sara; here, as in 16th-century German literature, the devil responsible for (marital) discord.

5393–5456 The first allegory: Prudence (Italian carnival figure) controls idle fears and vain hopes, permitting Victory (successful activity) to use Power, of which the elephant is a traditional symbol, effectively.

5457 Zoilo-Thersites the spirit of Mephistophelean anti-heroism and anti-idealism: Zoilus, a carping Alexandrian critic of Homer; Thersites, the scurrilous enemy of Achilles and Ulysses in the *Iliad* (and in Shakespeare, *Troilus and Cressida*).

5479 Pictorial model: Aldegrever, *Envy with Snake and Bats*.

5494–5708 The second allegory: things of the spirit, including poetry (Boy Charioteer), are not appreciated by a materialistic society (Mephistopheles as Sir Greed; greed of the Crowd). Pictorial model: elements from Mantegna, *The Triumph of Caesar*.

5649 Avarice traditional carnival (female) figure.

5801 Wild Hunt spectral hunters of folklore; here, as in heraldry, a group of Salvage (Savage, Wild) Men, who were often figures in masques even in the 18th century.

5840 Gnomes carnival and masque figures (here: miners).

5864 Men of Great Stature (Germ. *Riesen,* giants). These were often "Ethiopians." Pictorial model: Giulio Parigi (engraved by Jacques Callot).

5872 f. Pan Frequent symbol of the ruling prince in Renaissance masques (e.g., of James I in collaborative work of Ben Jonson and Inigo Jones). Pictorial model: Claude Gillet, *Pan with Attendants and Satyrs.*

5934 ff. Pictorial model: Matthäus Merian, the elder, *Pre-Lenten Fire at the Court of Charles VI* (showing the king's head and beard in flames). – Mock conflagrations were a popular Renaissance (and later) firework effect.

6025 f. Thetis a Nereid, mother of Achilles by *Peleus,* king of the Myrmidons.

6072 conjurors printers (allusion to the long popular identification of Faust with Gutenberg's associate Fust).

6216 Mothers despite Graeco-Roman analogues (e.g., Sicilian mothergoddesses), inventions of Mephistopheles (and of Goethe); they allegorize the eternal existence of (insubstantial) forms and ideas. In a conversation recorded by his friend Riemer, Goethe called the Mothers' realm of solitude a "sphere of dreams and magic" (cf. *3872*), an experience of "poetic reverie" in which Faust gains "the Idea of Beauty in the form of Helen."

6259 key The key (to Nowhere) is a traditional symbol of (magical) power—here: of Mephistopheles' hypnotic powers as much as of any power it may lend Faust.

6421 in priestly robe and wreath Pictorial models: Giuseppe Cesari, *Priest at Altar* (drawing); *Simon Magus* (Assisi fresco, attr. Giunta Pisano).

6436 sorcerer Faust both as Magus and as Poet staging a pantomimic drama. (Goethe first wrote *Dichter,* poet, which he later changed to *Magier,* magician, sorcerer, magus; the equation is traditional.)

6509 picture Sebastiano Conca, *Diana and Endymion* (other treatments known to Goethe include those of Guercino, Annibale Carracci, and a Graeco-Roman fresco at Herculaneum).

6557 doubly as not only created, but also rescued—from Paris—by Faust (i.e., transported from the sphere of the imagination, of the Mothers, into that of tangible realities).

6566–10,038 Acts II and III take place on the same night as does the scene Knights' Hall (cf. *7442, 7990 f.*)—i.e., in February or March and not, as Mephistopheles will suggest through Homunculus *(6940 f.),* on the anniversary of the Battle of Pharsalus (Aug. 9, 48 B.C.,—cf. *6955 ff.* and *7018*).

6566–7004 Rhymed (except for four lines *xaxaxbxb, 6596 f.*). Time: 16th century (with allusions to the 18th century—cf. notes to *6588* and *6736*).

6588 professor (Germ. *Dozent,* non-tenured professor—introduced as title in the later 18th century).

6634 Nicodemus a literal-minded person (cf. John 3, 4).

6635 Oremus "Let us pray."

6736 with nothing left up there (Germ. *nicht absolut*) i.e., an adherent of some form of philosophical absolutism, which was often condemned as atheistic by the religiously orthodox—possibly that of Fichte (cf. n. to *4347*), in which the Absolute Ego is God.

6879 Homunculus since antiquity an artificially produced diminutive man supposed to have great learning and magical powers. (Goethe said that the voice in the vial was to be projected ventriloqually—presumably here by Mephistopheles, since in this scene the homunculus seems to be the latter's spokesman.) Pictorial model: Pretorius-Illustrator, *Homo lunaris* (1666), and illustrators of books with bottle-imps (e.g., Le Sage's *Le Diable boiteux*).

6864 crystallized allusion to folklore accounts of Stone-people.

6903 ff. Description in style of Ariosto and his imitators. Pictorial models: Correggio, Michelangelo, etc.

6951 southeast to Thessaly.

6953 Peneus chief river of Thessaly.

6955 Pharsalus city in Thessaly (site of Pompey's defeat by Caesar, 48 B.C.—cf. *6957* and *7018 ff.*).

6961 Asmodeus cf. n. to *5378*.

6978 Thessalian witches the most famous witches of classical Greek folklore.

6994 to dot the i's to obtain substantial existence (like that which Faust has vowed Helen shall have).

6997 f. traditional benefits of the Philosopher's Stone (cf. n. to *1046*).

7005–8487 Classical Walpurgisnight (cf. n. to *6566–10,038*). Time is magically suspended. – Two stage sets *(7005–8033* and *8034–8487),* each representing several different places.

7005–39 Unrhymed (iambic trimeter, i.e., lines of six iambs without a marked caesura—the verse of dialogue in Attic tragedy). *Pharsalian Fields* are at first the battle field near Pharsalus, then other parts of the Thessalian Plain, which extends from the Pindus Mountains eastward to the Aegean Sea, and of Macedonia (cf. n. to *7463–68*). *Erichtho* is the most famous Thessalian witch (cf. Lucanus' epic, *Pharsalia*).

7018 battle cf. *6955 ff.* and note.

7077 Antaeus's strength depended on contact with the earth (his mother, Ge); a giant, he was slain by Hercules, who lifted him off the ground.

7083 Griffins half lion, half eagle.

7104 Giant Ants according to Greek folklore, as large as foxes.

7106 Aramasps one-eyed Scythian enemies of the Giant Ants.

7107 how far to Scythia.

7198 slain by Hercules a "labor" of Hercules invented by Goethe.

7199 Chiron a medically skilled centaur and teacher-sage whose most famous pupil was Achilles.

7210 restrained by ropes Homer, *Odyssey*, Bk. XII. Pictorial models: Pietro da Cortona, Annibale Carracci.

7220 Stymphalian birds the Stymphalides, man-eating birds with iron beaks and talons, slain by Hercules.

7227 Hydra serpent-monster slain by Hercules.

7235 Lamiae vampire-like ghosts.

7249 Peneus the god of the river, *6953*.

7276 once before cf. *9603–20*.

7277–312 No pictorial source, since Leda is not seen; the landscape suggests that in Leonardo da Vinci's treatments of Leda and the Swan.

7342 doesn't do so well Despite the help of Pallas Athena, who takes the form of Mentor, Telemachus' tutor, Telemachus' search for his father Ulysses is a failure *(Odyssey)*.

7371 Boreiads sons of Boreas (the North Wind), hence winged warriors helpful to the Argonauts in fighting the Harpies.

7377 Lynceus (cf. Gk. *lýgkeios,* lynx-like) proverbial for his keen sight; hence *9218 ff.* and *11,143 ff.* as name of a lookout or watchman.

7381 Hercules was an emblem of the model prince in Renaissance art (especially in France).

7403 f. for the commonplace, cf. Milton, *Paradise Lost,* IV, 844f.

7405–25 Chiron's assistance to Castor and Pollux in the Eleusian swamps near Athens when they rescue Helen from Theseus is Goethe's (Faust's) invention.

7434 ff. Pherae the Thessalian city to which Alcestis was returned after Hercules (Faust's "handsomest man," *7397*) rescued her from Hades. – The shades of Helen and Achilles were joined in marriage on Leuce (an island in the Black Sea sacred to Achilles), where a son Euphorion (cf. *9599, 9695 ff.*) was born to them.

7450 f. Manto daughter of the Theban soothsayer Tiresias and herself a prophetess, is here instead given Aesculapius, the god of medicine, as father, and is endowed with medical skill. (Her temple in Greece was at Delphi.)

7463–68 place Pydna (in Macedonia, just north of Thessaly), site of the battle in which the last Macedonian king was defeated (168 B.C.) by Roman legions under generalship of the Roman consul Aemilius Paulus.

7491 Olympus the mountain lies on the border between Thessaly and Macedonia (between Pydna and the Thessalian border).

7493 Goethe's (Faust's) invention.

7519 ff. Seismos. Earthquakes and emerging mountains on which vegetation appears were common theatrical effects in Renaissance masques. Pictorial models: Raphael cartoon and tapestry, *St. Paul Freed from Prison by an Earthquake;* Giulio Romano, *Fountain as a Giant.*

7533 ff. Delos, originally a floating island, was supposedly raised from the deep by Poseidon and subsequently anchored by Zeus to provide a secure resting place on which Leto could give birth to Apollo and Artemis. (Goethe—or Faust—conflates two myths and gives them a new protagonist.)

7562 ff. The ballgame is an invention of Goethe or Faust; the mountains were piled not on Parnassus, but on Olympus, by Giants seeking to scale heaven.

7622 Dactyls a race of metalworkers, here identified with Tom Thumb-like dwarfs (Gk. *dáktylos,* finger).

7646–53 In Greek myth the Cranes are enemies of the Pygmies because the latter have stolen their eggs; here Goethe or Faust invents a new motivation of the enmity.

7660 The Cranes of Ibycus legendary symbols of retributive justice (of guilt incautiously revealed—theme of ballad with this title by Schiller).

7680 ff. allusions to places in the Harz Mountains (cf. n. to *3835–4398*).

7732 Empusa a protean vampire (whose power of metamorphosis is transferred paramythically by Goethe or Faust—*7766–90*—to the Lamiae).

7813 Pindus the Thessalian mountain range.

7836 philosophers Thales (d. 546 B.C.), who regarded Water as the First Principle, and Anaxagoras (d. 430 B.C.), who gave great importance to Air (here arbitrarily equated with Fire, which in *Faust* is a Mephisthophelean element); the former represents Neptunism, gradual evolution, and conservatism; the latter, Vulcanism and impatient radicalism. (Neptunists were geologists who held that the major force in determining the earth's features was water; Vulcanists attributed more importance to subterranean fire.)

7855 Anaxagoras is said to have held that rocks represented condensed fire-vapors.

7873 Myrmidons here: the Giant Ants. (Myrmidon, a son conceived by Zeus when disguised as an ant, was the mythical ancestor of the Thessalian race, the Myrmidons.)

7914 f. disc not the moon, but a meteor.

7967 The Phorcides The Graiae (Phorcydes, Phorkyads, *sing.* Phorkyas) were sisters of the Gorgons (and hence of Medusa).

7989 Ops and Rhea Roman and Greek goddesses of fertility, usually considered identical.

8034–487 Water pageants were frequently used in Renaissance and Baroque masques.

8051 ff. Pictorial model (for bejeweled Nereids): Dürer, *The Rape of Amymone.*

8074 Cabiri minor deities of Samothrace whose form and significance were much disputed by German-romantic mythologists.

8082 Nereus sea-god, father of the Nereids, and famous for his prophetic wisdom.

8121 Pindus' eagles (cf. *7813*) Thessalian warriors—the victorious Greeks—who have gained Troy.

8137 the Graces of the sea, whom Doris gave me (Germ. . . . *die Doriden,* Engl. *Nereids*) daughters by Doris.

8140 ff. Pictorial model: Raphael, *The Triumph of Galatea.*

8146 Cypria Aphrodite (as worshiped at Paphos on Cyprus), who has long since ceased to be a marine deity (although she was born of the sea).

8152 Proteus prophetic sea-god who could assume different shapes (in the Renaissance a common symbol of Nature).

8170 Chelone's giant buckler the shell of (a nymph who was changed into) a tortoise; shell-shaped boats were often used in water pageants.

8275 Telchines metal-workers at Rhodes, credited with forging Neptune's trident and the colossal statue of the sun-god Helios.

8343 Paphos town on Cyprus celebrated for its temple of Aphrodite—cf. n. to *8146*.

8359 Psylli and Marsi tribes famous for their reptile lore (Psylli, Libyan dwarfs; Marsi, an early Italian people); here, Cyprian attendants of Galatea, the new Cypria. – Snake charmers and snakebite healers were figures in Italian Renaissance carnivals.

8371 f. Eagle . . . Crescent symbols of successive Roman, Venetian, Crusader, and Turkish sovereignty over Cyprus.

8424 Galatea . . . on her conch Pictorial models: Raphael (cf. *8140*), Domenico Feti, Annibale Carracci, L. Backhuyzen, F. Albani, etc.

8466 ff. water "on fire" was a popular pageant-effect from the Renaissance on.

8488–10,038 Three stage sets, but no pause in the action. Many echoes of Homer and of Attic tragedy, especially of the plays of Euripides. (The placing of the Chorus on the stage is ancient-Roman, not Greek, theatrical practice, however.)

8488–9191 Unrhymed verse: iambic trimeter (cf. n. to *7005–39*) alternating with ode-strophes and, occasionally, trochaic tetrameters (cf. n. to *8909*).

8492 Euros Eurus, the southeast wind.

8493 Phrygia The area of Asia Minor in which Troy is located.

8498 Pallas' Hill Athens (as here translated); the German text of *8497 f.* can also be read to mean: erected by Tyndareos near the slope of this hill sacred to Pallas Athena on his return (*sc.* from Aetolia in Asia Minor, where he married Leda).

8511 Cytherea's shrine the temple of Venus on Cythera (in the Ionian Sea, south of Sparta), the site of "The Rape of Helen" in the scene Knights' Hall.

8539 Eurotas chief river of Laconia (not navigable); Sparta lies inland on it.

8547 Lacedaemon founding king of Sparta (hence also called Lacedaemon).

8564 ff. Renaissance conceit.

8677 Pictorial model: the figure Sleep of Michelangelo's *Medici Tomb* (Florence).

8704 Discord the goddess Eris.

8763 Orcus Hades.

8812 Erebus Darkness (son of Chaos).

8813 Scylla here the Homeric monster with six heads.

8851 Aphidnus A fortified town in Attica held by a friend of Theseus.

8855 Pelides Achilles, son of Peleus and friend of Patroclus.

8873 in both Ilium and Egypt The legend that the "real" Helen was transported by Mercury to Egypt, leaving Paris with a double, is the premise of Euripides' *Helen*.

8876 ff. cf. note to *7435 ff.*

8888 classicistic paraphrase of "(ravening wolves) in sheep's clothing" (Matt. 7, 15), imitative of Renaissance Latin poetry on biblical themes (Vida, Sannazaro, etc.).

8909–29 Verse: trochaic tetrameter (eight trochees, often without the last unstressed syllable, and usually with a caesura after the fourth trochee); occasionally shortened in later passages to four trochees (e.g., *8970*) with omission of the unstressed syllable of the fourth trochee.

8928 f. The fate of the twelve women-servants of Penelope whose conduct was dishonorable (*Odyssey*, XXII).

8996 Taygetus (Tāȳgĕtŭs) a mountain range west of Sparta, extending southward from the frontier of Arcadia.

9014 heroes Achilles (*Iliad*, XXII. 346 ff.) expressing his hatred of the dying Hector.

9020 Cyclopean using irregular stone blocks without mortar (primitive Greek).

9135 Pythoness wise woman, soothsayer (in the Vulgate *pythonissa* is a witch; cf. Exod. 22, 18, and—for the witch of Endor—1 Sam. 28, 7).

9162 ff. allusion to the apple of Sodom (Dead Sea apple).

9170 ff. Pictorial models (for the canopy borne above Helen's head): painters of the Venetian school; Correggio, *Madonna of St. Francis*.

9192–376 Faust and Helen speak in blank verse.

9218–45 Verse: quatrains (rhymed *abba*—in Spanish drama of the Golden Age: redondillas). *Lynceus* (cf. n. to *7377*).

9273–332 Verse: quatrains (rhymed *aabb*).

9346–55 Verse: rhymed couplets.

9411–18 Verse: rhymed couplets.

9419–34 Verse: rhymed

9435–41 Verse: iambic trimeter.

9442–81 Verse: quatrains (rhymed *abab*).

9454 Pylos harbor-city on the west coast of the Peloponnesus.

9467–77 the provinces of the Peloponnesus (the capital Sparta represents Laconia).

9506–73 Verse: quatrains (rhymed *abab*).

9509 center Arcadia, the mountainous region north of Sparta.

9511 almost-island (Germ. *Nichtinsel*, non-island) The Peloponnesus—literally: Pelops' island—is a peninsula connected to mainland Greece by the isthmus of Corinth).

9538 Pan as originally, an Arcadian deity of flocks and shepherds.

9573 Arcadian idyllic (post-classical idealization of the harsh simplicity of life in Arcadia).

9574 Pictorial model (of stage set): paintings of Poussin.

9578 bearded elders the exclusively male spectators of the ancient Greek theater.

9587 idyllic as in love idylls of epic romances.

9594 f. belief in the possibility of a subterranean world was widely held well into the 19th century.

9603 Pictorial model: Raphael, in the Vatican *Stanze.*

9611 Antaeus cf. n. to *7077.*

9619 f. Pictorial models: Annibale Carracci, *The Genius of Fame;* Guido Reni, *Aurora.*

9644 son of Maia Hermes (Mercury).

9679–938 Rhymed verse (quatrains, couplets, opera libretto-like shorter lines, and—finally—*ababcdcd* stanzas).

9826 Pelops' island cf. n. to *9511.*

9901 Icarus traditional symbol of imprudence. Pictorial model: Cornelis Corneliesz.

9902 the *well-known figure* of the stage direction is Lord Byron, who had died in 1824 at Missolonghi (on the coast of the Greek mainland north of the Peloponnesus) as a commander in the Greek army fighting for independence from Turkey.

9939–44 Verse: iambic trimeter.

9945–54 Blank verse.

9955–61 Verse: rhymed.

9962–91 Verse: iambic trimeter and strophes.

9992–10,038 Verse: trochaic tetrameter. The four parts of the Chorus become respectively Dryads, Oreads (and Echo Nymphs), Naiads, and Vineyard Nymphs, corresponding to the elements Earth, Air, Water, and Fire. Pictorial models: Poussin, Giulio Romano, Annibale Carracci, Claude Gillot, Daniel Höpfer (for the Dryads: also Hans Bol; and for the Vineyard Nymphs: also H. van Balen).

10,039–10,782 Stage set representing a variety of locations.

10,039–66 Faust still speaks in unrhymed verse (iambic trimeter; this is the last passage of unrhymed verse in *Faust*). Time: again the 16th century.

10,061 image of love's dawn a cloud looking like Margarete.

10,092 princes of the air cf. Eph. 2, 2 ("the prince of the power of the air, the spirit that now worketh in the children of disobedience").

10,094 cf. also Eph. 5, 12 f.

10,131 cf. Matt. 4, 8.

10,176 Sardanapalus ancient Assyrian tyrant and voluptuary (subject of a tragedy by Byron).

10.212–17 echo of Vergil, *Aeneid,* XI. 624–28.

10,284 cf. Ps. 85, 10 f. (motto of 16th and 17th century Papal coins).

10,304 In the Faust legend, Faust's magic is supposed to have helped the Emperor Charles V win an Italian campaign.

10,321 Peter Quince the organizer of the miserable amateur actors in *A Midsummer-Night's Dream.*

10,424 prevision foresight, preparedness (Lat. *providentia,* a word in the mottos of Trajan and the Emperor Maximilian I).

10,439 Norcia town near the northern end of the Sabine Hills, which were the

Roman equivalent of Thessaly as a center of witchcraft.

10,488 footstool cf. Ps. 110, 1.

10,531 Quickloot (Germ. *Eilebeute*, Luther's translation of the second part of the Hebrew name in Is. 8, 1.).

10,547 ff. Phantom armies occur in W. Rowley's play *The Birth of Merlin* and in Calderonian drama—e.g., *La aurora en Copacabana*.

10,600 a light the Dioscuri cast St. Elmo's fire was regarded in ancient Greek folklore as an emanation of the spirits of Castor and Pollux.

10,624 f. Pictorial model: Giuseppe Cesari, *Roman Battle*.

10,719 ff. a popular stage effect (especially in masques and pageants).

10,849–11,042 Verse: alexandrine couplets (six iambs, with a caesura—normally—after the third iamb).

10,873–976 The honorific offices here created by the Emperor were actually established by the imperial Golden Bull of 1356; there were four secular and three clerical Princes Elector; one of the latter held the Arch-Chancellorship.

11,043–142 quatrains (rhymed or assonating *abab*).

11,059 and *11,069 Baucis* and *Philemon* in classical mythology an aged Phrygian woman and her husband, rewarded for entertaining Zeus and Hermes traveling in disguise (and granted their wish that they might die simultaneously of old age); here, symbols of hospitable helpfulness. Pictorial models: Adam Elsheimer; Matthäus Merian, the elder; J. W. Baur.

11,143–843 Stage set with view into Faust's palace; continuous time.

11,143 Lynceus cf. n. to *7377*. – Pictorial models: harbor scenes of Claude Lorrain; baroque gardens with canals or lagoons (and the canal of Pope Pius VI in reclaimed Pontine marshes).

11,167 Three Mighty Men civilian counterparts of the trio of *10,323*.

11,171 ff. Pictorial model: Corneille de Wael, *Unloading the Galley* (in his series of engravings, *The Galley Slaves*).

11,308 ff. Pictorial models: Netherlandish artists specializing in conflagration scenes (e.g., Jan van der Heyden).

11,384 f. cf. Milton, *Paradise Lost,* IX. 12f.

11,512 Lemures Roman nocturnal spirits (of the dead), represented in art—e.g., a bas-relief found near Cumae—as skeletons held together by mortuary wrappings and mummified sinews; here: supernatural grave-diggers.

11,531–38 and *11,604–11* cf. *Hamlet,* V, i, 67ff. (song of First Clown, digging Ophelia's grave).

11,594 cf. John 19, 30.

11,644 hell-mouth (still used as late as the 17th century in masques) Pictorial models: cemetery frescos, Pisa; Taddeo Gaddi; Michelangelo; Luca Signorelli; etc.

11,647 Flaming City Dis, not the god, but the city of that name in Dante's *Inferno,* VIII, 65–81.

11,662 my mark cf. Rev. 19, 20.

11,699 ff. Pictorial models: Luca Signorelli, *Angels Strewing Roses* (fresco, Orvieto); Lodovico Carracci, *The Miracle of the Roses*.

11,716 bellows-devils fire-spewing demons of Germanic folklore and statuary using such figures.

11,809 cf. Job 2, 7.

11,844 ff. Single stage-set; time overlap (*11,934* continues from *11,824*). Pictorial models: Taddeo Gaddi, *Thebaian Hermits* (frescos, Pisa); Roelant Savery; Titian (?), *St. Jerome;* etc.

11,854 Pater Ecstaticus title of various saints; here, a religious enthusiast and mystic.

11,866 Pater Profundus title of St. Bernard of Clairvaux; here, a somewhat earth- and sense-bound hermit.

11,890 Pater Seraphicus title of St. Francis of Assisi; here, a hermit and saint concerned with the welfare of others.

11,890 ff. Pictorial model: Correggio (cupola frescos in the cathedral of Parma.)

11,898 born at midnight reference to the popular belief that those born at midnight die in infancy.

11,956 even cremated (Germ. *wär' er von Asbest,* even if he were of asbestos) not to be purified by fire.

11,989 Doctor Marianus a hermit dedicated to the cult of (the Virgin) Mary, mother of Jesus and hence Mother of God.

11,994 f. the constellation Virgo (the Virgin).

12,032 Mater Gloriosa the Virgin in Glory. Pictorial models: Titian, *Ascension of the Virgin;* Murillo, *La Imaculata;* etc.

12,037 Magna Peccatrix "the greatly sinful woman" in the eyes of Simon, the Pharisee. Pictorial models: Michelangelo; Rembrandt; L. Cranach, the elder; Correggio; Annibale Carracci; Guido Reni; Carlo Dolci; Poussin; etc.

12,045 Mulier Samaritana the woman of Samaria.

12,053 Maria Aegyptica former prostitute who was supernaturally prevented from entering the Church of the Holy Sepulcher and therefore did forty years' penance in the desert where, as she died, she wrote in the sand a request that her father confessor pray for her soul. Pictorial model: Tintoretto (Venice, Scuola di S. Rocco).

12,104 mysticus mystic (the Latin avoids negative connotations—e.g., of mystifying obfuscation—of the German equivalent *mystisch*).

12,110 Woman, eternally (Germ. *das Ewig-Weibliche,* often translated "the Eternal Feminine").